W9-DAU-583

THAT NOBLE COUNTRY

The Romance
of the St. Clair River Region

by

Dorothy Marie Mitts

DORRANCE & COMPANY
Philadelphia

To the memory of my parents,
FREDERICK ERASTUS MITTS
and
ANNA CARRIGAN MITTS,
and of my brothers,

JOHN THOMAS MITTS
JOSEPH LESLIE MITTS
and
GERALD DeSALES MITTS

ACKNOWLEDGMENT

Much of the material in *That Noble Country* has appeared in vignette form in the author's weekly historical column, "Where The Wild Goose Flies," in the Sunday edition of the *Port Huron Times Herald,* and is used here with the kind permission of the President and Editor, F. Granger Weil.

CONTENTS

PART FIVE
WAR AND NEAR WAR ON THE ST. CLAIR

PART SIX
UNUSUAL SIGHTS AND SOUNDS ON THE ST. CLAIR

PART SEVEN
STORIED ISLANDS OF THE ST. CLAIR

PART EIGHT
PIONEERS! O PIONEERS

PART NINE

THE TWIN CITIES OF
PORT HURON, MICHIGAN AND SARNIA, ONTARIO

PART TEN
LEGENDS AND A TALL TALE OR TWO

INTRODUCTION

The St. Clair River, a part of the world's busiest waterway, is rich in historical lore. Seated at the head of the river are Port Huron and Sarnia, cities with a colorful heritage. The excitement, the romance and the drama of over 300 years of history in this border region has been captured by Dorothy Mitts in *That Noble Country.*

Forming, as it does, a scenic link in the world's longest unfortified border, the St. Clair River history has deserved a recounting. A procession of dignified and industrious peoples have settled and developed the area, making it prosper. The Indian and White occupations are contrasted and the vestiges of the Red Man's presence in colorful place names add a special flavor to this account.

With justifiable pride in the achievements of the peoples of the St. Clair River Valley and being impressed with the resources of the region, Miss Mitts here offers a series of accounts well worth the telling. She draws upon the extensive collections of original documents available for research and evidences all of her knowledge of the pertinent published material in writing her story. The comprehensive bibliography attests to her thoroughness. She utilizes the archaeologists' findings to tell of prehistoric St. Clair. The French and British occupation of the area come alive through her use of contemporary sources. The pioneer period and the beginnings of settlements are chronicled through the lives and labors of men and women. Not only the great and significant, but the many lesser important persons and events are remembered.

Great Lakes shipping and lumbering, which gave prosperity to the western shore of the St. Clair River are explained and examined through anecdotes and reminiscences.

In all, Miss Mitts brings alive to the reader a historic area in its several eras of development and enrichment. *That Noble Country* is an achievement in regional history.

James M. Babcock
Chief, Burton Historical Collection,
Detroit Public Library

. . . so that those who shall be so happy as to inhabit that Noble Country, cannot but remember with Gratitude those who have discovered the way . . . .

—Father Louis Hennepin

PROLOGUE

Across the clear, cerulean waters of the St. Clair River the Blue Water International Bridge stretches its great cantilever arms between Port Huron, Michigan and Sarnia, Ontario in a gesture of friendship between two great nations, and it spans a thoroughfare permeated with a history and a beauty rivaling that of any other spot in the world.

The traveler crossing on the Blue Water International Bridge looks down on a turbulence of waters rushing out of Lake Huron, fascinated and enchanted by their ever-changing bluish hues—from cerulean to sapphire, to indigo, to aquamarine, to azure—according to the mood of the heavens which they mirror. And he sees an artistic patchwork of well planned cities and pulsating industries sprawled along the American and Canadian shores, where once the explorer and the missionary and the pioneer saw only verdant meadows interspersed with luxuriant forest growths stretching far inland.

What the traveler may not be so aware of is the St. Clair River district's historic prestige. It is a prestige gained through its antiquity; through its fortified posts representing three nations and marking three centuries; through its famous shipbuilding days, when it controlled the commerce of the Great Lakes; through its natural resources and their early utilization; and through its pioneers whose accomplishments aided so materially in the development of the state of Michigan and the nation.

The antiquity of the region became known from the human bones and artifacts found in the remains of the numerous earthworks of that prehistoric race of men known as the Mound Builders. Traces of the earthworks and relics found in the St. Clair River region demonstrated the industry and other characteristics of those Lilliputian flatboned men to an extent unobserved in probably any other part of the continent.

Along the shores of the St. Clair River, a life-line of America and one of the world's busiest waterways, the sound of travel by white man has echoed for some three hundred years. Where 730-

foot freighters, foreign ships, and pleasure craft now travel—and where the great freshwater classic, the Port Huron-Mackinac races, are now held each year—La Salle's historic *Griffin* sailed in 1679.

Those giants of Michigan—Industry and Commerce—got their impetus from the pioneers of the St. Clair River region. On the shores of the St. Clair River was the primary site of the Great Lakes shipbuilding industry in the wooden boats era, when the shipbuilders and navigators of the St. Clair River region held sway over the commerce of the Great Lakes.

The St. Clair River district was blessed with great forests, which produced not only the spars and other timbers for its shipbuilding, but also the lumber to build many of the early cities of the Middle West. The first saw mills in the Northwest Territory were set up on the banks of the St. Clair River and its tributaries, several of them established long before the original Thirteen Colonies were declared free and independent of Great Britain.

The pioneers of the St. Clair River district were also the first to recognize the potential of Michigan's fabulous mineral resources and to carry out and utilize the first iron mined in Michigan.

The traveler crossing on the Blue Water International Bridge can, in his mind's eye, envisage the three forts which graced the banks of the St. Clair River on the American side and over which were unfurled the flags of France, Great Britain, and the United States. These forts not only played important roles in the strategic military and political events of three centuries but aided materially in the establishment of permanent settlements along the St. Clair River.

Historians tell us that if we want to learn the true story of America we must search for it in our own back yards. Perhaps nowhere in the country is this more clearly shown than in the St. Clair River district, for its story is the story of Michigan and of the Great Northwest Territory. It is, in fact, the story of America.

PART ONE

ORIGINS

... For today is the feast of the Abbess Claire;
And the corded priests, with chants and prayer,
Sprinkling the lake with holy water,
Name it after the Church's daughter.

—James V. Campbell

Chapter I

THE NAME ST. CLAIR

On a quiet August midday in the year 1679 a high-decked brigantine, with the figure of a griffin[1] at its prow and flying the white and gold flag of France, was becalmed in the St. Clair River just below the Rapids, at the foot of Lake Huron.

The world knows that brigantine as the *Griffin*,[2] the Sieur de La Salle's historic ship, first sailing vessel afloat on the Upper Lakes. It was on its way to the Mackinac country for a cargo of fur pelts with which the noted explorer and vassal of Louis XIV of France hoped to pay off his creditors in Montreal and secure funds for continuing his explorations of the Mississippi Valley.

The ship's company, too, is familiar to all. Besides La Salle[3] there was the Recollect missionary, Father Louis Hennepin,[4] the

---

[1] An emblem in the coat of arms of the Governor of New France, Louis de Baude, Count of Frontenac, friend and backer of La Salle.

[2] Cuthbertson in his *Freshwater* likens the design of the *Griffin* to a Dutch galiot, a vessel admirably suited for entering shallow harbors, such as the "shallow and narrow reaches of the Detroit and St. Clair Rivers." George A. Cuthbertson, *Freshwater, A history and narrative of the Great Lakes* (New York: Macmillan, 1931), pp. 44-45.

[3] René-Robert Cavelier, Sieur de La Salle, was born in Rouen, France, in 1643, son of the wealthy merchant, Jean Cavelier. La Salle was the name of an estate near Rouen belonging to the Cavelier family. He was educated by the Jesuits, and came in 1666, at the age of 23, to Canada to satisfy a craving for exploration. It was three years after sailing up the St. Clair River in the *Griffin* that La Salle travelled the Mississippi to the Gulf of Mexico, claiming the whole region for France and naming it Louisiana after Louis XIV. He was murdered by members of his party, March 18, 1687, in what is now Texas, after he lost his way while conducting colonists on a second expedition to the Mississippi.

[4] Father Louis Hennepin (1640?-1701), a Fleming, born in Ath, Belgium, was a missionary and explorer in the wilds of North America. A member of the Recollect Order (a branch of the Franciscans), he came to Canada as a missionary in 1675, serving at Fort Frontenac on Lake Orleans, and had

(Continued on page 4)

noted friar who earned an immortal place in history as an explorer and historian rather than as a missionary, and whose account of the voyage first publicized to the world (1683) the glories of the St. Clair River district. Also aboard, and among the ship's complement of 32 men, were two other Recollects, Fathers Zenobius Membré and Gabriel de la Ribourde, and the Italian officer Henry de Tonty,[5] brother of Alphonse de Tonty who was to accompany Cadillac at the founding of Detroit fifteen years later.

The world may also know how the *Griffin,* a few day earlier, sailing down from Cayuga Creek, just above Niagara Falls where she was built the previous winter and spring, had come upon a bulge in the strait between Lake Erie and Lake Huron. This

---

(Continued from page 3)

charge of scattered missions along the St. Lawrence. In 1680, after his expedition with La Salle through the St. Clair River country, La Salle sent him to the Mississippi, where he was taken prisoner by the Sioux, but was eventually rescued by the Sieur Du Luth. He returned to Quebec and then to France, where he wrote the first best seller on the doings of the French in America: *Déscription de la Louisiane Nouvellement Découverte,* published at Paris in 1683—a narrative which also told for the first time of the glories of the St. Clair River district. Father Hennepin discovered the Falls of St. Anthony, and he was the first European to describe Niagara Falls from actual view and publish a picture of them. His narrative was revamped and published at Utrecht in 1697 as *Nouvelle découverte d'un très grand Pays situé dans l'Amérique,* and again published in London in 1698 under the title, *A New Discovery of a Vast Country in America.* References in this work are to the Reuben G. Thwaites edition, a reprint from the second London issue of 1698, (Chicago: McClurg, 1903).

[5] Henry de Tonty, La Salle's friend and trusted lieutenant, was an Italian explorer, born about 1650. He was the son of the Neapolitan, Lorenzo Tonti, who invented the financial scheme (called the "tontine") from which the modern system of life insurance was derived. Tonty was with La Salle when that explorer descended the Mississippi to its mouth. It was Tonty who built Fort St. Louis for La Salle on the Illinois River, and there he remained until 1700. After La Salle's death in 1687 he assisted Iberville in Louisiana, where, it is said he died of the yellow fever in 1704. Tonty was also known by the sobriquet of "Tonty of the Iron Hand," because he wore an artificial (metal) hand in place of one he had lost in his youth on the battlefield in Spain. The metal hand was most effective in dealing blows to unruly Indians, and he came to be regarded as a medicine man with supernatural powers—"The Man with the Iron Hand."

widening of the strait was small, somewhat shallow, and round like a saucer. It was different from any other body of water La Salle and his companions had seen in this country or in the old.

It was the custom of the French explorers, when they beheld for the first time some distinguishing or prominent feature of the landscape, to bestow upon that piece of land or body of water the name of the saint to whom the day of discovery was dedicated in the church calendar. This christening was performed amid the most solemn ceremonies, which usually included a prayer, perhaps the offering of the Mass, and the singing of *Te Deum*.

The day being the twelfth of August, it was the feast day of Saint Claire, the celebrated foundress of the Franciscan nuns of the Thirteenth Century, known as "Poore Claires." Clara of Assisi, a friend and follower in poverty of St. Francis of Assisi, was the beautiful daughter of a nobleman of great wealth, and when she entered the convent of San Domiano in rich attire, it was Saint Francis himself who cut off her long hair and threw over her the coarse, penitential robes of the order.

This was the same Clara of Assisi who by means of a miracle saved her convent and the countryside of Assisi from being ravaged by the Moors and the Saracens. It is related, not by legend but by her contemporary biographers, that in 1234 when the army of Frederick II was devastating the Valley of Spoleto, the soldiers, preparatory to an assault upon Assisi, scaled the wall of San Domiano, spreading terror among the community.

Clara, then dying after a long illness, rose from her bed and, taking the ciborium containing the consecrated Host from the little chapel adjoining her cell, proceeded to face the intruders at the open window against which they had already placed a ladder. As she raised the ciborium, those who were about to enter the convent fell backward as if dazzled, and the others who were about to follow threw down their arms and fled. It is with reference to this incident that some of the great painters have represented St. Clare in their masterpieces.

One can imagine then, with what pleasure the Recollect, Father Hennepin, blessed the lake and christened it in honor of a member of his own related order. "We called [it] Lake St. Clare,[6] on account of our passing through it on that saint's day,"[7] Father Hennepin simply states in his narrative, and although we are not told just what were the imposing ceremonies accompanying the christening, we have a picture of what might have transpired that day in the following excerpts from the poem, "The Legend of L'Anse Creuse," written in 1879 by Judge James V. Campbell of Detroit for the occasion of the second centennial celebration of that historic event:

> . . . The bright warm rays of an August noon
> Hushed each sound but the locust's tune:
> But a gentle wind blew from the west,
> Dimpling with ripples the water's breast,
> And catching the swans' wings where they float,
> Drove each one on like a well-trimmed boat,

. . . .

---

[6] St. Clair River, St. Clair County, and the town of St. Clair all undoubtedly take their names from Lake St. Clair, named for St. Claire. The French *"Claire"* if properly Anglicized would be "Clare" (as it appears in most of the English maps for fifty years, beginning in 1710) and how it came to be spelled "Clair" remains a mystery. The spelling gives rise to the erroneous belief that the river got its name from Governor Arthur St. Clair, first governor of the Northwest Territory, which is without consideration since St. Clair was never in or near the district or even within the limits of Michigan. W. L. Jenks poses this possible explanation for the fallacy that the river was named for Governor St. Clair: "In 1810 Aaron Greeley, the surveyor of private claims, notes upon the survey of the claim just below the mouth of Pine River the location of Old Fort St. Clair,' indicating his ignorance of Patrick Sinclair and his fort. . . . The probabilities favor the idea that the people who began calling the river St. Clair did so with the belief that Gen. St. Clair, who was then governor of the territory, was the one whose name was being immortalized." William L. Jenks, *Scrapbook*, No. 1, *Port Huron Times Herald* clipping, undated, William Lee Jenks Room of Michigan History, and which will hereafter be referred to as the Jenks Collection, Port Huron Public Library. It might be pertinent to point out here, also, that St. Clair River was known for some forty years on maps and in documents as River Sinclair, the name originating from either Fort Sinclair or from Patrick Sinclair who built the fort on Pine River in present St. Clair. Capt. Alex Harrow in his *Journal* once referred to his farm as located on "the river Sinclair," but afterwards also used the form "St. Clair" and even "St. Clare." (Harrow *Journal*, Burton Historical Collection, Detroit Public Library) Hennepin gives the Iroquois name of Lake St. Clair as *"Otsi Keta."*

[7] Paré, op. cit., p. 70 quoting from Hennepin's *"Description de la Louisiane Nouvellment Découverte,"* Paris, 1683.

Just as the sun in his path on high
Stayed his course in the middle sky,
Speeding along with a foaming wake
A great ship sailed upon the lake:
And the loon dove down, and the white swans flew,
Scared at the sight of the wonder new:
For never had vessel along this shore
Cleft these quiet waves before.
No better craft was ever seen
Than brave La Salle's stout brigantine;
Out from the prow a griffin springs
With scales of bronze and fiery wings,
And the ship that earned so wide a fame
Bore on its scroll the Griffin's name.
. . . .

A gilded eagle carved in wood
On the crown of the quarter-deck castle stood.
And from the staff astern unrolled,
Floating aloft with its lilies of gold,
The great white flag of France is spread,
And the pennon decking the mainmast head
Bears the chieftain's arms on a field of red.
. . . .

But another standard is seen today
As the gallant cruiser wins the bay,
For the cross is raised and the censer swings,
And the seamen kneel as the mass bell rings,
For to-day is the feast of the Abbess Claire;
And the corded priests, with chants and prayer,
Sprinkling the lake with holy water
Name it after the Church's daughter.
Then in a trice the gunners catch
Each in his place the blazing match,
And the flame leaps out, and the trembling shore
Quakes at the terrible cannon's roar. . . .[8]

And then it was that, some days later the *Griffin*, after continuing up the strait was becalmed in the Rapids at the foot of Lake Huron, off what is now Pine Grove Park in Port Huron, Michigan.

There, one can imagine the ship's company coming ashore—La Salle in plumed hat and scarlet cloak trimmed with broad gold lace, Father Hennepin and the other friars in sandals and

---

[8] James V. Campbell, "A Legend of L'Anse Creuse," *Pioneer and Historical Collections, Mich.,* III (1881), 656-665.

the corded, grey robe and peeked cowl of the Recollects, and La Salle's uniformed lieutenant, all preceding the rest of the soldiers and sailors as they scaled the elevation of land above the Rapids.

One can see the oddly-assorted group, just as some Potawatomies and Ottawas may have seen them as they disembarked from the *Griffin*—a vessel that must have looked to them like a fantastic floating fort with its many cannons. One can see the explorers traversing the shores of the strait, admiring the luxuriant meadows and the great stands of virgin pine timber, the walnut and chestnut trees, the wild plum and apple trees, the great oaks smothered with festoons of wild grape vines, and the abundant wild game— all of which the adventurers helped themselves to, stocking the hold of the *Griffin* with the fruits and nuts, geese and turkeys, and hanging the bulwarks with the cut-up carcasses of small deer and perhaps a bear.

The country about the strait, Father Hennepin later wrote, was well situated, and the soil quite fertile:

> The banks of the Streight are vast Meadows, and the Prospect is terminated with some Hills covered with Vineyards, Trees bearing good Fruit, Groves, and Forests, so well dispos'd, that one would think Nature alone could not have made, without the help of Art, so charming a Prospect. That Country is stock'd with Stags, Wild Goats,[9] & Bears, which are good for Food, and not fierce as in other countries; some think they are better than our Pork. Turkey-cocks and Swans are there also very common; and our Men brought several other Beasts and Birds, whose Names are unknown to us, but they are extraordinary relishing.

And Hennepin continues:

> The Forests are chiefly made up of Walnut-trees, Chestnut-trees, Plum-trees, and Pear-trees, loaded with their own Fruit and Vines. There is also abundance of Timber fit for Building; so that those who shall be so happy as to inhabit that Noble Country, cannot but remember with Gratitude those who have discovered the way, by venturing to sail upon an unknown Lake for above one hundred Leagues.[10]

---

[9] Probably small deer.
[10] Hennepin, *op. cit.*, I, 111.

But it was not the intention of LaSalle to tarry longer than was necessary. As soon as the wind turned southerly the anchor of the *Griffin* was raised. And again one can picture how the savages must have fled into the woods in terror at the booming of the *Griffin's* cannon. As her sails swelled and the chanting of *Te Deum* drifted back to the shore, "with the help of twelve Men, who hall'd (the) Ship from the Shoar," the high-decked brigantine moved gracefully out into the lake—the first sailing vessel ever to ride the waves of Lake Huron.

Chapter II

THE DARK-SKINNED RACE THE WHITE MAN FOUND

When La Salle and his party passed up through the St. Clair River, they found inhabitating the countryside a race of men with bronze-colored skin called Indians,[1] whose ancestors may have been descendants of that aboriginal race inhabiting the region in pre-historic times, the Mound Builders.

Prevalent in historic times in the lower peninsula of Michigan were tribes of the powerful and extensive Algonquin family—the Potawatomies, Sauks, Foxes, Miamis, Ottawas, Mississaugas and Chippewas,[2] and, to some extent, the Wyandots who were of the Iroquoin language group. But the Indian was a great traveler, moving about with ease and rapidity from place to place in hunting and fishing season, or fleeing from the advance of the enemy in time of tribal wars, making it difficult to pinpoint tribes in definite locations for any particular length of time.

From weapons and tools found in the numerous Indian burial grounds in Port Huron alone, such as copper hatchets, double-pointed instruments of unknown use, beads which could have come only from the Lake Superior region, and flint arrowheads associated with the Indians living no nearer than central Ohio, we know that—as W. L. Jenks pointed out in his *St. Clair County, Michigan*—"a more extended commerce between Indian tribes perhaps existed than has been commonly believed."[3] From early maps and Indian treaties, however, one gathers a certain amount of knowledge as to the occupancy of general tribes in general places, although the stated names of tribes in some instances have not been positively identified.

---

[1] The inappropriate and misleading name of "Indian" was given by the Europeans to this race of men when they first came to North America in the mistaken idea that they were on the right course to the East and that the men they found along the way were inhabitants of outlying sections of India.

[2] Perhaps better known in Michigan as Ojibwas.

[3] William L. Jenks, *St. Clair County, Michigan; Its History and Its People* (Chicago: Lewis, 1912), I, 48.

At the time of Champlain's arrival in New France the country at the lower end of Georgian Bay was occupied by the Hurons, who remained there until the late sixteen eighties when they were scattered and almost annihilated by the Iroquois, while west and south of them were the Tobacco Nation. Still farther south and east of the Tobacco Nation were the Neutral Nation (or Neuters), extending from St. Clair River to the Niagara River. No doubt they occupied both sides of the St. Clair River, especially at the confluence of Black River with the St. Clair.

Nicholas Sanson's map of 1650, said to be based on the Jesuit *Relations,* and the first map to show all the Great Lakes, places the Nation of Fire, or Potawatomies, south of Saginaw Bay. The 1656 Sanson map shows the Couaeronon, or Sauk Indians, just west of the head of the St. Clair River. And a map made in 1660, which accompanied a history of Canada by Francois Du Creux[4] published in Latin in 1664, and which was also "largely composed from the Relations,"[5] indicates three tribes just west of the St. Clair River—the Assistoius, the Ondatouius and the Teoronius. This map also shows the Schenkioetonius, who were the Foxes, in the district east of Saginaw Bay.

The Teoronius seem not to have been positively identified, but the Couaeronon were the Sauk, and the Ondatouius were the Potawatomies (Ondatouatonde being the Iroquoin name for Potawatomi)[6] as were the Assistoius. Thus, if any Indians were in the particular region of the St. Clair River for the hunting or fishing season when La Salle made his historic passage in the *Griffin,* perhaps they were the Sauk, up from Lake St. Clair, or the Foxes, down from Saginaw Bay, or the Potawatomies, back from the central part of the peninsula to pay a visit to their old hunting grounds.

When Baron de Lahontan relieved Duluth in 1687 as commandant at Fort St. Joseph, in what is now Port Huron, a party of Hurons spent a considerable length of time at the fort. But these Indians were from Mackinac, where the Hurons and Ottawas

---

[4] Francois Du Creux, *Historiae Canadensis seu Nova-Franciae* (Paris, 1664).

[5] Thwaites note in his edition of Baron Lahontan's *New Voyages to North America* (Chicago: McClurg, 1905), I, 44—the edition to which reference in this work will be made.

[6] Marginal note in Jenks, *op. cit.,* I, 44.

had their villages, and were on their way to attack the Iroquois at Niagara.

It was Cadillac who, with a promise of protection from the then common enemy, the Iroquois, invited and encouraged Indians of all tribes to settle in or near Detroit. Included in the tribes who accepted the invitation was a new nation of the Algonquin family, the Chippewa, and a year after the establishment of Detroit, Cadillac reported that the Saulters[7] (Chippewas) and Mississaugas (a tribe closely related to, and forerunners of the Chippewas in the St. Clair River region) had "united in forming a village on the Detroit River."[8] These tribes occupied the St. Clair River area in hunting and fishing season.

In 1736 a small village of Mississaugas numbering about three hundred and fifty, including warriors, women and children, was situated at the north end of Lake St. Clair; and at the time of the Pontiac uprising, some twenty-seven years later, we know that the tribe encamped in what is now north Port Huron and who perpetrated the act of cannibalism in 1763 when the English survey party was murdered, was the Saginaw tribe of Chippewas.[9]

The Treaty of 1807 between the United States and the Ottawa, Wyandot, Potawatomi, and Chippewa nations, which gave the United States undisputed rights to the southeastern part of Michigan, provided for several reservations, including two in St. Clair County. One reservation comprised, substantially, the major portion of Port Huron south of Black River and north of Griswold Street; the other fronted on Lake St. Clair near New Haven, at the mouth of Swan Creek. The Indians making the cession are called in the treaty the Black River and Swan Creek bands of Chippewas.

Although the treaty was signed by seventeen Chippewa chiefs, five Ottawas, five Potawatomies and three Wyandots—probably representing the relative numbers of Indians affected in each tribe

---

[7] "Saulters were a Chippewa tribe, so named by the French from first encountering one of their band at Sault Ste. Marie." Thwaites note in Lahontan, *op. cit.*, I, 43.

[8] Jenks, *op. cit.*, I, 43.

[9] See PART TWO, Chapter IV, for story of murder and cannibalism.

—the two reservations in St. Clair County were claimed and occupied only by the Chippewas, and then only for periodic encampments. The Indians prefered to spend much of their time on the Canadian side of the St. Clair River, or in the Saginaw Valley, and came to the St. Clair River area primarily to hunt and fish.

By the Treaty of 1836, however, the Black River and Swan Creek bands of Chippewas ceded back to the United States their lands for a consideration of money and a considerable tract of land in Kansas, to which they removed; and the two Indian reservations in St. Clair County, Michigan ceased to exist.

On the Canadian side of the St. Clair River, the McKee Treaty of 1790 between Great Britain and the Ottawa, Chippewa, Potawatomi, and Huron Indians left the greater part of what is now Lambton County, Ontario still Indian land. In 1825 the Chippewas ceded their land to the Crown, and the formal transfer took place two years later. By that treaty four reserves were set aside for the Indians. Two were in Bosanquet, the Sauble Reserve and the Kettle Point Reserve. The third extended from a point a short distance south of present Sarnia, along the St. Clair River to the present Moore township line. The fourth reserve consisted of the entire area of Walpole Island.[10]

The Mound Builders

Of great interest, too, were the earthworks found in the St. Clair River region of that ancient race of men called the Mound Builders, who antedated the Indians of historic times and who were probably the ancestors of the Indians found inhabiting the same region by the first European explorers.

Of the more than eleven hundred mounds identified in Michigan some of the largest and most revealing were found within the present limits of Port Huron. They were situated at the head of St. Clair River and along Lake Huron, and on Black River. A great number of mounds were also located across on the Canadian side in Lambton County in the Province of Ontario.

[10] See PART SEVEN, Chapter XXVI, Walpole Island. See also Victor E. Lauriston, *Lambton's Hundred Years, 1849-1949* (Sarnia, n.d.) , pp. 3-7.

Perhaps one of the outstanding discoveries in the mounds found in Port Huron—according to a report made to the Peabody Museum of Archaeology and Ethnology in 1872—was that all the tibiae unearthed invariably exhibited to a greater degree the characteristics of the small, flat-boned, prehistoric platycnemic men, than was found in similar earthworks throughout the country.

These mounds were terrace-like embankments—which, unfortunately, were discovered and explored only after roads had been graded through the area and most of the artifacts scattered or destroyed—usually from ten to 20 and 25 feet in height, and ranging from fifty to five hundred or more feet in length. One of the most remarkable facts about the existence of these mounds is that in no instance was there evidence of the surrounding terrain having been disturbed or used in the building of them.

The mounds were built for living quarters—many fireplaces were found in them—as well as for burial grounds and protective hideouts from marauding enemies.

One mound along Black River near the vicinity of the Campau Tract exhibited not only a large number of human bones, pottery, and unusual stone implements of great length, but also a grave lined with pottery, a peculiar circumstance which archaeologists had not found in any other mound. The ornamented side of the grave was different, too, from any other specimens seen by the archaeologists; it was rough, with every appearance of having been pressed while plastic, with sand and pebbles adhering to it. The explanation attributed to the peculiar formation was the "coagulation and final hardening of blood," and to account for the presence of such large quantities of blood it was assumed that a battle had been fought in the vicinity.[11]

In one of the larger mounds near the site of Gratiot Inn at the foot of Lake Huron, the crumbled bones of a body were unearthed within two feet of its surface. Widening the excavation farther to the east and digging to a depth of six feet, the archaeologist

---

[11] For an extensive report on the mounds found in Port Huron made to the Peabody Museum of Archaeology and Ethnology, Harvard University, in 1872 by Henry Gilman, see Jenks, *op. cit.*, I, 50-58. See also Jenks' map, same volume, page 51, showing the numerous mounds at the head of St. Clair River, on Lake Huron and on Black River, and on the Canadian side in Lambton County in the Province of Ontario.

found the decayed stump of a great second growth, scarlet oak tree. The trench was then opened to the west, to the same depth, and the skull and bones of another dwarfish body were found (the bodies usually indicating that they were buried in a sitting position), with the decayed roots of the oak tree stretching above it. When these remains were removed a third body was discovered. The roots of the tree had penetrated the bones and burst them in several places, so that in many instances parts of the bone surrounded the roots.

One would have an idea of the antiquity of the mounds in Port Huron from the fact that ages after the mounds were abandoned second growth stands of centuries-old forest trees, like the scarlet oak, had taken root on them, reached their full growth, been cut down and, in some instances, their stumps long decayed when the white man first saw them.

But a more significant indication of the age of the mounds in Port Huron can be deduced from the coarse and rough markings on the pottery, or potsherds, unearthed in the mound on Black River, already referred to. The pottery was generally marked with the cord pattern, the marks made with a thick cord or small rope.

E. F. Greenman in *The Michigan Archaeologist* identifies pottery with surfaces roughened "by cord-impression" as Early Woodland Period (2700 B. C. to 600 B. C.). That being the case, the Mound Builders may have been living and building their earthworks in Port Huron more than four thousand years ago.[12]

------

[12] E. F. Greenman, "Prehistoric Detroit," Michigan Archaeologist. December, 1958, v. 4, no. 4, p. 92.

PART TWO

THE AMERICAN SHORE OF THE ST. CLAIR RIVER UNDER THREE FLAGS

Their swords are rust,
Their bones are dust,
Their souls are with the saints we trust.

—Author Unknown

Chapter III

THE WHITE AND GOLD FLAG OF FRANCE

Duluth Builds Fort St. Joseph

La Salle and his party were not the first white men on record to traverse the St. Clair River and to gaze upon its beautiful blue waters. Two other Frenchmen, the Sulpician priest, Father Francois Dollier de Casson, and René Bréhant de Galinée, a deacon of the same order, came up the river in the spring of 1670 on their exploration of the Great Lakes.

It is also true that a "Monsieur Jolliet"[1] came down the river the preceding year. That man, according to more recent research, was Adrien Jolliet and not Louis Jolliet, his brother, as has been generally assumed. An Iroquoin prisoner whom Adrien Jolliet had saved from torture at the hands of Ottawas[2] told him of a hitherto unknown passage from Lake Superior to Quebec, through the straits connecting Lake Huron and Lake Erie, and it was undoubtedly Jolliet who told the Sulpicians of the route they took in 1670.[3]

But it was another Frenchman, Daniel Greysolon, Sieur Du Luth, one of the most capable of the young Frenchmen to come to America during the reign of Louis XIV, who was to make the first settlement on the St. Clair River—a settlement in the form of a fortified post.[4]

---

[1] Rev. George Paré, *The Catholic Church in Detroit, 1701-1888* (Detroit: Gabriel Richard Press, 1951), p. 53.

[2] *Ibid.*

[3] *Ibid.*, p. 27. Since Sanson's map of 1656 shows Lake Erie in its extent and its connection with the Detroit River, Lake St. Clair and the St. Clair River, and locations of the Jesuit missions, Father Paré poses the possibility that Father Jogues or Father Chaumonot "came as far as Lake St. Clair during the mission to the Neutral Indians in the winter of 1640-41, and may have set foot in Michigan a few months preceding the visit of Fathers Jogues and Raymbault to the Sault."

[4] This was the third military post in Michigan. The first, Fort de Baude (later known as Fort Michilimackinac) was established at St. Ignace, around 1671. La Salle's Fort Miami, at the mouth of St. Joseph River was the second built by him in 1679 after he passed up the St. Clair River and Lake Huron in the *Griffin.*

19

In the latter part of the seventeenth century the French became apprehensive of the English encroachment on their monopoly of the beaver trade. Denonville, governor of New France, ordered Duluth to choose an advantageous spot on the strait (*detroit*) between the Toronto Portage and Michilimackinac and to build a fort to block further passage of the English between those points. The fort was also to serve as a refuge for the French and their Indian allies while hunting or marching against the hostile Iroquois.

The site of the fort chosen by Duluth was the eminence above the Rapids of the St. Clair River, at the foot of Lake Huron on the American side, and approximately where the Blue Water International Bridge reaches from Port Huron, Michigan to Sarnia, Ontario. When finished, Duluth named his post Fort St. Joseph, and Denonville, writing in November of 1686 to M. de Seignelay in Versailles, tells the colonial minister that he had word of "Duluth arriving at his post with fifty men."[5]

Fort St. Joseph was called a "bastioned block-house of logs,"[6] with stockade, similar in size and form, no doubt, to the one constructed by Cadillac in 1701 at the founding of Detroit. Duluth garrisoned it with *coureurs de bois* who, the following spring, busied themselves sowing bushels of maize, or Indian corn,[7] which was later to prove a godsend to the garrison.

Duluth's post, established in that year of 1686, although not intended as a permanent settlement in the strict sense of the word was, nevertheless, the first settlement of white men on the St. Clair. It is possible that from that year the St. Clair River district was not uninhabited by white settlers for any substantial length of time, as the evolution of its history, especially the stories of its saw mills and fisheries and military establishments, will bear out.

---

5 Jenks, *op. cit.*, I, 88.

6 Thwaites note in Lahontan, *op. cit.*, I, xviii. Parkman in his *La Salle and the Discovery of the Great Northwest* (Boston: Little, Brown, 1878), p. 275, calls it a "palisade fort." The English called it a "Castle"—See James V. Campbell, *Outlines of the Political History of Michigan* (Detroit, 1876), p. 43.

7 Lahontan, *op. cit.*, I, 139, calls it "Turkey-Wheat." Thwaites in a footnote, p. 140, writes that this was because of "a vague notion that it was first found in Turkey."

Duluth stayed at his fort only a short time, but Black River, running through Port Huron, carried the name River à de Lude (or duLuth) for many years,[8] a name by which it should still be known. There are documents in the Register of Deeds office in the County-City building in Port Huron showing deeds to property on which the name of Black River appears as River à de Lude. Special mention, then, should be made of the man who made this first habitation on the land that is the St. Clair River district.

Daniel Greysolon, Sieur Du Luth,[9] was a French explorer and fur trader, born at Saint-Germaine-en-Laye, about 1640.[10] As an officer in the French army, he had taken part in the campaign in Flanders, and was present at the Battle of Senef in 1674—a battle where Father Hennepin had also served, as chaplain.

In that same year of 1674 Duluth came to Canada where several members of his family had preceded him, including his brother, Claude Greysolon de La Tourette—for whom Duluth named Fort La Tourette on Lake Michigan in 1683—and his cousins, Henry de Tonty, who had accompanied La Salle on his voyage in the *Griffin*, and Alphonse de Tonty, who was with Cadillac at the founding of Detroit.

After establishing Fort St. Joseph, Duluth joined Denonville in the latter's expedition against the Iroquois, and later, in 1689, fought with conspicuous courage and success in the Iroquois invasion of Montreal. In 1695 he was in command at Fort Frontenac. Of his long years of exploration in the Northwest, twelve were spent in the Lake Superior and Minnesota regions. The city of Duluth, Minnesota perpetuates his name. He died in Montreal in 1710 and was buried in the Church of the Recollects.

This "king of the *coureurs de bois*,"[11] and one of the leaders of the French regime in America, was noted not only for his

---

[8] As late as the nineteenth century the name was still used. It was shown as "River DeLude" in the 1817-1818 Bayfield survey map of Lake Erie.

[9] The name has been spelled by the French writers of the time in various ways, including "de Lude," "du l'Hut," "Dulhut," "Du Lac," "Du Lud," "Du Lut," and "Du Luth."

[10] Authorities differ as to date.

[11] Thwaites footnote in Lahontan, *op cit.*, I, 73.

courage[12] but for his fair dealings with the Indians. His courage was exemplified by his order to shoot to death two savages of the Chippewa tribe who, as it had been proved at a trial, murdered two Frenchmen on Lake Superior, the execution being carried out in the presence of a great gathering of excited savages and only a little more than half a dozen Frenchmen. Because of his intrepidity Duluth had for some thirty years been able to keep the Indians under control and loyal to the French.

Fort St. Joseph was built none too soon. The previous year a party of thirty English traders, under the Dutch leader Rooseboom, with Iroquois guides had penetrated as far as Mackinac where they had been captured by La Durantaye and their furs confiscated. But it was evident that a second trip by the English to Mackinac would be attempted.

In the meantime, Denonville, determined to stop the Iroquois in their attacks on his Indian allies and to punish them for helping the English traders, put into motion a plan of invasion of that tribe. He sent out orders to La Durantaye, commanding at Michilimackinac; to Henry de Tonty at Fort St. Louis, on the Illinois; to Duluth at Fort St. Joseph, at the foot of Lake Huron; and to Nicholas Perrot, working among the Indians of the Mississippi and Lake Michigan regions, to muster as many Frenchmen and Indians as possible and meet him at the "place of the Senecas."[13]

Fort St. Joseph became the half-way rendezvous point of the gathering forces on their way to Lake Ontario, and, according to the *Memoire* of Nicholas Perrot, another party of thirty English and Iroquois, under the leadership of Colonel Patrick MacGregory, was stopped "at the fort of M. de Lude situate at 'the Detroit.' "[14]

As it turned out Tonty sent his lieutenant, de La Forest, to

---

[12] Lahontan speaks of Duluth as a "Lions Gentleman, who is a Person of great Merit, and has done his King and his Country very considerable Services." *Op. cit.*, I, 133. Charlevoix referred to him as "one of the bravest officers the King has ever had in this Colony." See Parkman, *op. cit.*, p. 274.

[13] The Seneca village in Denonville's time was east of the Genesee River in Ontario Co., N. Y., and just south of the present city of Victor. The permanent village of the Senecas was near Niagara. See note by Thwaites, Lahontan, *op. cit.*, I, 127, 137.

[14] Jenks, *op. cit.*, I, 89.

communicate with other leaders and to advance with them, while he led his forces of *coureurs de bois* and some two hundred Indians across country by land to a point lower down near Lake St. Clair. Duluth, while waiting for word of his arrival at that place, played host to the converging leaders and their parties.

The St. Clair River region had never seen, with perhaps the exception of La Salle's party, and would never see again such a gathering of notables of the French regime in America—such men as La Durantaye, Nicholas Perrot, de La Forest, de Lisle, Duluth, the latter's lieutenant, de Beauvais, and the Jesuit, Father Jean Enjalran.

Added to this colorful array of Louis XIV's liegemen was the motley crowd of some one hundred and eighty *coureurs de bois* and many hundreds of Indians, including the Ottawa, Huron, Winnebago, Fox, Menomonie, Kickapoo, Sioux, and Mascoutin tribes. Moreover, also at the fort was Rooseboom's captured party of twenty-nine white men and five Mohawks and Mohicans brought down by La Durantaye from Mackinac, and MacGregory's captured party, including his Iroquois guides and a considerable number of Ottawa and Huron prisoners whom the Iroquois had captured.

It was typical that the capture of the Englishmen and the Iroquois should be an occasion for celebration by the Indian allies of the French while mobilization was going on at Fort St. Joseph. Fortified by the rum and brandy found with the English trade goods taken with the captives, the savages celebrated for several days with continuous panegyrics intermingled with wild dancing, singing, drumming and unearthly yelling—a constant, uproarious din that echoed and reechoed across Lake Huron and the St. Clair River.

Finally, the distraught Duluth—tired out with the confusion and uproar of the savage and unpredictable celebrators, whose ranting and yelping might easily, at the slightest provocation, turn into war-whoops against the French—received and welcomed the word sent up to him by canoe from Tonty that he had arrived on the strait.

Giving orders to advance immediately, the great flotilla of canoes was made ready for the descent of the St. Clair River to the final

23

mobilization on Lake Ontario. And as the flotilla glided down-stream, accompanied by the shouts of the Indians and the chanting of the rowers, the little bastioned Fort St. Joseph remained in peaceful silence in charge of a handful of *coureurs de bois* to await the return of Duluth and Tonty, and the coming of Baron Lahontan, who was to be the fort's second and last commandant.

Lahontan at Fort St. Joseph

After the expedition against the Iroquois, which was moderately successful in that it destroyed the Seneca villages, Denonville, having other plans for Duluth ordered the youthful explorer Baron Lahontan[15] to take over command of Fort St. Joseph. He would accompany Duluth, who was returning to see to the crop of Indian corn he had had planted the previous spring, and to pick up supplies he had left in the fort. Denonville's reason for Lahontan's appointment, according to Lahontan himself, was that he "understood the Language of the Savages."[16]

This order to take command of Fort St. Joseph was a bitter disappointment to the Baron, who had but recently been promised a leave by the Ministry at Versailles to go home to France to look after the tangled affairs of his estate. But there was nothing for Lahontan to do but to comply with the governor's wishes. This was fortunate for posterity. Had he not taken the command, we should have been deprived of the lively account of the young explorer's adventures in the wilds of North America, and in the St. Clair River district in particular. His various accounts, mostly in the form of letters to an anonymous correspondent, were published in 1703 under the title, *New Voyages to North-America.*

---

[15] Louis Armand de Lom d'Arce, Baron de Lahontan, born in 1666 in the old province of Bearn, South France, was a French soldier, writer, and explorer in North America, and a "Hunts-Man" according to his own description. He came to Canada in 1683, being billeted in Beaupré and Montreal, and before assuming command at Fort St. Joseph had taken part in La Barre's unfortunate expedition against the Iroquois near the mouth of the Famine River (Salmon River). In 1693 he quit his post as "King's lieutenant" and returned to his native Bearn, after which he spent the rest of his life in exile, mostly in Holland and Portugal, dying in 1715.

[16] Lahontan, *op. cit.*, I, 132.

Duluth and Tonty tarried but a few days at the post before going on—Duluth to a further scouting expedition up the Ottawa against the Senecas, and Tonty to Fort St. Louis on the Illinois, where he was to learn for the first time of the murder (in Texas) of La Salle, his friend and leader, which had occurred in the spring of that year.

The young twenty-one year old commandant, even though under compulsion, rather enjoyed his stay at Fort St. Joseph. An avid sportsman, he had his fill of hunting the deer and bear, catching whitefish with hooks and nets in both summer and winter —in the latter season cutting holes in the ice as they do today in the Anchor Bay region—and bringing down the wild turkey, the teal, the swan, and the partridge.

He also spent much time in reading. A student of the classics, he enjoyed, through their writings, "the company of the honest old Gentlemen that liv'd in former Ages"[17]—the works of such as Homer and Anacreon and his "dear Lucian," whom he called his "inseparable companions." He should have had the works of Aristotle with him, too, he laments, had not his canoe been too crowded to allow the bulky works of that gentleman. A remarkable library in the wilds at the foot of the Lake of the Hurons in the seventeenth century.

While at the little Fort St. Joseph the young baron no doubt faithfully kept his *Journal,* drew many of the sketches, planned his maps and made copious notes for his letters sent out later from Michilimackinac—all of which appeared in his *Voyages.*

Lahontan's somewhat cynical philosophy, it has been said, was at least a generation in advance of his time, precluding that of Voltaire or Rousseau. In fact, Rousseau, as well as the later French romanticist, Chateaubriand, are said to have borrowed some of their ideas from Lahontan.[18]

His famous account of his explorations, entertaining if not always in good taste, and informative if not always accurate—as with his claim to have discovered the mythical River Long—not only adds greatly to our knowledge of the Indians, but gives interesting additional sketches to the literary portraits of some

---

17 *Ibid.,* p. 116.
18 Thwaites note, *op. cit.,* I, xlviii.

of the renowned French leaders, and provides us with the little we know of life at Fort St. Joseph and its environs.

Of great interest, too, are his maps accompanying *Voyages*, which show the location of Fort St. Joseph at the head of the St. Clair River on the west side. On one which shows Lake St. Clair, he wrote the name with the feminine spelling, "Claire," which most French travelers and writers used. And like Hennepin and the Sulpicians and Cadillac, and all the early travelers on the St. Clair River, Lahontan felt constrained to write about the beauty of the strait and the abundance of wild fruit and game in the region.

> You cannot imagine the pleasant prospect of this Streight, and of the little Lake; for their banks are cover'd with all sorts of wild Fruit-Trees. 'Tis true, the want of Agriculture sinks the agreeableness of the Fruit; but their plenty is very surprising. We spy'd no other animals upon the Shoar, but Herds of Harts, and Roe-bucks; And when we came to little Islands, we scour'd 'em, in order to oblige these Beasts to cross over to the Continent, upon which they offering to swim over, were knock'd on the head by our Canow-men that were planted all around the Islands.[19]

With the coming of an early and severe winter, however, and with rumors of impending Iroquoin raids, some apprehension began to mar the commandant's days, causing restlessness. When Lahontan had first taken over command at the fort he had sent two canoes to Mackinac, under guard of two soldiers, with tobacco—"a great Roll of Tobacco of 200 weight"[20]—to procure more corn and other necessities for himself and his detachment. Duluth had given him the tobacco before he left, telling him that soldiers could more easily purchase corn from the Indians in exchange for tobacco than for any other commodity.

The soldiers did not return from Michilimackinac until late November, and had it not been for the "Turkey-Wheat" harvested earlier, and for four young Canadians who had stopped to pass the winter with him and who were expert hunters, the garrison might have suffered from hunger.

---

[19] Lahontan, *op. cit.*, I, 139.
[20] *Ibid.*, p. 140.

26

The soldiers when they returned also brought back with them Father Claude Aveneau,[21] the Jesuit who was to be noted for his twenty-five years of labor instructing the Miamis. That provisions throughout the winter remained somewhat scarce at the post might be deduced from Lahontan's wry observation that Father Aveneau "found no occasion to trouble himself with preaching up Abstinence from Meat in the time of Lent."[22] One would also infer from the observation that Father Aveneau spent the winter of 1687-88 at the head of the St. Clair River as chaplain at Fort St. Joseph—the first "resident" priest in the St. Clair River district.

In December a party of Hurons who had successfully attacked an encampment of some sixty Iroquois beaver hunters in the vicinity of Fort Niagara, stopped at the fort with their prisoners, and from one of the captives Lahontan was given to understand that the main body of Iroquois, to the number of eight hundred, and who then blocked Fort Niagara, intended to appear at Lahontan's post "without delay."[23]

This inforation greatly irritated the young commandant, not so much that he feared being attacked by the Iroquois—for as Lahontan himself said, although the "Savages never (fought) fairly, neither (did) they ever attempt to pull up Palissadoes"—but he knew that their close presence might starve them out by "cramping their Huntsmen in their due range."[24]

He used precaution against running out of provisions by persuading the Hurons to assist his own hunters in providing meat and fowl, but as soon as the Hurons took their leave the hunting was at an end and the gates of the fort were kept shut.

As it turned out the expected invasion of the Iroquois never materialized, nor did much of anything else in the way of diversion or excitement for the young adventurer, and by the end of the long and severe winter the bored Lahontan had made up

---

[21] Father Claude Aveneau came to Canada in 1685 and was assigned the next year to the Ottawa mission at Mackinac. "He passed the remainder of his life in the West, for many years serving in the Miami mission, and finally dying at Quebec in 1711." Thwaites note, *op. cit.*, I, 140.

[22] Lahontan, *op. cit.*, I, 140.

[23] *Ibid.*, p. 142.

[24] *Ibid.*

his mind to go to Michilimackinac on the excuse of having to buy corn from the Hurons and Ottawas to replenish the fort's supplies. He accordingly left some soldiers to guard the fort in his absence and started out on the first day of April for Michilimackinac, arriving there seventeen days later.

On the second of June Lahontan set out from Mackinac for Sault Ste. Marie to secure the needed corn. But once there his love for adventure persuaded him to join with the Ottawas, Hurons, and a tribe of the Chippewas called the Saulters, in a rather questionable raid into the country of the Iroquois, stopping, on the way, at Fort St. Joseph long enough to leave the sacks of corn and to rest for a day.[25]

The incursion into the country of the Iroquois continued during July and most of August, and at the end of the forays, Lahontan, accompanied by his detachment and the remnants of the raiding tribes, started back for Fort St. Joseph, arriving there on August 24. Also accompanying the aggregation back to the fort was a party of Miami prisoners who had been retaken from the Iroquois.

Lahontan, on landing at the Rapids, was surprised to see his fort "cramm'd with Savages,"[26] including a party of eighty Miamis under the command of Michitonka who had returned from the Fort of Niagara. The Miamis, in turn, were astonished—and delighted—to see their own countrymen arrive with the delegation. In fact, so happy were the countrymen to see one another that the greetings continued in a great celebration well on into the night.

Lahontan later wrote about the meeting to his anonymous correspondent:

> The joyful Meeting filled the Air with Acclamations, and Panegyricks rung all about to an extravagant degree. I wish, Sir, you had been there to partake of so fine a Show: had you been present, you would have join'd with me in owning that all our French Rhetorick cannot reach such pithy and significant Figures, especially upon the score of Hyperbole's, as made up the bulk of the Harangues and Songs that these poor People utter'd with Rapture and Transport.[27]

---

[25] July 1, 1688.
[26] Lahontan, *op. cit., I*, 161.
[27] *Ibid.*, p. 162.

The chief of the Miamis, Michitonka, had brought news to Lahontan of the disastrous scurvy epidemic at Fort Niagara, and of that fort's possible abandonment, as well as the rumor that Fort Frontenac had been equally hard hit by the scurvy. He had also brought the news that Denonville was negotiating a peace with the Iroquois.

Fort St. Joseph Abandoned

Lahontan considered at length the news reported by the Miamis and concluded that it would be expedient for him to abandon his post and embark for Mackinac—the summation of his conclusions having been given in this wise in his *Voyages:*

> Being informed of all these Circumstances, I consulted with the three different Nations that were then posted in my Fort. After a mature Reflection upon the Intelligence that was laid before 'em, they came to this Resolution; That since the Marquis de Denonville had a mind to clap up a Peace, and the Fort of Niagara was abdicated, the Fort I then commanded would be of no use: that since I had neither Provisions nor Ammunition for above two Months, I should be oblig'd at the end of these two Months to retreat to the Place from which I now write; that at that time of the Year our Navigation would be uneasy and dangerous: that in regard I lay under an indispensable necessity of making my Retreat, 'twas of no great moment whether I march'd off two Months sooner or later; and, in fine, that since I had receiv'd no fresh Orders, nor no Succors, 'twas my Business to go off along with them. This Resolution, which was a sufficient Argument to sway me, afforded matter of joy to the Soldiers, who were afraid of being oblig'd to a more rigorous course of Abstinence in that Post than they had formerly undergone; for the measures of a critical Abstinence do not sit well upon a Soldiers Stomach. In fine, pursuant to our joint Resolution, we set fire to the Fort on the 27th, and embarked that same day . . .[28]

Although Lahontan wrote that he set fire to Fort St. Joseph there seems to be no record to show that it actually burned down. It is conceivable that a rain storm, following the firing of the

---

[28] *Ibid.,* p. 163.

post, may have prevented it from being completely destroyed. And it is possible that if it did burn, it was repaired. In any event, contrary to the general assumption that Lahontan's abandonment and firing of the post ended the Franch occupation at the mouth of Lake Huron, there are indications that this fort which was originally erected by the Sieur Duluth in 1686, may have continued well on into the turn of the century.

Several instances have been cited showing a possible continuation of the fort. In a French memoir, written about 1689 and quoted in Jenks' *St. Clair County, Michigan,* there is the note:

> If the Iroquois be in the English interest, it will be almost impossible to maintain the establishment at the Detroit without very considerable expense, to garrison it two or three hundred picked men at least, would have to be sent thither.[29]

And in 1691, in a French document recommending measures for the better defense of Canada, and also quoted in Jenks' history, is the advice:

> It is well to preserve the posts we occupy in their country, namely, Fort St. Louis of Louisiana, Detroit and Michilimaquina. These can be kept up at a very trifling expense, which will not be of less utility to us than if it were more considerable.[30]

Mr. Jenks himself, in posing the possibility of Fort St. Joseph being in continuation at least until 1700, states the following:

> In 1694 at a conference or council between the French and Indians, the Detroit is spoken of as a fine rendezvous and in 1700 a council is held by M. de Longeuil, commanding for the French king at Detroit with the four nations belonging to his post, these four nations being the Ottawas, Hurons, Potawatomies and Mississauges. It must be remembered that the word Detroit at that time had no reference whatever to the locality of the present city of that name, but covered the whole waterway from Lake Erie to Lake Huron, and these references make it probable that there was a continuance until 1700 of the post erected by Duluth.[31]

---

[29] Jenks, *op. cit.,* I, 90.
[30] *Ibid.*
[31] *Ibid.*

There are those who contend that these references are in relation to a post established at the lower end of the Strait—at or near the present city of Detroit—about the same time that Fort St. Joseph was built.[32] Reports of Tonty and of La Salle are also cited to clinch the probability of such a military station.

In any event, the next famous Frenchman to traverse the St. Clair River was Antoine Laumet de Lamothe, Sieur de Cadillac, on his way from Montreal to found the city of Detroit in the summer of 1701. Ordinarily the route from Montreal to Detroit would have been up the St. Lawrence, across Lake Ontario to the Niagara River, over the portage at that point and then along Lake Erie to the Detroit River—the route Madame Cadillac followed a few months later to join her husband. But to avoid stirring up the temperamental Iroquois the Cadillac party was ordered by the ministry to take the Ottawa River route. And so it was that the twenty-five heavily loaded and brightly colored bark and cedar canoes containing Cadillac's "hundred men"— priests, officers, soldiers and colonists—came down through Lake Huron and the St. Clair River.

There is no conclusive evidence that Cadillac and his retinue beached their canoes and came ashore to visit the ruins of Fort St. Joseph, but it certainly would not have been a visit of idle curiosity if he had stopped. On the contrary. Had not a fellow countryman, Daniel Greysolon, Sieur Duluth, built and commanded the fort fifteen years before? And had not a brother Gascon, Baron Lahontan, commanded there, too?

Certainly Alphonse de Tonty, second in command of the expedition, had a special interest in visiting the spot. His brother, Henry de Tonty, had been at the fort with Duluth and Lahontan, and had also walked on the same shore over twenty years before with La Salle and Father Hennepin when the *Griffin* was becalmed very near there in 1679. In addition to that, the Sieur Duluth was his cousin.

One wonders what was in the mind of Cadillac as he gazed about him that July day, and one wonders, too, why he did not choose that end of the Strait for his future colony—his planned dynasty. But the consensus of authorities is that the astute Cadillac

---

[32] See "Date of the Detroit Settlement," by James V. Campbell in *Pioneer and Hist. Coll., Mich.,* VIII (1885), 412-415.

realized that the region at the upper end of the Strait did not lead across by portage trail (as did the lower) to the more distant tribes of Indians he hoped to bring to trade at Detroit. And this advantage, as one historian pointed out, was what later "created Detroit as a great freight and manufacturing entrepôt."[33]

The expedition, if it did stop, did not tarry long; it was imperative that Cadillac reach his destination, make a clearing, and build a stockade and dwellings before the winter set in. One can imagine the command given to resume the voyage, and picture the canoes once more gliding swiftly and noiselessly down stream, the wet paddles catching and flashing the sun, the strokes timed to the cadence of a gay boating song. With the completion of that journey the history of Detroit was to begin.

Beaver Dams and Fossil Trees

An interesting feature of one of Lahontan's maps[34] accompanying the 1703 edition of his *Voyages* is the number of times he designates locations for beaver hunting, indicating to us the prevalence of the beaver in the St. Clair River region, on both the American and Canadian sides.

Wherever a brook trickled through a valley the beaver would bar its course with a strong, compact dam, to secure sufficient backwater for a pond on which to build his home. This was discernible as late as 1884, in Port Huron especially. There the beaver had built dams to obstruct the flow of Indian Creek, which had its source in the southwest end of town near the Grand Trunk Tunnel Depot and which meandered northeasterly to its outlet in Black River near Seventh Street Bridge.

One of these dams, said to be no less extensive than the great dams in the Upper Peninsula and in Nova Scotia, commenced near the junction of what are now Chestnut and Eleventh streets,[35] curved in its serpentine course across Chestnut to White and Twelfth streets, and then continued toward Thirteenth Street

---

[33] Agnes G. Laut, *Cadillac* (Bobbs-Merrill, 1931), p. 137.

[34] Lahontan, *op cit.*, I, facing p. 156.

[35] Chestnut and Union Streets, etc., still show elevations made by these dams. Although Indian Creek disappeared long ago, many residents still remember the floods caused by this creek during the spring freshets, and also that foot bridges were required on several streets over the deeper depressions.

where it was lost in the fields and sand hills beyond; the dam is believed to have flooded most of the area of Port Huron south of Union Street.

The antiquity of this dam can be imagined by the fact that trees had sprouted and died on its summit after reaching an age of perhaps half a dozen centuries. The pioneers at the turn of the nineteenth century found stumps on the edge of the ridge of the dam, in the vicinity of Union Street, which showed over 300 annulations of yearly growth, and yet the dam itself must have been centuries old before the seeds from which these trees grew took root.

Ruins of a series of dams were also found along the banks of St. Clair River at the foot of Lake Huron (probably seen by Lahontan) at what is now Pine Grove Park, and reported by James D. Doty, a member of the Schoolcraft Expedition of 1820, who referred in his report to the strata of blue clay, sand and fossil wood as "made land."[36]

At that time the bank of the river just below Fort Gratiot was thirty to 40 feet high and nearly perpendicular. The rapidly flowing current, aided in winter and spring by immense masses of sharp ice forced against the shore, had slowly gouged out the bank and opened to view a number of trees which had been felled by the beaver centuries before, and which appeared to be in a perfect state of preservation.

Ten years earlier an anonymous poet, evidently impressed by his discovery of these same trees, wrote a lengthy poem entitled "The Fossil Trees," which was published in the Detroit Gazette in the spring of 1830. The following are stanzas from that poem:

At Huron's foot there is a lofty bank
Some thirty feet or more of elevation,
Which worn away by chafing waves has sunk
And left a wall of sand on clay foundation.

These chafing waves have rent the seal away
Which through long centuries has kept from view
The changeful freaks of earth's primeval day,
When land and water other bounderies knew.

---

[36] Doty's report in H. R. Schoolcraft's *Narrative Journal of Travels*, ed. by Mentor L. Williams (Michigan State College Press, 1953), p. 405. Schoolcraft, and others, also mention the same formations.

Here where alluvial sands a bed have found,
Usurpers o'er the clay or yielding waves;
Trees that in earliest ages wav'd around,
Are slowly peeping from their ancient graves.

C. M. Stockton, pioneer resident of Port Huron, visiting the same site with officers from Fort Gratiot in the 1850s, found uncovered in the blue clay, "a tangle of cedars varying in diameter from four to twelve inches, in excellent condition and minus the outer bark."[37] And, as late as 1939, a number of these fossil trees were found when the piers of the Blue Water International Bridge were laid on the American side of the St. Clair River.

---

[37] Newspaper clipping, "Report of the annual meeting of the St. Clair County Pioneer Society," (Clipping undated, probably 1897). Also in article by C. M. Stockton, "Reminiscences of Port Huron," *Pioneer and Hist. Coll., Mich.,* XXVIII (1897-98), 111.

Chapter IV

THE CROSS OF ST. GEORGE AND ST. ANDREW

There has been a general belief that since Fort St. Joseph was but a transient military station there was no continuance of habitation by white man in the area after Lahontan's abandonment of the post. In fact, it has been stated that after Fort St. Joseph ceased to exist, "nearly a century passed before the site of Port Huron was again occupied."[1]

But later sources have come to light showing that there was a saw mill on Black River as early as 1749,[2] and where there was a mill there must have been a certain amount of habitation within the district. It is also certain that there was a saw mill on the St. Clair River, at what was later known as Bunce Creek, prior to 1740, and tradition has it that there was a mill on the same spot about 1690.[3]

Let us look ahead now, however, to the St. Clair River area under a new power, Great Britain, and see how a settlement in the form of a fortified post, on Pine River at its confluence with the St. Clair, came to be.

The Treaty of Paris (1763), following the surrender of Quebec and Montreal and other French possessions to Great Britain, brought an end to the French and Indian War. But in the aftermath of that war, the Indians also chose this time most forcefully to assert their rights to the lands of the Great Lakes area—an area which as part of the Northwest Territory had also come into the hands of the British.

The Indians were led in their attempt to regain their lands from the hated English by the Ottawa chief Pontiac. It was an ambitious plan; on a given signal, with one great concentrated effort, every

---

[1] Jenks, *op. cit.,* I, 139.
[2] To be dealt with later, at length, under PART THREE, The Lumbering Era.
[3] *Op. cit.,* I, 364.

35

British garrison on the Lakes would be destroyed. The uprising began with the murder of several Englishmen on the St. Clair River bank close to the site of old Fort St. Joseph. Pontiac himself was in charge of the abortive attempt to take the fort at Detroit, while several parties of his warriors were encamped in numerous and advantageous points along the Detroit and St. Clair Rivers. The fort on Pine River (in present St. Clair) was the result of that uprising.

Murder and Cannibalism on the St. Clair

In early May of 1763, just a few weeks before the massacre at Michilimackinac and but a day before Pontiac's attempt to take Gladwin's fort at Detroit, a large bateau, followed by a dugout canoe, came up the St. Clair River carrying a party of Englishmen taking soundings in the river. In the bateau were Capt. Charles Robertson of the 77th Regiment, six soldiers, two sailors who manned the bateau, and a seventeen-year old Scot tourist, John Rutherford, who had accepted Robertson's invitation to accompany them.[4] In the canoe were a nobleman, Sir Robert Davers, on a "voyage of curiosity," and his Pawnee slave, a young boy.

Robertson was under orders from Major Gladwin, commanding at Detroit, to determine whether the St. Clair River route to Lake Huron was navigable for vessels of greater burden than the bateau, vessels which could more quickly and conveniently provide the distant posts, such as Michilimackinac, with provisions, troops, and military stores.

The English party on its way up the river had passed several Indian villages, but as there were few, if any, Indians in sight it

---

[4] The story of the murders and act of cannibalism perpetrated at the head of the St. Clair River was later told by Rutherford in a letter to his cousin, Sir John Nesbit, who was in New York. The original manuscript seems to be missing, but three copies of it were made before it was lost. First published obscurely in the nineteenth century, John Rutherford's *Narrative of a Captivity* appears with *The Siege of Detroit of 1763, The Journal of Pontiac's Conspiracy*, ed. by M. M. Quaife (Chicago, Donnelly, 1958) (The Lakeside Classics). It was published recently in the April, 1958 *American Heritage*, IX, No. 3, 65-81. Some details of the affair were also told in signed statements, following the uprising, at proceedings of a court inquiry held by Major Gladwin. See "Gladwin Manuscripts," *Pioneer and Hist. Coll., Mich.* XXVII (1896), 605-680).

was supposed they were out on hunting parties. They were, in reality, congregating at prearranged locations along the strait to intercept any traveling parties of English. Many of the Saginaw Chippewas had already assembled at the mouth of the St. Clair River on the eminence overlooking the Rapids.

On the early morning of May 6, the party stopped at a point on the river now known as Bunce Creek in present-day Marysville, and which Rutherford called *"La Pinnierre,"*[5] to deliver a few barrels of flour to French Canadians who were building a saw mill. These men were joined by several other wood-cutters who had been felling pine timber in the distant woods—men by the names of Clairmont, Campeau, Massack (Marsac), and Desnoyers—who told that a number of Indians had been there in the early

---

[5] Many sources, including Dr. Quaife, say that *La Pinnierre* was the pinery on Pine River. I prefer to think it was at Bunce Creek, for several reasons. This spot was favored for a saw mill by a number of generations of Frenchmen. Tradition has it that there was a mill there as early as 1690. Judge James V. Campbell in one of his articles speaks of a saw mill well known on the site prior to 1742, and Duperon Baby built one there in 1780. In his *St. Clair County, Michigan,* Mr. Jenks wrote that there were still traces (1912) of two dams in evidence older than the Bunce dam (1818), which were probably those of the latter two mentioned. Patrick Sinclair who owned the pinery on Pine River did not arrive in Detroit until 1763 to take charge of the navigation of the Lakes, and it is highly improbable that with all of his important duties he would have found time to begin building his saw mill as early as May of that year. But what is more significant, Rutherford, in his *Narrative*, says that since it was still morning Captain Robertson, despite the warnings of the Frenchmen, decided to go "six miles farther," and take soundings at the mouth of the river. It is of interest to note that the distance from Bunce Creek to the mouth of the St. Clair River is about six miles, while it is around seventeen miles from St. Clair (the site of Sinclair's Pinery). And to further stress the likelihood that the saw mill was at the site of Bunce Creek, a Mr. Clairmont, testifying at a court of inquiry before Major Gladwin, in the presence of Captain Grant and Lieutenant Hay, told that he was one of the wood-cutters at the pinery when the English arrived around eight o'clock in the morning and were warned about the Indians. About two hours after they continued on the journey up the river, Clairmont testified, he "heard the report of some guns toward the Lake," and between three and four o'clock in the afternoon the Indians came down to the pinery and "brought their scalps." The report of guns could hardly have been heard if the woodcutters had been at Pine River. The Clairmont quotes are from "The Gladwin Manuscripts," *Pioneer and Hist. Coll., Mich.,* XXVII (1896), 663.

hours of that morning and that they had "sung a War Song" in the cabin of Mr. Massack.[6] With evident concern they warned the British party that "all the nations of Indians around were in league to take up the hatchet against the English," that they were, in fact, aware of Robertson's journey up the river, and that at that very moment "were waiting six miles up the river to seize and destroy them."[7]

In spite of the warning and the still further protestations of the French Canadians, Captain Robertson decided to go the six miles to the mouth of the river before returning to Detroit. The order was given to ply the oars, and when they reached a point about where the Civic Center is now in Port Huron, the Englishmen saw that some three or four hundred Indians had congregated along the river bank. The swift current in the rapids forced the rowers to keep close to the shore, making little time; in fact, the Indians seemed able to walk along the shore faster than they could row.

The savages—men, women and children—crowded close to the riverbank shouting greetings, calling the Englishmen "Brothers," and urging them to come ashore and get some of the fish and maple sugar that the squaws, pressing forward, held up for them to see. The Englishmen refused the invitation but did give them some of their bread and tobacco when the Indians asked for it.

This demonstration of friendliness, as the Englishmen were to find out to their horror, was only a ruse to distract them, for while the women and children were crowding forward, creating a sort of curtain which hid what went on behind them, the men had filed silently away. When out of sight the warriors had removed their blankets and ornaments and were now naked and painted red and black, making a hideous sight, and had posted themselves on the bluff or elevation above the Rapids[8] by the time Robertson's party reached that point.

Then it was that the squaws and children, who had been following along, ran off as fast as they could, and as soon as they

---

[6] *Ibid.* The name more commonly appears under the spelling "Marsac," but also appears as "Marsacre" and "Marsaque."

[7] Rutherford, *op. cit.*, p. 220.

[8] Near the southeast end of Pine Grove Park in present-day Port Huron.

were out of the way the Indians began firing upon the Englishmen, killing two of the soldiers. Captain Robertson was wounded by the first volley of shots, and was giving orders to sheer off when a second bullet killed him.

Young Rutherford took the helm and endeavored to bring the boat around, but the remaining soldiers and sailors, in a panic and trying to shield themselves from the enemy's fire, were unable to ply the oars. The Indians, seeing that Robertson was killed and that all was in confusion, rushed forward and boarded the bateau, yelling their terrible *"death hollow."*

Rutherford, and the others not killed, were seized by the hair— each by his "future master"[9]—and dragged from the boat, through the water and up onto the shore, along with the bodies of Robertson and the two soldiers. The Indians then scalped Robertson and the soldiers and stripped them naked, and one of the savages, presumably the one who killed Roberston, then dressed in the captain's clothes.

In the meantime Sir Robert Davers had attempted to flee to the opposite shore in his canoe but was brought down by the rifles of two savages firing simultaneously. His body fell into the river but was dragged out and brought ashore where it was decapitated. The Indians then buried the body of Sir Robert, and also his head after the scalp was taken off. His Pani (Pawnee) slave was taken prisoner. Young Rutherford, who was also taken prisoner, was claimed by the Chippewa chief Perwash,[10] who had first seized him, and was taken by him to his hut where he was made a slave of the chief's wife.

That evening Captain Robertson's body was cut up, roasted and eaten[11] at a great celebration amidst hideous yelling, dancing and singing. Later that night some of the Indians, including the one dressed in Captain Robertson's clothes and now drunk from the liquor plundered from the bateau, came to Perwash's hut and tried to seize Rutherford—the *"English dog"*—but he was

---

[9] According to the custom of the Chippewas "whoever first seizes a captive by his hair, to him he belongs, and none may take him from him." See Rutherford's *Narrative.*

[10] Rutherford calls him "Peewash."

[11] There was a superstition among the Indians that the eating of the flesh of the slain would give them great courage and success in battle.

protected by the chief's wife and hid by her until he could be smuggled into another hut to await the end of the orgy.

The next morning Perwash's son brought a small piece of Robertson's body to the hut, and Perwash, after roasting it on a stick at the fire, tried to persuade Rutherford to eat it. But with a surprising amount of diplomacy and discretion in one so young—Rutherford telling Perwash that he wanted to obey him in everything, and would do so even in that instance if he insisted, but that eating Robertson's flesh would be repugnant to him since he had been his friend—he avoided doing as he was requested by his master.[12]

What was the ultimate fate of the remaining soldiers taken captive with Rutherford seems to be shrouded in mystery, but it is presumed that they were murdered, along with hundreds of other prisoners, during the atrocities later committed at Detroit, where they were all eventually taken.

In the weeks that followed Rutherford's capture he had been made, to all appearances, a full-fledged savage, having undergone many terrible experiences.[13] By the end of May, Perwash—who in the meantime had formally adopted Rutherford into his family in place of a son who had died—and the other Indians made preparations to leave their village at the head of the St. Clair River and join the rest of Pontiac's savages encamped within a few miles of Detroit. After a four-day journey, they reached the encampment.

There Rutherford's life was no less arduous. His duties included the planting of a large field of maize, pumpkins and other vegetables in the broiling sun, with but a breechcloth on, getting his back and shoulders so badly burned he was "one continuous blister." And here, too, he was a witness to such atrocities as the murders of eight Englishmen, including a 12-year-old drummer boy of the Rangers, all of whom were shot or tomahawked to death, after which their bodies were thrown into the water so they

---

[12] The soldiers captured with him had not fared so well, for, according to what one of them told Rutherford while they were still in the Indian village, he was forced to eat of Robertston's body.

[13] One of these was a seven-day siege with dysentery due to a diet consisting only of fish, without bread or salt, which weakened him to the point of being helpless, and during which time he was consoled by the assurance of his captors that he would not be eaten if he died while suffering from such a disorder.

would float down past the fort where their countrymen would see them.

Rutherford made one more journey with his "family" to the Indian village at the mouth of the St. Clair River where he had first been taken prisoner—this because of the scarcity of provisions at Detroit. But on the return to Detroit, near the end of August and after further near-tragic adventures, he made his escape on the sloop Michigan, which was eventually wrecked near Catfish (Eighteen-Mile) Creek on the south shore of Lake Erie. There, again eluding pursuing Indians, he made his way to Niagara and finally to his uncle, Walter Rutherford, in New York, where he decided he would never again "tempt fortune" in the woods.[14]

Patrick Sinclair Builds a Fort

In the meantime, after the atrocities at the head of the St. Clair River, Lieutenant Patrick Sinclair took action. He persuaded the British auhorities that a fort midway between Lakes Huron and St. Clair would facilitate his duties of providing supplies for the forts, would control the river as far as the Indians were concerned, and serve as a trading post as well.

Lieutenant Patrick Sinclair, who had entered the British army as ensign in 1758, had come to America in 1760 and three years later was in command of transporting supplies between Detroit and Mackinac. Singularly enough, Sinclair got along very well with the Indians, and on one of his early trips to Mackinac his appreciation of the beauty of the St. Clair River country, and his still greater appreciation of the value of its pine lands, prompted him to obtain a deed from the Indians of land two and a half miles along the St. Clair River, and the same distance in depth.

The land was described in the deed[15] as being on the northwest side of the St. Clair River between Lake Huron and Lake St. Clair, one mile above the mouth of Pine River and ending one

14 Little is known of Rutherford's later life. He is said to have enlisted in the famed 42nd Highland Regiment (Black Watch) after he returned to New York, and to have fought with that regiment in the American Revolution, attaining the rank of captain. After thirty years of service as a career officer he returned to Scotland, where he died in 1830 at the age of 84.

15 The dead, dated July 27, 1768, was signed "by Massigiash and Ottawa, chiefs of the Chippewa nation, in the presence of 15 Indians of that Nation and

(Continued on page 42)

mile below Pine River. The area encompassed within these boundaries would have been four thousand acres.[16]

Colonel John Bradstreet, who arrived in Detroit in August of 1764, authorized Sinclair to build the fort "for the Security and convenience of Lodging and Provision for the Vessels which may hereafter Navigate on Lake Huron,"[17] and the spot chosen by Sinclair was just south of the mouth of Pine River on his tract of land. This fort, which was "to be abandoned at the peace to be completed"[18] between Great Britain and the United States

(Continued from page 41)

of George Turnbull, Captain of the Second Battalion of the 60th Regiment, George Archbold, Lieutenant, and ensigns Robert Johnson and John Amiel of the same Regiment, John Lewis Gage, Ensign of the 31st Regiment, and Lieut. John Hay of the 60th Regiment, Commissary of Indian affairs." "The deed was not registered and when Sinclair returned to England (1785) he took the deed with him." See W. L. Jenks, *Patrick Sinclair* (printed pamphlet) (1914), p. 10, in Jenks Collection, Port Huron Public Library. Same biographical sketch is also in *Pioneer and Hist. Coll., Mich.,* XXXIX (1915), 61-85.

[16] In the disposition of Sinclair's estate on Pine River when it was sold at auction (1788) and bought by Meldrum & Park, a firm of merchants and traders of Detroit, the latter obtained another deed (purportedly in confirmation of the original deed) from twenty-six Chippewas, conveying a tract of land "ten miles along the St. Clair River by four miles in depth or about six times as much land"—which is why many sources quote Sinclair's tract of land at 24,000 acres. The Meldrum & Park deed was not recognized by the United States as a conveyance of title but "the possessions taken under it enabled Meldrum & Park and their grantees to obtain patents from the United States in 1810 to nearly five thousand acres." See W. L. Jenks, *Patrick Sinclair,* pp. 10, 13. Actually, Sinclair's original deed did not convey any legal title, either. King George III of Great Britain in his proclamation of October 3rd, 1763 establishing the province of Quebec, had "expressly prohibited the obtaining of deeds from the Indians except under special license, and through certain officials." Sinclair's deed did not meet with these particular specifications. See *Ibid.,* p. 11.

[17] Bradstreet letter to Sinclair, September 10, 1764. Letter in William Clements Library, University of Michigan.

[18] Governor St. Clair in a letter to John Jay, Dec. 13, 1788 (*St. Clair Papers,* I, 101) says that Lord Dorchester had ordered "a Fort they call St. Clair on the American side of the strait, between the lake of that name and the Huron, which had been begun during the war and abandoned at the peace to be completed." See Jenks, *St. Clair County, Mich.,* I, 94, marginal notation. Sinclair later insisted that General Gage, commander-in-chief of the British forces in America approved of the fort and that it was "Impliedly assented to by the English government." *Ibid.,* 92.

and which was in existance for about twenty years before it fell into decay, had consisted of two barracks, one for soldiers and one for sailors, at least one brick building,[19] two blockhouses for cannon and small arms, and a wharf for drawing out and careening vessels.[20] All was enclosed within a stockade, and over the fort flew the flag bearing the cross of St. George and the Scottish cross of St. Andrew.

In 1768 Lieutenant Sinclair returned to England, where he was made a captain of his regiment, and where in 1775 he was appointed lieutenant-governor of Mackinac. However, owing to political complications and a ruling of the Continental Congress in 1776, it was not until 1779 that Sinclair reached his post at Mackinac to take over his duties—four and a half years after the date of his commission.

Sinclair was at Mackinac[21] until 1782, when he was recalled to Quebec to explain the extraordinary expenditures incurred during the removal of the fort from the mainland to the Island under his supervision, and he was never again to return to the St. Clair River area.[22]

---

[19] Rev. O. C. Thompson said that when "Judge Brewer came into the county" he saw a "chimney of one of the old fort buildings standing, twenty feet high." *History of St. Clair County, Michigan* (Chicago, 1883), p. 254. And W. L. Jenks quotes Judge Zephaniah Bunce as saying that when he came in 1817 there were "2 large chimneys standing." Jenks, *op. cit.*, 92, marginal note.

[20] Sinclair had built the fort more or less at his own expense, and when he requested the British government to reimburse him, General Gage, commanding at Detroit, refused, informing him that the government had not directed the construction and that Sinclair "could do with the improvements what he saw fit." Jenks, *Patrick Sinclair*, p. 29.

[21] While at Mackinac Sinclair had negotiated with the Chippewas for a deed which he obtained in May, 1781, and in which the chiefs of the Chippewa nation relinquished "to Lieut. Governor Sinclair for the behalf and use of the English King, the Island of Michilimackinac" for the consideration of £5,000, which was equal to $12,500. Jenks, *Patrick Sinclair*, p. 29.

[22] Sinclair took up his residence on the Isle of Orleans, where he remained until 1784 (pending the investigation of his accounts—the details of which were complicated and the outcome somewhat obscure, but which ended, presumably, by the Government paying the debts) when he was allowed to return to England. His difficulties here and in England seemed not to have interferred with his advancement in the British Army, as he became, in turn, major, lieutenant-colonel, major-general, and, lastly, lieutenant-general. This rank he held at the time of his death, which occurred at Lybster, Scotland, January 31, 1820 at the age of 84. See Jenks, *Patrick Sinclair* and Jenks, *St. Clair County, Michigan*, I, 92-94.

In all this time, however, and while at Mackinac, Sinclair had kept in touch with his properties on the St. Clair River, to which he referred in his correspondence as the "Pinery," or, as his "farm." There seems to be no record of who might have been looking after the property for him from 1769 to 1779 when he arrived at Mackinac, but in 1780 Francis Belcour, the British Indian agent at Detroit, was in charge. In May of that year Major E. S. De Peyster, the commanding officer at Detroit, advised Sinclair that his man was "at the Pinery," and that he would remain there "until a Vessel from Michilimackinac passes."[23]

Belcour was evidently not giving satisfaction, especially in regard to relations with the Indians in the vicinity, for in July of 1780 Maskeash,[24] one of the chiefs who had signed Sinclair's deed, with his wife and several other Indians of his band went up to Fort Mackinac on one of the government's vessels (probably the *Wellcome*), commanded by Alexander Harrow,[25] to ask that Jean Baptiste Point de (or du) Sable be appointed to take charge of the properties in place of Belcour.

The request was granted and we find Lieut. Gov. Sinclair, in a letter to a Mr. Guthrie, ordering him to "take charge of the Sloop *Wellcome*" from Mackinac to Detroit and to land "the Chief Markeash with his Band where he may require" after they got into the St. Clair River, and to "land Baptiste Point de Sable at the Pine River."[26]

Jean Baptiste Point de Sable,[27] who was referred to as a mulatto, and who called himself a "free Negro," had engaged in trade with Miami Indians in the region of Lake Michigan for many

[23] De Peyster letter to Sinclair dated May 18, 1780, *Pioneer and Hist. Coll., Mich.,* IX, 582.

[24] Also spelled "Massigiash," "Massigayash," "Musquash," "Mashquiash," "Maskiash," and "Markeash."

[25] To be dealt with, later, at length. See PART EIGHT, "Pioneers! O Pioneers!"

[26] Letter dated July 31, 1780, the Haldimand Papers, Letters of Sinclair, De Peyster, and others, *Pioneer and Hist. Coll., Mich.,* IX, 605.

[27] According to Dr. Milo M. Quaife, although Point de Sable's parentage was not known, there was "considerable reason for believing that he belonged, on his father's side, to the family of Dandonneau *dit* du Sable, one of the most noble in the annals of New France." Editor's note in Mrs. J. H. Kinzie, *Wau-Bun,* (Lakeside Press) (Chicago: Donnelly, 1932), p. 220.

years, until captured by the British and detained at Mackinac for being too sympathetic to the American rebels. His conduct while at Mackinac rather impressed Sinclair, it seems, and when the request came from Maskeash to send him to Fort Sinclair, he did so.

Although John Kinzie seems to have acquired the posthumous honor of "Father of Chicago,"—an honor which could easily go to Capt. John Whistler who built the first Fort Dearborn, the real beginning of civilized Chicago—Point de Sable is another logical candidate for the claim.

It was after Point de Sable's tenure at Fort Sinclair, where he held a position of considerable authority on the St. Clair River, that he engaged in trading at Peoria and Chicago (1784-1800), acquiring a considerable estate,[28] and also giving rise to the ancient local jest that the "first white man in Chicago was a negro."[29]

Point de Sable was at Fort Sinclair from the summer of 1780 until May of 1784, according to entries in an old Day Book and Ledger of the "Adventure" (or Enterprise) at the Pinery, which lists names, and dates, and items charged to accounts.[30] In the meantime, while Sinclair was living on the Isle of Orleans, he gave a power of attorney to Nicholas Boulvin (Boilvin) to take care of his estate on Pine River, and Boulvin, when he accepted the appointment of Indian agent for the United States Government, turned over his power of attorney to David Ross. Under the latter's supervision the property was sold at public auction to Meldrum and Park, Detroit merchants, who obtained a con-

<hr>

[28] The itemized bill of sale of Point de Sable's property to Jean Lalime of St. Joseph (property later acquired by John Kinzie), drawn at St. Joseph, May 7, 1800, discloses that he had a surprisingly complete domestic establishment, including "stables, horsemills, dairy, bakehouse, henhouse, workshop, and a large quantity of livestock of various kinds," and household furniture which included "a couch, a bureau, four tables, a stove, mirrors, spits, and, to crown all, 'a cabinet of French walnut 8 by 4 with 4 glass doors.'" "Detroit and Early Chicago," *Burton Historical Collection Leaflets*, V, no. 3, p. 35.

[29] Mrs. Kinzie in her *Wau-Bun* says, "In giving the early history of Chicago, the Indians say, with great simplicity, "the first white man who settled here was a negro," pp. 219-20.

[30] Day Book and Ledger, relative to the "Adventure" at the Pinery on Pine River, is in the Burton Historical Collection, Detroit Public Library.

firmation of that grant of land by another deed from the Chippewa Indians, signed by twenty-six chiefs.

There are numerous salient associations connected with Fort Sinclair other than as a fort, which were involved in the history of the Great Lakes and of the St. Clair River area in particular. One of these is the fact that Sinclair's Pinery, or farm, including the fort buildings and wharf, was probably the first great estate in Michigan. When Sinclair gave Nicholas Boulvin a power of attorney to take care of his four-thousand-acre farm on Pine and St. Clair Rivers, there were listed his "stock, houses, barns, orchards, gardens, timber and every other article thereto appertaining,"[31]—constituting an outlay of holdings comparable at the time to those of a laird of Scotland or a duke of England.

Patrick Sinclair was certainly one of the important historic characters in the early history of Michigan, and it seems surprising as well as regrettable that his name has not been honored and perpetuated in either Mackinac or in the St. Clair River area with proper memorials.

Pioneering of the Schooner *Gladwin*

Of special interest also is the schooner *Gladwin's* association with Fort Sinclair and with its builder. Next to La Salle's *Griffin*— the first sailing vessel to move on Lake Erie and Lake Huron— the *Gladwin* was perhaps the most historic and most important Lakes vessel, for that schooner was the first vessel we know of to make the trip from Detroit to Mackinac *and return*— making her, as Goodrich in his *First Michigan Frontier* has pointed out, "the vessel marking the true beginnings of sail above Detroit."[32]

The schooner *Huron,* by order of Major Gladwin, had set out from Detroit in September of 1762 to take a detachment of troops to Sault Ste. Marie, but had to put back because of low water in Lake St. Clair. In the meantime, Pontiac's conspiracy—which resulted in the massacre at Fort Mackinac, and also at the River Raisin after the unsuccessful attack at Detroit—curtailed any further attempted navigation on Lake Huron. But in September of 1764, immediately after Bradstreet's negotiations for peace, we

---

[31] Jenks, *Patrick Sinclair,* p. 12.

[32] Calvin Goodrich, *First Michigan Frontier,* (Ann Arbor: University of Michigan Press, 1940), p. 283.

find him ordering Lieutenant Sinclair, commanding the schooner *Gladwin,* to take stores to Michilimackinac "at the beginning of May next."[33] This was evidently a follow-up of a previous order which was fulfilled, for in a letter of Capt. William Howard's to Bradstreet, dated October 16, 1764, at Michilimackinac, Howard says "This day the Vessell arriv'd."[34]

Reports show that at the close of the 1764 season and on his return from Mackinac to Detroit, Sinclair laid up the *Gladwin* in Pine River,[35] and no doubt she was utilized to house the soldiers and sailors and artisans who were building Fort Sinclair and otherwise working at Sinclair's Pinery.

But perhaps the most interesting and significant of Fort Sinclair's associations, in regard to the St. Clair River area is its connection with the early lumbering history of the community. Sinclair was not the first to make inroads on the pine lands of the St. Clair River district, as an excursion into the history of lumbering in the area will disclose. But the industry of Sinclair's "Adventure," of which we have actual records, adds immeasurably in any attempt to show a continuous habitation in the St. Clair River district from about the time of the establishment of Fort St. Joseph in 1686.

Before examining this lumbering "adventure," however, we must first look into the reason for the establishment of the third fortified post on the St. Clair River—the post over which flew the Stars and Stripes of the United States of America.

---

33 Bradstreet order to Sinclair, dated Sept. 12, 1764. In William L. Clements Library, University of Michigan.

34 Howard letter to Bradstreet, dated at Michilimackinac, Oct. 16, 1764. Letter in William L. Clements Library, University of Michigan.

35 An entry under date of November 5, in *The Diary of the Siege of Detroit in the War with Pontiac,* pub. by Munsell and edited by Franklin B. Hough, page 113, says that "This morning Capt. St. Clair (clearly a mistake) arrived here from Michilimackinac after laying up the Schooner *Gladwin* in a small river near the head of the River Huron." The River Huron was, of course, the St. Clair River, and the "small river" was evidently Pine River. The *Diary* is in *Burton Historical Collection,* Detroit Public Library.

The trader, John Porteous, in his *Diary* (1765-66), also makes several references to the *Gladwin* and Fort Sinclair, and to Captain Sinclair, as does Capt. John Montresor in his *Journals* (*New York Hist. Soc. Colls.,* 1881).

The Montresor *Journals* and the Porteoeus *Diary* are in the Burton Historical Collection, Detroit Public Library, and a copy of a part of the Porteous *Diary* is also in the Jenks Collection, Port Huron Public Library.

Chapter V

THE STARS AND STRIPES OF THE UNITED STATES

Captain Gratiot Builds a Fort

The dusky allies of George the Third were still rampant on the St. Clair River even after Perry's and Harrison's victories ended American-British hostilities on the northwest American border in the so-called War of 1812. Because of this situation, and the fact that the British still held Mackinac and the small trading post at the Sault,[1] the American authorities deemed additional protection necessary for the St. Clair River-Lake Huron area, and General William Henry Harrison, commander of the Northwestern Army, ordered a fort built for the double purpose of keeping the Indians in check and controlling the water connection between the lakes.

On the morning of May 14, 1814, twelve bateaux, each flying a pennon, and a sloop carrying a cannon, arrived at the foot of Lake Huron. The boats carried a detachment of forty men, directed by Major Thomas Forsyth, with Capt. Charles Gratiot as engineer; and they were joined on the 6th of June by a battalion of Ohio Militia under a Major Dawson who had been ordered to "march (from Detroit) to the head of the Rapids of the River St. Clair"[2] for the express purpose of keeping the "Indian foes" in check while the fort was being constructed.

Captain Gratiot with a discerning eye chose an advantageous spot about one thousand feet[3] below the entrance from the lake to the river, on the west bank, twenty feet above the water. The elevation and the narrowness of the channel enabled the small

---

[1] North West Company.

[2] From a letter by Major Dawson published in the *Weekly Intelligencer,* Phila., Pa., July 9, 1814.

[3] From indications in some surveys it was "located about 1,300 feet south of the 43rd parallel of latitude, and on the edge of the high bank which ran substantially parallel with the river." See W. L. Jenks, "Fort Gratiot as a Fort," Clipping, *Port Huron Times Herald,* February 14, 1914, in Jenks Scrapbook, Jenks Collection, Port Huron Public Library.

cannon of that day to command the situation. The spot was approximately the same one which Duluth had chosen for Fort St. Joseph one hundred and twenty-eight years earlier as a place of protection against the English and the hostile Iroquois.

No plan of the original fort as constructed by Captain Gratiot has been preserved in the War Office, but some of the surveys and individual reports made about that time indicate that the fort was "165 feet in width through the bastions at the north end and perhaps three times that distance in length (with numerous angles), the faces at the upper and lower ends commanding the approach on the river from either direction."[4]

The fort was built of logs with earth filling on the north, south, and west sides, and with picket stockade. One small, but protective cannon[5] commanded the eminence overlooking the narrow channel and the neighboring country of Canada, and over this fortified post flew the Stars and Stripes of the United States. One can imagine the joy and relief which the early settlers, long beleaguered by the insolent Indians, felt in the building of the fort and in the presence of troops in that frontier settlement.

When finished, the fort was named for its builder, Captain Gratiot, and Gratiot's name has also been perpetuated in Michigan by Gratiot County, as well as two townships, avenues in Detroit, Mt. Clemens, and Port Huron, and by the Gratiot Turnpike (U.S. 25) between Detroit and Port Huron.

Charles Gratiot

Charles Gratiot, a young man of twenty-eight, and but eight years out of West Point when he took over the job of building the fort, was born August 29, 1786 in St. Louis (then a small town in the Spanish Colony of Louisiana), the son of distinguished and influential parents. His mother was Victoire Chouteau, sister of Auguste and Pierre Chouteau, the founders of St. Louis; his father,

---

[4] W. L. Jenks, "Fort Gratiot and Its Builder, Gen. Charles Gratiot, *Michigan History Magazine,* IV, No. 1 (Jan., 1920), 141-155.

[5] During most of the later years of the fort's existence the armament consisted of four 3-inch guns which were used only for salutes and as sunrise and sunset guns. The guns, which were of brass and kept highly polished, were covered with tarpaulin when not in use. See Jenks, clipping cited.

Charles Gratiot, a descendant of French Hugenots, was a wealthy trader who gave valuable assistance to the Americans in the Revolution, and when the United States took possession of Louisiana Territory it was from his house that the American flag was first raised as a signal of authority over that vast region.

Charles Junior and his cousin, a son of Auguste Chouteau, were the first two appointees, by President Thomas Jefferson, from Louisiana to the newly established Military Academy at West Point. After graduation Gratiot achieved acclaim both in battle and as an engineer. The building of Fort Gratiot was his first independent engineering assignment.

Captain Gratiot was not long at his fort. It was hardly completed when, in July, the Croghan-Sinclair expedition, on its way to attempt the recapture of Mackinac from the British, stopped at the fort for troops to assist in the venture, and Gratiot himself accompanied the expedition from that point.

On the return of the troops Captain Gratiot was appointed brevet colonel of the Michigan Militia, and the following year promoted to major of the Corps of Engineers. He was then transferred to the East, where he eventually superintended the construction of the fortifications on the Delaware River and the important defenses at Hampton Roads, including Fortress Monroe and Fort Calhoun—engineering feats which were to bring him fame.

In 1828 Gratiot was promoted to colonel (being breveted brigadier-general the same year for meritorious service) and made Chief Engineer of the United States Army, a position he held for ten years. It was while he was chief engineer that the military road between Detroit and Fort Gratiot—Gratiot Turnpike (U.S. 25)—was constructed.[6]

At this point Gratiot's career took a tragic turn. He was in a position of great authority and responsibility, and it became necessary for him to allocate and disburse millions of dollars on a single project. In 1838 he was dismissed from the service by President Van Buren for claimed irregularities in his financial relations with the government. Gratiot petitioned Congress for vindication of his stand in the matter, and for reinstatment in

---

6 1828-1833.

the army, but before anything was done in that quarter the Government brought suit against him in the United States Court at St. Louis to the amount of some thirty-one thousand dollars. For fourteen long years the case went on—through the administration of six Presidents, from Van Buren to Fillmore, through decisions of the Court and reversals of decisions by the United States Supreme Court.

Finally—and unfortunately for Gratiot—although the judiciary committee of the United States Senate reported highly on Gratiot's character and ability, it claimed no authority existed in Congress to undo the action of President Van Buren.

In the meantime (1840) the now General Gratiot was given a position in the General Land Office in Washington, D.C., which he held until he returned to St. Louis a short time before his death in 1855, at the age of 69.[7]

Distinguished Officers at the Fort

Fort Gratiot graced the north end of Port Huron for 65 years— from 1814 to 1879—and was an integral part of the area's development from a frontier settlement to a flourishing city; its many facets of military occupation were deeply interwoven with the economic and social life of the city. The fort, with its group of buildings hugging the multi-toned greens of the great pine woods in the background, and looking out onto the glittering blues of the St. Clair River, has been called the most beautiful log fort in Michigan.

Captain William Whistler,[8] uncle of the American painter, James Abbott McNeil Whistler, and son of Captain John Whistler, builder of Fort Dearborn (Chicago) in 1803, signed the earliest report on file (1815) in the War Department relating to Fort Gratiot.

---

[7] For a biographical sketch of General Gratiot, and for a detailed report of the suit involving him and the Government, see W. L. Jenks, "Fort Gratiot and Its Builder, Gen. Charles Gratiot," *Michigan History Magazine*, IV, No. 1 (January, 1920), 141-155.

[8] Capt. William Whistler's wife and his mother (Mrs. John Whistler) are said to have been the first white women to set foot on the site that is now Chicago.

Lieutenant James W. Webb was another of the early officers at the fort (1820). This was the same James Watson Webb who later exercised an extremely powerful influence on the politics of the United States, both as editor of the New York Courier (and later of the Courier and Enquirer) and as Minister to Brazil, when he was instrumental in securing the withdrawal of the French from Mexico, owing to his friendship with the French Emperor, Napoleon III.

Throughout the years many other officers who served at Fort Gratiot were distinguished in the history of the United States, some twenty gaining sufficient recognition to be included in the National Biographical Dictionary of Americans.

At least two officers had attained fame before arriving at the fort. One of these was Dr. Alfred E. Fechét, a young French physician who, while serving as a junior medical officer in the French Army of Occupation in Algiers, had become involved in the military conspiracy to restore the Bonapartes. When the plot was discovered and his companions were caught, tried and sentenced, Fechét, due to a timely warning, evaded his pursuers and escaped to the United States. Here he took advantage of the Government's call for young doctors to serve in the Seminole War in Florida, and when the war was over his command was stationed at Fort Gratiot.

After a short service at the fort (1839-41) he resigned from the army and remained in Port Huron to practice medicine for 30 years, until his death in 1869, and was the first practitioner in the St. Clair River district to specialize in surgery.

Dr. Fechét's eldest son, Captain Edmund G. Fechét, was the man who, at the time of the Indian Uprising of 1890, while stationed at Fort Yates in North Dakota was ordered to arrest and bring into the fort the Sioux chief Sitting Bull.[9] The death of Sitting Bull by the Indian Police a few hours before Fechét reached the chief's house is well known history.

The other officer of early fame, and commandant at Fort Gratiot in 1817, was Lieutenant-Colonel John McNiel,[10] a hero of the

---

[9] A buckskin jacket Sitting Bull wore in parades in the Midwest while a member of Buffalo Bill's Wild West Show, is now one of the historical items in the Museum of the Port Huron Public Library.

[10] McNiel's wife was a half-sister of President Franklin Pierce.

War of 1812. Although he was severely wounded in the Battle of Lundy's Lane—and as a result was lame for the rest of his life—he continued on in the battle, and with such bravery that he was twice breveted for gallant conduct.

While at Fort Gratiot McNiel evidently became impressed with the future prospects of the St. Clair River district, for he later became a large stockholder in the Huron Land Company, the real estate corporation that owned the Town of Huron,[11] in present-day Port Huron.

Besides serving at Fort Gratiot, McNiel commanded at Mackinac, Green Bay, and Chicago, and he was one of the U.S. commanders who in 1829 made important treaties with the Indians at Prairie de Chien. He resigned from the army in 1830, when President Jackson appointed him surveyor at the port of Boston, a post he held until his death in 1850. McNiel Tract and McNiel Creek in Port Huron perpetuate his name.

A second post surgeon worthy of special notice was Dr. Zina Pitcher (1828-30), who later became one of the best known men of the state of Michigan. Noted in medical, educational, historical, and political circles, Dr. Pitcher was three times mayor of Detroit, a member of the Board of Regents of the University of Michigan (1837-52), and founder of that university's School of Medicine.

He was also one of the charter members, along with such Territorial figures as Gov. Lewis Cass, Father Gabriel Richard, and Henry R. Schoolcraft, of the first Michigan State Historical Society.[12] This was the same Dr. Pitcher who saved the arm, and probably the life, of a young boy who was later to become one of the Upper Peninsula's most famous citizens and a legend in his own time—Marquette's Peter White.

The incident occurred when Dr. Pitcher was City Physician of Detroit and when Peter White, then a lad of 16, had fractured his left arm on the propeller *Chicago* while working his way from Bay City to Detroit. By the time the *Chicago* had passed Port Huron and had reached Detroit the boy's arm was swollen to three times its normal size, and after a cursory examination by

---

[11] To be dealt with later in PART NINE, Chapter XXXVI.

[12] Dr. Pitcher presented to the Michigan Historical Society, as one of its first gifts, a pair of antlers of an elk killed near Fort Gratiot.

the attending physician it was decided that amputation of the arm was the only means of saving his life.

It was customary in those days for doctors to invite their fellow surgeons to witness such an emergency operation, and among the interested spectators was Dr. Pitcher. The makeshift operating room was redolent with the fumes of coal tar, intermingled with the smell of the stiff shot of whiskey given to the terrified boy strapped in a reclining chair—there were no preventives against either infection or pain.

The operating surgeon was about to select his instruments when Dr. Pitcher suddenly demanded of his confreres if anything had been done to reduce the swelling in the boy's arm. When the reply was in the negative Pitcher insisted that the condition of the arm could not be determined until the swelling was reduced, and suggested that the amputation be postponed for at least a day or two. The operating surgeon acquiesced, allowing Dr. Pitcher to take over the case.

Pitcher then directed that equal parts of whiskey and water, as hot as could be endured, be poured over the boy's arm at 15 minute intervals for the next 24 hours. As the arm at the end of that time showed a marked improvement, the treatment was repeated for another 24 hours, and the arm gradually reached its normal size. Dr. Pitcher then set the broken bone, and after some months in splints Peter White's arm was as good as ever.

Many of Fort Gratiot's officers[13] became distinguished in the history of the United States through their outstanding services in the Civil War. These included Major Gabriel J. Rains (1851-52), a native of North Carolina, who resigned from the army of the United States when war was declared and entered the Confederate army, where he became noted for his work with explosives; Lieut. Samuel Heintzleman (1828-30, 1846), who distinguished himself at Seven Pines and at Williamsburg; and Lieut. Silas Casey (1835-36), a hero at Fair Oaks, and author of the 2-volume *System of Infantry Tactics,* adopted by both the United States Army and the Confederates. Another officer and

---

[13] For a more complete list of officers at Fort Gratiot see Jenks, *St. Clair County, Michigan,* I, 99-105. Also additional information in Jenks, *Papers,* Jenks Collection, Port Huron Public Library.

writer was Lieut. Randolph B. Marcy (1838-39), author of "best sellers" in his day, of which his *Border Reminiscences* was perhaps best known. Lieutenant Marcy later became Chief-of-Staff for his famous son-in-law, General George B. McClellan.[14]

Croghan-Sinclair Expedition Stops at Fort Gratiot

It has been said that from Fort Gratiot a hostile shot was never fired in all the years it was garrisoned. But although it was not a theater of war where actual battles took place, it was a stage for many spectacular events, all serious in their scope, and some a part of larger events important in the history of Michigan and of the nation.

The first of these events occurred when Fort Gratiot was hardly finished, and it presented a picture rarely seen on the Lakes, with the exception, perhaps, of the Battle of Lake Erie. The troops, having arrived at Fort Gratiot in May of 1814, had by the first week in July laid up strong earthworks, cut sufficient timber from the nearby forests for the several buildings and picket stockade, and had barracks ready for habitation. But barely had the artisans put on the finishing touches of construction when word was received that the Croghan-Sinclair expedition was ready to start on its attempt to recapture Fort Mackinac from the British, and that on its way it would stop at Fort Gratiot and take on the Regiment of Ohio Volunteers to assist in that undertaking.

Then on the morning of July 12, a shout went up from one of the workers, and the soldiers hurried to the river bank and watched from their vantage point on the elevation above the Rapids as five of the proud old fleet of Captain Oliver Hazard Perry at Lake Erie, now completely reconditioned and with banners flying, sailed majestically up the St. Clair River to anchor off the fort.

Leading the squadron as it came around the bend in the river was the trim schooner *Scorpion* bearing its swivel guns, followed by the *Caledonia* with its long "three 24's," and close behind advanced the impressive *Tigress* with its one great projecting gun silhouetted against the sky. Hard by rode the gallant *Lawrence*

---

[14] See PART TEN, Chapter XXXX (3), for story of the Marcy family and the daughter who later became Mrs. George B. McClellan.

with twenty guns—the brig which had been Perry's flagship, her deck now washed clean of the blood-stained sawdust resulting from the carnage of that famous battle on Lake Erie, and with her once shattered bulwarks, spars, and rigging all made new again.

Last of all came the proud *Niagara*, which, after the crippling of the *Lawrence*, had borne the commodore's great blue banner carrying the words, "DON'T GIVE UP THE SHIP," and the same brig upon which Perry had written his famous message to General Harrison—"We have met the enemy and they are ours: two ships, one schooner and one sloop. . . ."

The squadron was in the charge of Captain Arthur Sinclair, and it was accompanied by a land force of five hundred Regulars and two hundred and fifty Militia under the command of Lieut. Col. George Croghan, the gallant defender of Fort Stephenson and a nephew of the famed George Rogers Clark, with Major Andrew Hunter Holmes—who was to lose his life in battle at Mackinac—second in command.

The squadron had needed a pilot to guide it safely through the St. Clair River and on Lake Huron and so had secured the services of Capt. William Thorn, a pilot of pre-Revolution days, who had secured land on the St. Clair River (at Cottrellville) as early as 1785. Captain Thorn at that time was suffering from a dislocated hip and was unable to climb a ladder or mast. He was taken aboard ship in a chair just below Roberts Landing (north of Algonac), and during the low fog which was later encountered on the river and on Lake Huron he was securely strapped in his chair and hoisted with pulleys to the masthead from which he did his piloting.

After stopping to pick up Captain Thorn, the squadron continued on up the river but anchored again off Fort Gratiot to take on the regiment of Ohio Volunteers, leaving only a part of Major Dawson's command and the small force of Regulars under Captain Cobb at the post. The next morning the expedition continued on, Captain Gratiot sailing away with it, and the historic squadron was soon lost to sight on the broad expanse of Lake Huron.

William Brown Saves the Garrison

A second event followed shortly upon the time of the Croghan-Sinclair expedition to Mackinac. The regiment of Ohio Valunteers which accompanied the expedition from Fort Gratiot did not return to the fort until late in August, and in the meantime troublesome Indians, made more bold by the unsuccessful attempt of the Americans to recapture Mackinac, continued to disrupt the usual tenor of pioneer life along the lakes and rivers with their plundering and vicious forays.

Because of this, provisions and supplies were not received at the fort from Detroit as expected. Furthermore, both the soldiers and civilians found it impossible to fish or to hunt game or to gather the wild fruits and nuts to supplement their fast-depleting stores, because of the Indian snipers, who used both arrow and deadly stone slung from buckskin slings in their stealthy forays.

Finally a courier made it to Detroit with word of the garrison's plight. He also informed Colonel A. H. Butler, in charge at Detroit, that the settlers along the St. Clair River were flocking to the fort for something to eat—their cattle having been run off, or killed, and their gardens denuded by marauding Indians.

William Brown,[15] one of the St. Clair River district's most enterprising and capable pioneers, was living in Detroit at the time and helping to rebuild the fort destroyed by the British. He was chosen by Colonel Butler to convoy a train consisting of 40 men and 60 head of cattle to Fort Gratiot.

Brown led the train out from Detroit early the next morning, each man carrying a gun and a heavy pack of supplies on his shoulders, and reached Point Aux Trembles, below Algonac, at nightfall. And although hampered by showers of stones from the slings of lurking Indians, and by the repeated attempts of the savages to stampede the cattle with both stones and their blood-curdling yells, the relief party remained intact.

The route from Point Aux Trembles to Fort Gratiot was considered equally dangerous for the convoy. The narrow trail led

---

[15] Brown was the son-in-law of Capt. William Thorn.

through forests and around swamps, and large numbers of Indians were known to hide in the woods, often times dropping like a flock of birds out of the trees onto unsuspecting travelers.

But Brown knew well the ways of the savages and knew many of their hiding places. He knew, too, that they could be cowards at times, easily outwitted, and when the train passed possible hiding places Brown would have the men cry out with unearthly wild yells, as if there were hundreds in the party, and at the same time rush the men and cattle by the danger spots, successfully discouraging any of the Indians who might be lurking there.

After fording Belle and Pine Rivers, Brown led his convoy across Bunce Creek and hurried on up the trail to Black River, the 40 frontiersmen trudging along behind with their packs, and the hoofs of the cattle raising a great cloud of dust on the trail which is now Military Street in Port Huron.

On reaching Black River a Frenchman by the name of Jean Baptiste Desnoyers ferried the men across in a canoe, the cattle swimming in tow of a rowboat. Black River was the last obstacle Brown and his train had to overcome, and they reached the overjoyed garrison at Fort Gratiot by nightfall.

Cholera Is Brought to the Fort

Perhaps the most tragic event associated with Fort Gratiot, one which brought terror to the people along the St. Clair River, occurred while the Black Hawk War was in progress in Illinois (1832), when troops from the east were ordered by way of the Lakes to Fort Dearborn at Chicago.

Gen. Winfield Scott, in charge of the troops, chartered four steamboats at Buffalo to carry the troops and supplies—the *Henry Clay,* the *Sheldon Thompson,* the *Superior* and the *William Penn.* When the overcrowded *Henry Clay* stopped at Detroit on the evening of July 4, a soldier who had been stricken with cholera (then sweeping westward and southward from New York) died, and many new seizures followed. Alarmed, General Scott, in a vain attempt to save Detroit from an epidemic, ordered the *Henry Clay* to Hog Island (Belle Isle) where it was brought additional medical supplies, and from which point it was then to go on to Mackinac with orders to remain at Bois Blanc Island if the spread of the disease worsened.

But the scourge pursued the *Henry Clay,* and the vessel got no farther than Fort Gratiot at the mouth of the St. Clair River. So many of the soldiers were ill that the crew refused to continue the voyage, and there on the bluff overlooking the rapids, the troops disembarked, the sick being carried ashore.

The facilities of Fort Gratiot were inadequate for so great a number—many of them young officers fresh from West Point—and many had to fend for themselves. Those unable to find room in the fort buildings—or in the crowded makeshift hospital that was the fort barn—wandered down the trail along the St. Clair River with their knapsacks on their back, some of them dying within six hours after being stricken with the disease, their bodies in many cases devoured by the wolves and hogs. In the end, more than half of the troops either died or deserted. Of one detachment of 208 recruits, that of Colonel David F. Twigs, only nine remained, thirty having died of cholera and the rest reported missing.

In a letter written at Fort Gratiot on July 10 by a Mr. Norval to a friend in Baltimore, Maryland, and published in the Philadelphia Inquirer, it was stated that the dead bodies of soldiers were "literally strewed along the road between here and Detroit," and also that "a person on his way from Detroit here passed six soldiers lying under a tree groaning with the agonies of the cholera, and saw one corpse by the road, half eaten by the hogs."[16]

In the same letter Norval wrote that no one dared give the cholera victims relief of any kind—"not even a cup of water"—but this was not always the case. Generally speaking, the settlers living

---

[16] This letter and others, postmarked at Detroit, first appeared in the *Philadelphia Inquirer,* and extracts were reprinted in the *Niles* (Mich.) *Weekly Register,* July 28, 1832. Sixty-five years later the *Port Huron Weekly Times,* July 15, 1897, printed excerpts of the letters from copies of that paper which were in the possession of Mrs. E. G. Spalding, then living in Port Huron.

In addition to the soldiers put ashore at Fort Gratiot, the officers and men of the Niagara garrison, on board the William Penn, were disembarked indiscriminately near St. Clair according to a Norval letter, some eighteen of them dying on the trail while attempting to get back to Detroit.

along the river did panic and met the soldiers' pleas for assistance with frightened refusals. This was not surprising in the wake of such a plague, but there were many instances where help and compassion were shown.

At that time the Louis Facer family was living in Port Huron on the north bank of Black River, about where the river is now crossed by Military Street Bridge. Mr. Facer, on the influx of the cholera-infested troops, barred the doors and boarded up the windows, and, with admonitions to his wife and son not to let anyone in, left for St. Clair to get a boat to take his family up to Lakeport.

But the poor soldiers came in such numbers, begging for something to drink, that Mrs. Facer was unable to refuse their pleas. She had her son break away part of a window, and all day long she passed out to the steady stream of soldiers cups of hot, strong coffee. The soldiers in gratitude for this kindness paid liberally by throwing back in through the window quarters, half-dollars, and dollars. By the end of that day the sum of seventy-two dollars had been left by the grateful soldiers.[17]

A sidelight to this incident gives an indication of treatments prescribed in fighting disease of that day. Mrs. Facer did contract the cholera. When her husband returned from St. Clair with the boat that evening he started at once with his family up the lake for Lakeport to escape the plague-ridden area, but by the time they reached there Mrs. Facer was already ill. He immediately sent back to St. Clair for Dr. Harmon Chamberlain[18] and in the meantime "fed (his) wife cayenne pepper and all the tea she

---

[17] W. D. Facer reminiscences, *Miscellaneous Papers*, Jenks Collection, Port Huron Public Library.

There were other instances of compassion and kindness shown to the cholera victims, such as that expressed by Peter F. Brakeman and his wife when several stricken soldiers who had wandered down the trail as far as their farm (a few miles north of Algonac) took refuge in an old log shanty on the premises. The shanty was without a door, but Brakeman improvised one by hanging a large boat sail over the doorway. He also brought in straw for bedding and furnished the soldiers with provisions and cooking utensils. Eventually the ailing men recovered, and when the Brakemans refused any payment for their services the men insisted on leaving them books and other little presents that they had in their possession.

[18] Facer, Letter cited.

60

could drink." The treatment proved successful, for when the doctor finally arrived—two days later—Mrs. Facer was recovering. Her son quoted the doctor as having said he "could have done no better for her than was done."[19]

It is also worthy of mention in regard to this cholera epidemic that one of the young officers who died at Fort Gratiot was Lieutenant Clay, a son of Henry Clay, the Kentucky statesman.[20] His remains rest in Lakeside Cemetery, to which the bodies of all the soldiers were removed from the old Post Cemetery when the military reservation was divided and sold, but the name on his marker has long since been obliterated by time and the elements.

An Incident of the Patriot War

Perhaps the most exciting event at Fort Gratiot, and as close as the fort ever came to being the scene of hostile shots, took place at the time of the Patriot War in Canada. This was a popular revolution—a large body of Canadians in arms against alleged misgovernment, with special grievance against the excessive privileges of the upper classes. The attempt on the part of the rebels to assert their rights to a more equitable administration of justice found many hot-headed Americans sympathizing with their Canadian neighbors to such an extent that they came close to violating our proclamation of neutrality.

"Squads" of these Americans were raised, and secret meetings were held in out-of-the-way cabins, called Hunters' Lodges. The recruited Patriots were found throughout Ohio and New York State, and even as far south as Kentucky; but Michigan led them all, with Lodges stretching from Detroit to Port Huron, where

---

[19] Surgeon Josiah Everett, one of the two doctors trying to cope with the epidemic at the fort, was then seriously ill and died within a few days. There was no other doctor closer than Dr. Chamberlain of St. Clair. See also PART TEN, Chapter XXXX (2), for the story of Dr. Chamberlain and the founding of Pontiac, Mich.

[20] "John Drew, then of Old Mission, Michigan, wrote to the (Detroit) *Free Press* that he built the 2nd steam saw mill on Black River, about 3 miles above mouth . . . . Also says the only grave stone in the Fort Gratiot Military Graveyard was that of a son of Henry Clay." Marginal note in Jenks, *op. cit.,* I, 366.

crossing the Rapids was a favorite way of getting into Canada, by way of Sarnia.

The wild excitement occasioned by the activities of the Patriots, such as the rumor that a band was intending to cross over from Sarnia and take away the munitions at Fort Gratiot, prompted the United States government to take drastic measures to avert clashes between Americans and His Majesty's forces, and one of these was to prevent the confiscation of military supplies from American forts.

Although Fort Gratiot had been without garrison since the previous June (1837)—one of the three times it was temporarily abandoned—it held great stores of military supplies. These valuable stores, which included several pieces of brass artillery, some forty kegs of powder, a great quantity of shot and shell, numerous caissons, and a large collection of small arms, muskets, sabers, and side-arms, were in the charge of a single United States ordnance sergeant.

One unsuccessful attempt had already been made by the Port Huron Patriots to take away a cannon from the fort grounds, and in November of 1837, to prevent any further attempts at confiscations, as well as to avert any embarrassing complications with the Canadian Government, such as using the fort as a base from which to invade Canada at Sarnia, General Hugh Brady ordered half a dozen of his Guards to proceed to Fort Gratiot and bring back to Detroit the entire supply of military stores, with the admonition "not to return without them."[21]

Headed by Lieuts. A. S. Williams and A. T. McReynolds, the small force of Brady Guards steamed up the St. Clair River aboard the *General Macomb,* and when they landed near the Rapids they found a great crowd gathered in and about the fort grounds. Not only were a large number of Patriots there, but also hundreds of residents of Port Huron and vicinity who insisted that they would resist by force the removal of the stores, which they needed to "protect their property from a threatened attack from the Canadians at Port Sarnia."[22]

---

[21] Geo. C. Bates, "Reminiscences of the Brady Guards," *Pioneer and Hist. coll., Mich.,* XIII, 535.

[22] *Ibid.*

62

Here indeed was a hostile and warlike situation—open resistance to the lawful authority of the United States. Certainly the small force of Brady Guards could not hope to beat back and overcome by force of arms the crowd of "some 600 or 800 desperate men";[23] neither could they return to Detroit without the property.

Many stories are told of the altercations that followed—ranging from fist fights to threats by the Guards "to sweep the vagabonds from the parade grounds with grape and canister," as was done on a similar occasion involving the arsenal in Dearborn, at a cost of fifteen lives. But probably the truest version was that told by a participating Brady Guard, of how Lieutenant McReynolds called "a council of war" and with his "Irish wit and pleasantries negotiated and treated and parleyed," with the mob of excited men until they yielded to the orders of their government.[24]

At any rate the supplies were finally loaded on board the steamboat without bloodshed, and the *General Macomb* steamed away from the fort on that afternoon in late November, only to get stuck fast in the ice of Lake St. Clair. By noon the next day, however, by rolling the vessel from side to side a passage way was made through the ice and the *Macomb* put back to St. Clair. The supplies had to be brought ashore, and all available teams and wagons in the village and surrounding district were commandeered to transport the caissons, guns, kegs of powder, and other equipment overland to Detroit.

Taking advantage of the situation was Wesley Truesdail, shipbuilder, mill owner, and cashier and manager of the Bank of St. Clair,[25] a county bank, situated in St. Clair. Fearing for the safety of the bank's funds at the hands of the Patriots, Truesdail persuaded the Guards to take along under their protection the entire specie amounting to $14,500. The coins were packed in boxes, piled

---

[23] *Ibid.*

[24] Geo. C. Bates, "Bygones of Detroit," *Pioneers and Hist. Coll., Mich.*, XXII, 318.

[25] It is of interest to note that the Bank of St. Clair was one of the few banks in the United States which continued to pay specie for its notes during the general bank suspension of 1837. See *Fifty Years of Banking in Port Huron, Michigan: First National Exchange Bank (1871-1921)*, Privately printed, pp. 70-71.

on top of the fort supplies, and the military train, half a mile in length, reached Detroit safely the next day.

There the guns and ammunition and other military supplies were stored away at the fort, and the specie was deposited in the vaults of the Farmer's and Mechanics Bank,[26] where it remained for several months until the disturbances of the Patriots had quieted down.

Although this incident just about ended the Patriots' activities in Port Huron, a troop of Regulars (100) was sent the following month from Buffalo and stationed at Fort Gratiot a short time to keep the hot-headed Patriots in check. It was not long, however, before the home government in England righted the alleged injustices in the Dominion, and peace reigned once more along the St. Clair River borders.

The handling of this affair was one more instance where common sense prevailed in a dispute and kept intact the friendly relations existing between the United States and Canada along the Michigan border. These cordial relations are exemplified today by such events as the Detroit-Windsor International Freedom Festival, held annually in July as a joint celebration of Dominion Day and Independence Day, as well as by such means of travel as the seventy-seven year old St. Clair Railroad Tunnel under the St. Clair River (connecting the United States, at Port Huron, with the Dominion of Canada at Sarnia, Ontario) and the handsome Blue Water International Bridge—that "perfect emblem of peace"[27]—both giving quick and easy access to life-long friendly neighbors.

[26] *Ibid.*, p. 69.

[27] Quote is from the late Louis A. Weil, editor of the *Port Huron Times Herald*, in his dedicatory speech at the formal opening of the Blue Water International Bridge, October 8, 1938.

Chapter VI

PROMINENT INDIANS OF THE FORT GRATIOT ERA

When the Americans came up the St. Clair River to build Fort Gratiot they found living on the Indian Reservation the half-breed, John Riley, a figure prominent in Territorial affairs and whose name is perpetuated in the Township of Riley[1] in St. Clair County.

Riley's house, near what is now the southwest corner of Military and Water Streets, was the only house on the so-called Black River Reservation, although there were numerous other houses in the settlement—homes of the Frenchmen, Francois Leviere, Louis Moreaux, Baptiste Levais, Pierre Brindamour (Brandimore), Michel Gervais, Anselm Petit, Jacques and Louis Campau, Denis Caslet (Causley), Francois Boyer, Pierre Bonhomme, Jean Baptiste Deschamps, and others—all of whom had come before Fort Gratiot was built, and some as early as the seventeen eighties.

Riley, one of three brothers, John, James and Peter, came from a prominent, well-to-do family of Schenectady, N.Y. His father was James Van Slyck Riley, a one-time postmaster in Schenectady; his mother, a Chippewa woman from Saginaw. All of the Rileys were of great assistance to the Americans on many occasions during and after the War of 1812, as valuable Rangers, as interpreters, and serving on numerous diplomatic missions.

It was John's brother James who, as interpreter, was with the Cass exploring expedition in 1820, and who accompanied Governor Cass to Chief Sassaba's lodge where he (Cass) daringly tore down the British flag and trampled it under foot. John himself was one of the official interpreters at Detroit in 1815; and at the treaty with the Saginaw Chippewas made in 1819 there were reserved for his use six hundred and forty acres of land near what is now Bay City.

John Riley, according to his contemporaries, was a large, hand-

---

[1] Also by Riley Center in same township.

some man of commanding appearance, well educated and well mannered. There is a story told concerning the wife of an officer at Fort Gratiot. The officer, who was walking with his wife, met Riley on the "Parade green" one evening. Carelessly using the Indian mispronunciation of the Frenchman's "bon jour," they both greeted him with a friendly but patronizing "Bo jo" and were somewhat taken aback when Riley, after acknowledging the officer's greeting, bowed with dignity, and added, "Good evening, madame!"

Territorial Judge James Witherell tells of the time when John, courageous as he was fine looking, was living with his brothers in Detroit during the British occupation and was commanded by a British officer to work on a highway. He refused. When the soldiers were ordered to flog him, he dared them to do it, and the British major in charge, surprised and impressed by Riley's appearance and his courage, let him go.

It was John Riley who successfully obtained the release of the 11-year-old boy, Archie McMillan of Detroit, from the Saginaw Chippewas who had kidnapped him after they had killed his father, Ananias McMillan, on the commons outside the fort grounds (near LaFayette Avenue and Wayne Street and where a plaque now memorializes the event). And it was Riley who negotiated a peaceful settlement with the Canadian relatives of the Indian murdered at the Sun Dance by the warrior Akockias (better known as Black Duck), on the bluff overlooking the north bank of Black River in Port Huron.

At this Sun Dance, the usual feasting, drinking of the white man's whiskey, and speech making were carried on. In one of his harangues, the Canadian Indian had boasted of all the Americans he had scalped and slain, and Black Duck, in an equally emotional harangue, berated the Indian for having killed his friends, and then plunged his tomahawk into the offender's head.

The ceremonies of the Sun Dance were abruptly ended, and Black Duck, somewhat sobered, realized the seriousness of the killing, knowing full well that the relatives of the victim would immediately meet in council and demand vengeance for his death. These repercussions were prevented, however, by the intervention of John Riley. He sought and obtained the assistance of Col.

John McNiel, in command at Fort Gratiot, who placed Black Duck in the fort for safety and detailed a guard against any attempt of the Canadian Indians to abduct him.

Through Riley's influence also, the matter was placed before Governor Cass and the affair settled when the "avengers of blood" accepted a selection of goods in payment and 40 quarts of whiskey —the latter they considered necessary to "soften their hearts and cause tears to flow more freely over their dead relative."[2] The order for the whiskey was drawn on Aura P. Stewart of China Township, and the Indians arrived for it with their faces blackened with charcoal in mourning for their dead. After the "mourners" returned to Canada Black Duck was released from the fort.

Riley continued to live on the Reservation until it was ceded to the United States in 1836, and then he moved to what is now Riley Township, where his sister was living on land owned by their father, and where he was in the habit of hunting and making maple sugar. There he opened a store, but extended too much credit to his white friends and soon lost his goods and money. After that he mortgaged and then sold his property and moved to Canada, where he died in 1842.

As well known as Riley to early, and later, settlers was old Mother Rodd—who lived to be over a hundred years old. Mother Rodd, of full Indian lineage, was the granddaughter of Maskeash, one of the prominent chiefs along the St. Clair River, and one who signed many of the deeds of land given by the Chippewas. Both she and her husband, Alexander Rodd, a halfbreed, were fond of the Americans and gave their loyalty to them rather than to the British—a loyalty which cost Rodd his life and Mother Rodd great sorrow and privation.

It was at the time of the War of 1812, when the majority of the Indians were giving their allegiance to the British, that Rodd refused to do so, incurring their (the Indians') enmity. They never forgave Rodd and bided their time for revenge. Soon after the close of the war, a band of Saginaw Chippewas who had settled in Canada came across the river and, under cover of friendly

---

[2] "Recollections of Aura P. Stewart," *Pioneer and Hist. Coll., Mich.*, IV (1881), 346.

overtures, hired Rodd (who with his family was making maple sugar near what is now Riley Center in Riley Township) to guide them on a hunting expedition some distance inland, west of Port Huron. In the party were Chief Wawanosh (a very prominent Indian Chief in Lambton County, Ont.), Wapoose, a medicine man, and four other Indians.

Starting out along the south bank of Black River, the Indians, as was their custom, followed along in single file with Rodd in the lead. Just beyond what is now Wadhams the Indian immediately behind Rodd stepped out of line to the right, and the Indian behind him shot Rodd in the back. Another one shot him in the side, while a third shot him in the head. They buried Rodd where he fell and then took his coat, with the hole showing in the back, to his wife. To make their revenge complete, the Indians took her and her family into captivity for a year or more before they were eventually allowed to return to the Sarnia Reservation.[3]

Although her home was on the Sarnia Reservation, Mother Rodd—or "Granny Rodd," as she was sometimes called—spent most of her time on the American side of the St. Clair River, camping along the beach in the summer time, and in the woods in the winter, since it was warmer there; the trees, as she explained, gave protection from the cold north winds.

In the woods she gathered hickory "timber" for brooms and ash for baskets, and her brooms and baskets and mats were always well made and in demand by the settlers, as were her berries and maple sugar squares. Mother Rodd, in her younger days, had one trait, especially, in which she was akin to her white sisters. She was unusually conscious of wanting to look her best and to make a good impression on occasions. When she peddled her wares she invariably dressed in her best clothes, and always carried her berries and maple sugar in bright, clean tin pails. She told one of the pioneers that she "made a more ready sale" when she and her wares looked their best.[4]

[3] Reminiscences of Mrs. Peter (Nancy) Brakeman, who said that Mother Rodd told her the story. *Brakeman, Papers,* Jenks Collection, Port Huron Public Library.

[4] *Ibid.*

She was considered a good "doctress" by the pioneers, who recorded many cures due to her expert knowledge and use of herbs, roots, and barks. Her "grave clothes," including gaudy, bright red leggings trimmed with ribbon and beads, had been made for twenty years before her death (1871), and part of that time Mother Rodd had left them in the care of Mrs. Peter Brakeman's mother, Mrs. William Brown. Her totem was the turtle, and it was wrought with red yarn in the corner of the great white blanket she wore wrapped around her in cold weather.

Contemporaneous with Riley and Mother Rodd were many chiefs and other Indian personages familiar to the St. Clair River pioneers. There was Okemos, the nephew of Pontiac (therefore part Ottawa although he had been made a Chippewa chief), who during the War of 1812 led a scouting party against the Americans, and no doubt took part in many ferocious attacks. After the war, however, he took the oath of fealty to the United States and rendered many services to the Americans.

Okemos and his wife and family were frequent visitors to the St. Clair River district on their annual trips from their home near the mouth of Red Cedar River, in south-central Michigan, to Malden (Amherstburg) for their annuities, and the early settlers remember him especially for the consideration he showed his wife.

One winter on the trek to Malden with his family he stopped over night at the home of Peter Brakeman (then living in Port Huron), where his wife became gravely ill. He attended her with great solicitude, carrying her to the canoe which was to take them across to Sarnia enroute to their destination. She died before reaching Malden, and Okemos returned with her remains and took them to her home in what is now known as the village of Okemos, near East Lansing.[5]

Okemos' antithesis was the arrogant and cruel Chippewa chief, Kishkauko, a dreaded tyrant along the St. Clair River for decades, who not only broke the white man's law but the code of the Indian as well—a man who lived by his own law. The story of how one of his crimes finally caught up with him and how he dealt with the situation is well known. He had killed one of

---

[5] *Ibid.*

his own tribe on a street in Detroit, and after being convicted and sentenced to be hanged, he cheated the hangman out of his job by committing suicide in his cell in the Detroit jail, presumably by poison smuggled in to him by one of his wives during a visit.

This was the same Kishkauko who stalked out of the Council at Sault Ste. Marie in 1820—when Governor Cass was endeavoring to obtain a cession of land there on which to build a fort—and led the other chiefs, including Sassaba, in a revolt which might have been disastrous had it not been for the intervention of the daughter of another Chippewa chief, Wabogish, Mrs. John Johnston.

And this was the same Kishkauko who once gave a severe whipping to Sally Ward of Marine City, sister of Eber Brock Ward, the great Michigan industrialist. According to Sally's father, Eber Ward, Kishkauko passed down the St. Clair River on his way from Saginaw to Detroit at least twice a year, and it was his habit to make himself at home in any white man's house and take whatever he wanted. He usually had with him a bodyguard of armed braves, and he himself invariably carried a tomahawk in the crook of his left arm.

On one occasion when Eber Ward was away from home, Kishkauko and his braves entered his house and demanded whiskey of Sally. When she told him there was none he strode to the vinegar barrel in a rage and pulled out the spigot, letting all the vinegar run out. He then ordered the braves to take what bread and other food they could find, and as he was leaving he pulled the rod from one of the brave's rifles and with it brutally whipped the girl.[6]

Other frequent visitors to the St. Clair River settlements were Maskeash, already referred to as one of the important chiefs during the British occupation; Naykeeshig (Driving Cloud), who was a cousin of Mother Rodd and a grandson of Maskeash, and who was often employed by Judge Zephaniah Bunce; and Animikans (or Nimekance), who served under Patrick Sinclair at his fort on Pine River.

---

6 *Autobiography of Eber Ward, in Pioneer and Hist. Coll., Mich.,* VI (1883), 473.

But of all the warriors the Potawatomi chief, Maconce, was perhaps most often mentioned by the pioneers. His name appears under many spellings—Maconce, Manconse, Macsunse, Macompte, Mascoonse, and even Cumekumanow—but the St. Clair River district pioneers called him Francois Maconce.

Maconce, who kept a hotel at Swan Creek, where many of the early Detroit judges and lawyers stayed on occasion, was well liked and admired both by his own people and the pioneers. He spoke English very well and was quite civic-minded, attending all the "bees" and other affairs of early days. One of his activities was his appearances at the Thompson Academy in St. Clair, where he talked to the students and teachers just as guest speakers address the assemblies in high schools and colleges today.

On these occasions Maconce, who was noted for his fine physique, would be dressed in a sort of compromise of Indian's and white man's wear—black frock coat tied around the waist with wampum, fringed calico hunting shirt, vest, broadcloth leggings profusely decorated with porcupine quills and silver ornaments which jingled with every step, buckskin moccasins, and a plug hat ornamented with a broad silver band. There was a silver ring through his nose, and in each ear five or six silver ear-bobs. The students, it is recorded, were always fascinated with the tales that Chief Maconce related—tales which no doubt would have made equally fascinating Americana had they been recorded for posterity.

Indian Place Names

Oddly enough, considering the prevalence of the Indian in the St. Clair River area, there are few Indian place names. In fact there is only one bona fide Indian name, that of Kenockee (Township), a Chippewa name meaning crooked, suggested by Daniel B. Harrington and probably referring to the tortuous course of Mill Creek which traverses the township.

Oddly enough, too, one of the most Indian sounding of the place names—that of Algonac—did not have its origin in any descriptive words the Indians themselves applied to it. Rather, it was a name prefabricated by the white man. The people of the settlement called Manchester (now Algonac) wanted the name

71

changed and asked Henry R. Schoolcraft, the Indian agent and philologist, to suggest for them an aboriginal name.[7] Schoolcraft selected a name composed of *Algon,* from the word Algonquin, and *ac,* meaning "land" or "earth," the word thus formed meaning the land or place of the Algonquins.

And incongruous as it may seem, the one place name selected to honor and perpetuate the name of a regional Indian—that of John Riley (Riley Township and Riley Center)—does not carry an aboriginal name but one of Dutch-Irish origin, Riley's father's name being James Van Slyke Riley.

Many of our pioneers, however, carried Indian names. The pioneers at times depended on the red man to supply them with the necessities of life—such as sugar, wild game, and fruits, roots, canoes, and woven rushes for mats and carpets—and in their dealings with the white man the Indians, it seems, were accustomed to call their white friends by some name or title characteristic of them.

Jeremiah Harrington, father of Daniel B. Harrington, was known as Keosaonena or "Hunting-man," and Samuel Wilson, one of the soldier-settlers, was given the name of Abatauwachuan, or "Half-way-man," for the simple reason that the house in which he lived was half-way between the mouth of Black River and the Ignace Morass mill, which was situated at the mouth of Indian Creek.

John Thorn bore the title Sonsagaunsa, or "Little Village," because of his being the first purchaser of lots (1818) in the "new" town on the St. Clair River (St. Clair). John W. Canfield, the shoemaker in Port Huron, was called Moconica, or "Shoemaker", and Anselm Petit, who had his toes amputated because of frostbite, was called Cis-ces-it, or "Cut-feet."

Peter Brakeman, an early fur trader who later bought the mercantile firm of Verhoeff and Jasperson (the largest general store on the St. Clair River), had several Indian names, the most interesting perhaps being Ah-tong-ganee, "the Borrower," for when he first acquired the name he was clerking for Peter F. Verhoeff and selling goods on commission. The Indians would sometimes want him to trust them, but he would refuse, saying the goods

---

[7] Jenks, *op. cit.,* I, 265.

were borrowed, hence the name; Mrs. Brakeman they called Ah-tong-gomer-ah-que—"Borrower's Woman."

Mr. Verhoeff wore glasses, and the Walpole Indians called him Nee-win-ah-skee-zhick, "Four-eyed Man," and so they called Brakeman, Nee-win-ah-skee-zhick-ah-neeteh-kee-nah-see, or "Four-eyed Man's Friend."

Other names indicate a decided sense of humor in the Indian. Joseph Campau of Detroit, who was well known all along the St. Clair River and the father of Daniel J. Campau, original owner of the land in the west section of Port Huron called the Campau, was given the name Che-mook-ke-mon, which meant "Big Knife" (American), or "Great White Man"—a cognomen probably comparable to our slang expression, "Big Shot." Peter (Pierre) Brandamour was named Thongodos, or "Brave-Big-Talking-Man," because he was always telling grand tales about his prowess in the hunt or his skill at logrolling. One can well imagine the chiefs and warriors around the campfires telling tales of their dealings with the Big Shot, Campau, and hearing their guffaws when retelling the stories of the braggart, Brandamour.

Black River, according to Mrs. Peter Brakeman, had the Indian name, Muck-a-ta-see-bing, and the Michigan & Wisconsin map, by Johnson & Browning, gives it Skoo-taw-gur-mish. St. Clair River had two Indian names, Waikai-go-sing, and Chis-so-wee, or "Big River," and Marine City was called She-ban-me-to-go-se-bing. Lake St. Clair, according to W. L. Jenks, had other Indian names besides the familiar Otsi-keta ("Sea" or "Salt water," a name given because of the prevalence of salt springs) —Oiatinatchiketo and Oiatinon-chikebo—probably given by the Wea or Miami Indians, and Wahawehyahtahnoong, used by the Missisaugas.[8]

Indian Idiosyncrasies and the Pioneer Woman's Courage

The Indian for the most part was neither the inveterate blood-thirsty villain nor the noble creature of nature, as he is so often characterized. Rather, he was like the pioneer himself—a complex human being with many virtues as well as faults, and always un-

---

[8] Jenks, *op. cit.*, I, 24.

predictable. Stories told by two of the St. Clair River area pioneers are illustrative of these facts.

That the pioneer never quite knew what to expect from the savage is exemplified in the story told by Mrs. John (Nancy) Howard,[9] who as a young girl had left Painsville, Ohio with her family in an open boat in 1811, to settle in Detroit.

Nancy was soon experiencing the horrors of the War of 1812 and witnessing atrocities committed by the Indians under the British General Henry Proctor after Governor William Hull surrendered Detroit to the British. Her family lived close to the fort, near Proctor's house, and she often saw the Indians bringing in their white prisoners captured in the Ohio campaign, to be sold back to their own people for tobacco and whiskey.

At that time Proctor was said to have a standing offer of five dollars for every American scalp and the Indians would bring them into his yard to collect their rewards. Nancy would often peek through the slats of Proctor's fence into his yard, and once she saw as many as twelve Indians come with their scalp trophies. They formed a circle around one of their number, who beat on his drum, and they danced and shouted their war whoops as they pushed their trophies higher and higher into the air on long sticks.

But probably the most frightening incident that Nancy told about was of a time when, after her father's death, the family was on their farm in Grosse Pointe, where the widowed mother was trying to harvest the wheat. One day in the late fall Nancy saw a canoe full of Indians coming near to the shore. Hurrying to the house she told her family and they all watched from a window to see what the Indians might do. And as they watched they saw a squaw emerge from the bush onto the road and beckon to the Indians. They sprang from the canoe, ran to the fence enclosing the yard, leaped over it like deer, and continued running on up to the house.

Nancy's older sister rushed to the door and her first impulse was

9 "Reminiscences of Fifty-four Years Spent in Michigan," by Mrs. John Howard. Manuscript is in the Jenks Collection, Port Huron Public Library. Mrs. Howard was the wife of John Howard, mill owner and prominent Port Huron pioneer, whose name was associated with the lumbering industry for half a century.

to bolt it, which she did. But then she withdrew the bolt and, opening the door, spoke in a friendly manner to the Indians in French, asking them to come in and get warm. They shouted unintelligible words at her and she turned and walked into the kitchen where her mother and the rest of the children were sitting around the fireplace.

The Indians followed and surrounded the family, presenting a terrifying picture in their red and black war paint, brandishing tomahawks and scalping knives as they argued among themselves. It was obvious that they were not certain that the family was English and not American since the girl had spoken to them in French, and therefore were undecided about killing them.

But while they discussed the situation Nancy's sister picked up the baby and walked out the back door. The mother, marshalling Nancy and the rest of the family ahead of her, followed, all forcing themselves to appear unhurried as they walked across the fields to the nearest French neighbors.

Before the Indians left the premises they plundered the house— even to breaking all the dishes—and drove away a span of horses from the barn. The plundering was complete except for one thing. They left intact and unharmed the clothing of the girl who had spoken kindly to them in French, and they could have identified the clothing only by the size of it.

*   *   *

Living on the "Flats" along the banks of the St. Clair River near Black River, and not far from John Riley's home, was Anselm Petit, a native of Quebec who came to the St. Clair River (Port Huron) in the latter part of the eighteenth century, and whose son, Edward, platted the "City of Peru," the first recorded plat in Port Huron.

Petit, a fur trader, lived in a log house on what is now Third Street, and in his house there occurred an incident indicative of Indian ways and character—and also of the worries and difficulties to which the early settlers, especially the women, were subjected.

Of Anselm Petit's eight children the first two boys were twins, and when one of them died—at the age of two—he took the body to Detroit to be buried in consecrated ground in St. Anne's church-yard. He made the trip by bateau and was accompanied by his neighbor, John Riley.

But two days after he left, the second twin became ill and died later in the night. Mrs. Petit, left alone in her grief, was further anguished when she looked out the next morning to find that hundreds of Indians had arrived in the night and were encamped on both sides of Black River near its mouth. Their canoes were drawn up on the shore and from the mast of each, swinging back and forth crazily in the wind, were hung the trophies of the braves—the matted, bloodstained scalps of men and women and children they had killed.

This incident also occurred during the time of the War of 1812, after Governor Hull had surrendered Detroit to the British, and the Indians were not only extremely troublesome but committing many atrocities against the white man.

The first thing Mrs. Petit saw the Indians do was to come into the yard and kill one of her cows. They then dragged it away toward what is now Water Street, where they cut it up and cooked it over an open fire and then had a feast.

Later in the day three more Indians came to the house, armed with hatchets and scalping knives. They walked into the house and one of the braves snatched the lace kerchief from Mrs. Petit's head, accusing her of being a Yankee. But when one of the Indians aimed a blow at her head, another one, who seemed more in authority, held off the weapon to question her further.

He was impressed that she showed no fear, but was curious, too, at her demeanor, for it was apparent she had been crying. He asked her, "Why do you weep, if not from fear?" Mrs. Petit motioned them to follow her and then she drew aside the cover on the bed in the corner of the room and showed him the body of her dead son.

The attitude of the Indians when they saw the dead boy changed instantly. They bowed their heads for a few moments and then, with the Indian expression of grief, each one put his hand over his mouth and filed silently out of the house.

In a short time their squaws came to the house carrying food with them—food which included, of course, barbecued steaks

76

from her own cow. The squaws stayed and made fires and carried in extra wood for her. In their Indian fashion they did everything they could for the grieving mother, and kept watch with her day and night in her lonely vigil, until her husband returned home.

Mrs. Petit was never to forget how, on the banks of the St. Clair River, in the wilderness settlement that is now the city of Port Huron, there was performed by the savages, with primitive dignity, one of the great Christian works of mercy.

PART THREE

THE LUMBERING ERA

Those were the days in Michigan,
The good old days, when any man
Could cut and skid and log and haul,
And there was pine enough for all.

—Douglas Malloch

Chapter VII

A DISTRICT RICH IN TIMBER TREES

The frontiers and territories of a new nation have natural resources which attract the venturesome, called pioneers, and it is in the conquering and making use of these resources by the pioneers that villages and cities and states develop. Official records, letters, memoirs, newspapers, and tradition relate the story of their development, and the story of the St. Clair River area is excelled by that of no other section on the continent in the romance of its beginnings.

To be sure, the beaver trade was directly and indirectly responsible for the early habitation—mainly in the form of forts—along the Michigan frontier ports. But the amazing development of that part of North America known as the Northwest Territory, with its resultant permanent settlements, was due primarily to its vast forest reserves.

These forests were rich in pines, which included, besides the white and Norway varities, blue spruce, tamarack, white cedar, red cedar, juniper, and hemlock, and they also abounded in oak, ash, gum, poplar, elm, beach, birch, chestnut, walnut, sycamore, maple, and many others.

Of all these timber trees the pine and oak were the most valuable, and, singularly enough, St. Clair County, stretching along the St. Clair River and lower Lake Huron, was particularly rich in both, as well as being blessed with most of the other varieties mentioned. And it is interesting to note that Patrick Sinclair's holdings on the St. Clair and Pine Rivers, with its considerable tract of pine, marked on the East side of Michigan the Southern line of the great pine section of the Lower Peninsula. The oak, ash, maple, walnut, and other hardwoods covered the lower part of St. Clair County and extended through the northern part as well.

To the pioneer the white pine was the most important product the forests of a new country could furnish, because of its light-

81

ness and ease in cutting and handling, its strength and durability, and, most of all, its adaptability to the wants of man. No other wood could so adapt itself to the building arts and commercial uses, from the manufacture of shingles and packing cases and matches, to bearing timber, and the finer finishes for interior decoration.

Along the St. Clair River and within the limits of St. Clair County was the finest white pine found on the continent. Traces of that white pine can still be seen today, lone majestic sentinals here and there, extending a few miles on Mill Creek in the vicinity of Abbottsford and Avoca. But, majestic as they are—like the famous Hartwick pines in the state park north of Grayling—they are as dwarfs in comparison to those which were cut and sent hurtling down Mill Creek and Black River in the early days, when *"Timber-r-r"* was forever the cry.

Chapter VIII

FIRST SAW MILLS IN THE NORTHWEST TERRITORY

The first saw mills of the great Northwest Territory were set up on the St. Clair River and its tributaries, with at least eight erected before the year 1800—three on Black River (Port Huron), two on Bunce Creek (formerly Baby Creek, Marysville), one on Meldrum Creek (later Mack Creek, Marysville), and two on Pine River (St. Clair).

The great lumbering waterways—the Saginaw and the Au Sable Rivers, the Muskegon and the Manistee, the Tittabawassee and the Shiawassee—are famous for the lumber barons they produced, and for the rollways of logs which corrugated their banks in the boom days of lumbering. But none has the ancient prestige of St. Clair River, or of Black River, the stream which gets its source in the swamps of northern Sanilac County and flows through the city of Port Huron to empty into the St. Clair.

Tradition has it that there was a saw mill on the St. Clair River in 1690,[1] and Judge James V. Campbell, in his "Early French Settlements in Michigan," says there was a saw mill "in the pine region on St. Clair River near Lake Huron," which was "well known before 1742."[2] If these mills existed they were probably at the same point where Duperon Baby erected a mill on the St. Clair River near present-day Marysville in 1780, and where Antoine Morass operated one on the same site six years later, for, according to W. L. Jenks in his *St. Clair County, Michigan*, there still existed as late as 1912 traces of two dams older than the original Baby and Morass dams which Judge Zephaniah Bunce used before he built his water power mill a short distance below.

But we do know for sure that long before Patrick Sinclair built a saw mill at his Pinery at Fort Sinclair on Pine River in 1763-64, there was a saw mill on historic Black River. We know this from an entry in the *Journal* of the celebrated French military engineer,

---

[1] Jenks, *op. cit.*, I, 364.
[2] *Pioneer & Hist. Coll., Mich.*, II, 102.

Chaussegros De Léry,[3] who supervised the building of early Detroit, and who wrote (at Detroit) in 1749: "There is no cedar or pine here. For these one must go about 25 leagues to the River Dulude[4] where there is a large pinery and a saw mill belonging to Mons. Gervais, habitant at Detroit."[5]

The Gervais mill was no doubt at the mouth of Indian Creek (once known as Rivière Gervais), which emptied into Black River (south bank) a short distance west of Seventh Street Bridge in present-day Port Huron.

After the British took possession of the territory, and when in 1764 an enlargement of the fort at Detroit (called the Citadel) was found necessary to house additional soldiers in the Pontiac War, Captain John Montresor of the Royal Engineers wrote in his *Journal* that the pine timber used in putting up the Citadel was brought "from the pinery on the opposite side of Lake St. Clair."[6] This reference was obviously to Patrick Sinclair's pinery and saw mill on Pine River.

During the British occupation, which lasted until 1797 in Detroit, the French mills of Duperon Baby and Antoine Morass operated on the St. Clair River, as did the Meldrum & Park mill on Meldrum Creek in the seventeen nineties, and as did the small shingle manufacturing plants of the Frenchmen who had settled along Black River in that decade. But the great fire of 1805 which destroyed Detroit created a greater demand for timber and shingles, and saw mills on Black River and Mill Creek later began to operate.

The Ignace Morass[7] mill, built on Black River near its junction with Mill Creek—at a place later to be called Abbottsford[8]—supplied the United States Government with spars and ship timbers during the War of 1812. Fine tracts of pine land surrounded the

---

3 De Léry was the builder in 1725 of the famed Fort Niagara, still standing today, as a monument of goodwill between the U. S. and Canada.

4 This was Black River in present-day Port Huron.

5 Letter of M. M. Quaife to W. L. Jenks, Nov. 25, 1932, *Jenks Papers,* Jenks Collection, Port Huron Public Library.

6 C. M. Burton, *The Building of Detroit* (pamphlet, 1912), p. 18.

7 Ignace Morass was the son of Victor Morass of Detroit.

8 Abbottsford was named for James Abbott, merchant, trader, and judge of Detroit, who acquired the Morass mill.

mill, and here Morass, under contract with the government, selected and cut large "sticks" of pine timber. In midwinter, with men and teams, it was drawn on trains down Black River and St. Clair River, then across Lake St. Clair and down the Detroit River —all the way on the ice to the shipyards. With only crude axes for tools, and oxen for beasts of burden, fulfilling that contract proved to be an amazing undertaking.

Settlements began to increase in the Northwest Territory, and so did saw mills as the demand for lumber and shingles grew. The next mill in point of time on Black River was that of Judge Zephaniah Bunce, built in 1818. This was followed by the Robert Smart mill at Clyde Mills (Wadhams), in 1825 by the Palmer-Jerome[9] mill on Pine River (St. Clair), in 1827 by the Knapp mill in the Township of Burtchville in 1828, and in 1830 by the Ai Beard mill at Ruby.[10]

The year 1832 marked the establishment of the historic Black River Steam Mill, the first steam mill in the Northwest Territory, and the following year the first John Howard mill was built on Black River—about three miles above its mouth—beginning a lumbering era associated with the Howard name in Port Huron which lasted for almost three-quarters of a century.

In 1835 other cities in the territory that is now Michigan, Wisconsin, Minnesota, Ohio, and Illinois began to spring up, and they, too, needed white pine and oak and all the other timber necessary for building. In the eighteen thirties the lumber from the Ai Beard mill at Ruby literally built the early city of Milwaukee, Wisconsin. The lumber was floated down Black River in rafts to its mouth and shipped in boats to its destination.

Those were the days in Port Huron of the shrieking, crunching noise from the log jams in the spring river drives, of the hoarse shouts of the rivermen, and of the constant whining of the mill saws, all blending with the blows of the caulkers' hammers in the shipyards along the Black and St. Clair Rivers. Those were the days in Port Huron when the atmosphere was permeated with

---

[9] Thomas Palmer of Detroit, father of Senator Thomas W. Palmer, and Horace R. Jerome also of Detroit, father of David H. Jerome, Governor of Michigan.

[10] For a more complete list of the many saw mills in St. Clair County, see Jenks, *op. cit.,* I, 362-374.

the odors of pitchy tar from the shipyards and the resinous saw-dust from the mills, when great "sticks"[11] for vessel spars drawn by six span of horses rumbled through the streets, and when those spars eventually marked the skyline on finished ships after being launched in colorful ceremony with great civic pride.

The mills continued to hum, and the logs continued to flow down the rivers—in 1869 more than sixty-four million feet of logs floated down Black River alone[12]—and the forests were worked until they were depleted, the lumbering era reaching its peak in the St. Clair River area in the late eighteen seventies.

Saw Mill (and City) Builders

Many other distinguished Michigan names besides Gervais, Baby, Palmer, Jerome, and Morass were associated with the St. Clair River district saw mills. When Robert Smart of Detroit, together with Ralph Wadhams, John Biddle, and others of that place became interested in the pine lands along the Black and Pine Rivers in Kimball Township, Smart's mill, on Black River, at what is now known as Wadhams, was built for him by William Allen Burt.[13] This was the same Burt who was Michigan's famed inventor, surveyor, and legislator.

Burt was the inventor of the first writing machine in America, the typographer, prototype of the present-day typewriter. But he was perhaps more noted for his solar compass[14]—the instrument

---

[11] In one of those "Boss loads of timber" were two "sticks" of white oak, measuring 222 cubic feet, which were said to have been 2,264 foot board measure and about seven tons in weight. One spar from the Beard mill at Ruby measured 22 feet in diameter at the bottom and was "103 feet from the butt." Fred A. Beard "Reminiscences" in *St. Clair County Pioneer Society Scrapbook and Minutes*, p. 211. Jenks Collection, Port Huron Public Library.

[12] W. L. Jenks, *op. cit.*, I, 372. Marginal notation.

[13] Burt first came to Detroit from Massachusetts (1823) as a young man with hopes of engaging in public land surveys. The surveying prospect being none too promising, he engaged in construction work as a millwright, first in Auburn, Oakland County, and then in Washington, Macomb County. During that time, and as a member of the firm of Burt & Allen, millwrights, he built many of the early mills in Oakland, Macomb, and St. Clair counties.

[14] He also invented the equatorial sextant.

which detected in 1844 the important outcrop of iron ore near the present site of Negaunee, where the Jackson mine was opened two years later to be the first iron mining operation in the state.

It was with Dr. Douglass Houghton, Michigan's first State Geologist, that Burt surveyed the Upper Peninsula, later completing the important reports on the geology of Michigan after Houghton's untimely death by drowning in Lake Superior. And it was this same early millwright who, as Territorial legislator, and with the help of Eber Brock Ward and others, was so instrumental in securing the necessary legislation which made possible the construction of the ship canal at Sault Ste. Marie.

One other mill which carried a name prominent in Detroit and the Territory was the Knapp mill, owned by Thomas S. Knapp, one-time sheriff of Wayne County. The Knapp mill was on Black River, about one-half mile south of Jeddo, and Knapp at that time also had a trading post on the north bank of Black River (in Port Huron) near its mouth. In addition, he owned, with John Thorn (son of Capt. William Thorn) , the land known as Thorn Plat, or the Village of Gratiot—one of the four plats that made up the town of Port Huron in 1837.

Thomas S. Knapp was sheriff at the time Stephen G. Simmons, tavern owner in Detroit, was sentenced to be hanged for the murder of his wife, whom he killed with a blow of his fist while intoxicated. Knapp refused to act as hangman because of his strong convictions against capital punishment, so Benjamin Woodworth,[15] popular proprietor of Detroit's famed Steamboat Hotel, who later retired to his farm on the St. Clair River near St. Clair, was appointed acting sheriff by Governor Cass and willingly dispatched the job.

The scene of the hanging was the Wayne County jailyard, the site of the downtown branch of the Detroit Public Library, on the triangle formed by Gratiot Avenue and Library and Farmer Streets. Knapp's attitude in the controversy, and Simmons' impressive demeanor of contrition on the scaffold that day before crowds that filled the jailyard and the roofs of surrounding buildings, helped to create the strong reaction against capital punishment which

---

[15] Benjamin Woodworth was the brother of the poet Samuel Woodworth, who wrote the popular doggerel, "The Old Oaken Bucket."

swept the state and resulted in the eventual abolishment of the law in 1846.

Judge Bunce operated the mill for Knapp for a year (1828) before Knapp sold it to Francis P. Browning of Detroit (owner of the Black River Steam Mill) and his associates, the sale occurring a few years before both Knapp and Browning died of cholera in 1834. Both men died the same day that thirty other prominent Detroit citizens succumbed to the disease—including Gen. Charles Larned, and the territorial governor, George B. Porter, whose death brought to the fore the controversial figure of the "Boy Governor," Stevens Thompson Mason.

The Mill That Altered the Course of Black River

Probably one of the most interesting facts concerning the history of the Knapp mill was how it affected the course of Black River. At the point at which the mill was situated, south of Jeddo, Black River made a sudden detour to the east, and, after making a circuit of about a mile and a half in extent, it doubled back almost to the place where it deflected. The place of departure and the point of return were hardly fifteen rods apart.

Where the river made the sudden detour there existed a ridge of land—the pioneers called it a "hog back"—measuring from sixty to eighty feet in height. The stream was dammed just below the deflection, the hog back being cut down a sufficient width to admit of doing so, and Knapp erected his mill in the cut.

All went well for some eight or nine years. The dam furnished plenty of water and the fall was sufficient through the cut to give greatly increased force and power. But the architect of the mill had miscalculated the strength of old Black River.

In the spring of 1835 a freshet of more than ordinary height and velocity developed. The water of the river washed its way under the raceway leading to the mill, and, eating its way under the mill itself, carried away the entire structure. From that time on Black River has continued to flow in the channel it made for itself that spring, and steadily, for all these years, the waters have washed over the grave of the Knapp mill.

First Steam Saw Mills in the Northwest Territory

It was also on Black River that was set up the first steam saw mill in the Northwest Territory. This was the Black River Steam Mill, established in 1832 by Francis P. Browning of Detroit, on the north bank of the river near the site of present-day Seventh Street Bridge in Port Huron.

Not only did this mill have historic distinction in itself, but it was the nucleus around which a settlement[16] clustered, along the higher ridges to the north and including the site known as Erie Square. It was a settlement complete with houses, stores, a two-story rooming house and a boarding house, a grist mill, barns, carpenter shop, dry kiln house, wharf, and even a school for the children of the mill hands—the first school building in Port Huron.

There is nothing in the history of the mill to indicate that there was a church, but anyone knowing the history of the man responsible for the mill and the settlement would feel certain that had he lived there would have been a church of the Baptist denomination. Francis Browning, called an "ardent" Baptist by his contemporaries, built in Detroit (1829) the first Baptist Church; this took place at the time of reconstruction following the disastrous fire of 1805.

Fortunately, many of the ledgers of the Black River Steam Mill, beginning with that of 1832, have been preserved,[17] and their contents are a great source of information pertaining to the early history of the St. Clair River district.

The entries in those ledgers—made by a young bookkeeper in buckskin pants, semi-frock coat, and white ruffled stock, as he sat on a high stool at a built-in pine desk—provide a record of not only the names of the early settlers, with their occupations, but also of their food and apparel. They tell of some of the earliest vessels that sailed our lakes and rivers, and of the men who commanded them; they tell of efforts to provide educational facilities, and they tell of noted men of Detroit and the Territory who

---

16 This was a different settlement from the one at the mouth of Black River in 1778-1800, and the one centered around Fort Gratiot after 1814.

17 The ledgers are in the Jenks Collection, Port Huron Public Library.

affiliated themselves with the St. Clair River district—all this in the days when nearby Detroit was virtually the capital of the great Northwest Territory and when everything centered there, even the headquarters of the Military.

The items charged to the settlers in the ledgers ranged from dry goods and medicines to groceries and cord wood, and from hardware and writing paper to lumber and whiskey. And the names of the purchasers ranged from some of the most important Territorial personages to the lowliest of the fishermen and woodcutters. Such famous Territorial judges as Solomon Sibley and James Witherell were listed, as were Oliver Newberry, merchant and shipbuilder of Detroit, and James Abbott, the noted trader— the first Englishman to establish a trading post in Detroit.

The "Captain Vidal" entered in one of the earliest ledgers refers to Captain Richard E. Vidal, one of the British naval officers who settled along the Canadian side of the St. Clair River in Sarnia, Ontario. This Captain Vidal was the man who, together with George Durand and Malcolm Cameron, founded the city of Sarnia, then known as The Rapids.

The C. L. Hannah to whom "tallow, corn beef and bread" were charged, was the father of Perry Hannah,[18] one of the founders of Traverse City. Perry Hannah, the guiding force of the historic lumber firm of Hannah, Lay and Company—the firm which also bought up the site of Traverse City and platted it—came with his family to Port Huron from Erie, Pennsylvania in 1838, at the age of thirteen. For ten years he worked in the woods and rode logs down Black River for John Wells, mill owner and merchant, and finally became a clerk in Wells' store. It is one more instance in a long line of records showing that there were but few of the noted pioneers throughout the state of Michigan who had not at some time been significantly associated with the St. Clair River District.

The eccentric and erudite George McDougall, famed Detroit

---

[18] When Perry Hannah left Port Huron, at the age of twenty-three, he went first to Chicago where he worked for A. Tracy Lay—the beginning of a friendship and a business career which culminated in the Hannah, Lay and Company lumbering empire in the Grand Traverse region. And it is of interest to note that after Hannah's "Big Store" was established in Traverse City he sent for his friend and one-time fellow clerk, Smith Barnes, then clerking for Dowling and Company, Port Huron's leading mercantile establishment at the time, and made him manager of his store.

lawyer and territorial figure, who was Chief Justice in 1807 and Aide-de-Camp to Territorial Governor William Hull, was another registered debtor to the firm—for what was listed as "sundries." McDougall was the first Fort Gratiot Lighthouse keeper (1825), a position he held until his death in 1842, and he was the first post-master in the St. Clair River district, the post office being estab-lished in January of 1826 at his Fort Gratiot headquarters, under the name of Huron Light House. George McDougall was also the first resident lawyer in St. Clair County, a familiar figure try-ing cases in the then county seat, St. Clair.[19]

McDougall had evidently long since used up his inheritance — including his share of the £1,594 he and his brother John Mc-Dougall received for the sale of Belle Isle to William Macomb (1794) [20]—and he needed, in his later years, the salaries from the two offices which he managed to get through political pull.

---

[19] McDougall, like Joseph Campau, Duperon Baby, James Abbott, and many other prominent men in early Detroit, was a slaveholder. During his residency in Port Huron as the Fort Gratiot Lighthouse keeper, he was a frequent guest at the Exchange Hotel in St. Clair—a favorite gathering place for lawyers, judges, military officers, and political leaders in the Territory when on business in the district—and he was always accompanied by a Negro boy, his valet. Friend Palmer, in his *Early Days in Detroit*, gives a striking picture of the over-weight and aging McDougall (whom he likened to Dickens' Mr. Pickwick) in that hotel where he would be the center of a crowd: ". . . Seated comfortably in the bar-room of the hotel, his gouty foot resting easily on a cushioned chair, with his brandy toddy at his elbow, and his valet combing, oiling, and brushing out his voluminous wig (for he was as bald as a billiard ball), and cracking his jokes and making witty comments on the passing show, he was a pleasure to behold."

It was to George McDougall (while he was tender of the Fort Gratiot Light) that the famous toast was drunk, at the annual bar dinner after the session of the Supreme Court each February, at Woodworth's Steamboat Hotel in Detroit, and where Judge William Woodbridge presided: "Brethren of the Bar: We drink now to the Nestor of our bar, George McDougall, who in early life shed the light and brilliancy of his genius over our profession in beautiful Michigan, but who now, in his old age, illuminates the dark waters of Lake Huron with his magic lantern, and so guides the tempest-tossed mariner safely through storms and dangers of the lake down to the silvery streams of the St. Clair." In Friend Palmer's *Early Days in Detroit*, (Detroit, Richmond: Backus, 1906), p. 218.

[20] McDougall's father, Lieutenant George McDougall of the Royal Navy, having obtained the grant of land from George III, obtained a deed to the land from the Chippewa and Ottawa Indians with goods valued at about £194.

One entry charges tobacco, whisky and cornmeal to Jeremiah Harrington, referring to the father of Daniel B. Harrington, proprietor, with Fortune C. White, of the Village of Desmond, one of the four original plats, or villages, which made up the town of Port Huron in 1837. And, interestingly enough, at the time of the Harrington entry the ledger was headed "Desmond", instead of Black River, as before, no doubt honoring the name that White and Harrington had given their plat.

An entry in one ledger charges bread, wine, cornmeal, and a box of soda powders to Captain John Burtis, the man who commanded the steamboat Argo, the first regular passenger steamer to run on the St. Clair River between Detroit and Port Huron. The Argo's hull was composed of two immense whitewood logs, hollowed out and joined together, with a deck upon which was the small engine which operated the side-wheels. Her speed was about two miles an hour, and, unable to carry sufficient fuel for a trip from Detroit to Port Huron, she would be obliged to stop at Stromness Island in the North Channel of the St. Clair River and take on a supply of wood—usually fence rails.

The Argo was what the passengers called a "cranky" boat, and she required her load to be carefully distributed. In this connection there is the story told about the portly Thomas ("Uncle Tom") Palmer of Detroit (father of Senator Thomas W. Palmer), who was a frequent passenger going to and from his property in St. Clair, then called Palmer. It is said that in his moving around the deck, his weight so affected the boat that Captain Burtis had frequently to call out, "Trim ship, Uncle Tom!" to keep her from tipping over.

John Clark, to whom a pair of shoes, two yards of calico, a box of candles, and a pound of rice were charged, was the Captain Clark of East China Township who commanded the steamboat General Gratiot, the second passenger steamboat to run regularly on the St. Clair River between Detroit and Port Huron, and which was then owned by Francis Browning.

Captain Clark, who, after the death of Browning, became one of the directors of the newly organized Black River Steam Mill Company, was prominent in the St. Clair River area for many years and was the pioneer who named Casco and China townships, taking those names, it is said, from similar ones in Kennebec County, Maine, where he lived as a boy.

The simple entry of "crackers, tea, and molasses," charged to Sam Ward,[21] recalls the man who made history at the opening of the Erie Canal, and who, together with his nephew, Eber Brock Ward, controlled the commerce of the Great Lakes in the wooden boats era.

In August of 1834 there was recorded the somewhat pathetic—and revealing—credit entry of "Cash Dr. to School House for amount received for rent of shoes during the winter months." Some of the entries charged to the Steamboat General Gratiot—one of which included "three-fourths of a yard of green flannel and one yard of red flannel"—gives us a picture of the Captain using the flannel for wristbands and chest protectors, and for lining his cap in bitter-cold weather.

A quaintly-worded entry in one of the ledgers illustrates the pioneer clerk's deference toward the settlers' wives. It was an account charged to the mill owner, John L. Baby (and spelled in the ledger as it was then pronounced—Beebee). Provisions such as cinnamon and raisins, a pound of tobacco, and a pint of wine, are charged just to John L. Beebee. But items for his wife—three yards of lace, one raw silk shawl, and one pair of worsted stockings—are charged to "John L. Beebee for his Lady."

The young bookkeeper, or clerk, who recorded the entries in many of the Black River Steam Mill Company's ledgers, and who became the mill's manager in 1842, was John Miller, later one of the first and most prominent of Port Huron's bankers. Miller also served the village of Port Huron as president, was mayor of the city three times, and served the district twice as Representative in the State Legislature.

Miller's entries in the ledgers of that historic Black River Steam Mill are now bits of Americana—particular items concerning not only the St. Clair River district but Michigan Territory as well—invaluable little gems in the annals of history.

One other bit of historic interest pertinent to the Black River Steam Mill is the fact that it used sawdust as fuel—the first steam

---

[21] See PART FOUR, THE ERA OF SHIPBUILDING, for Sam and Eber Brock Ward.

mill in Michigan Territory to so utilize that residue from the forest. And what sawdust was left over was used to fill in and raise low sections of land along the north bank of Black River, principally along Quay and River Streets and the lower end of Huron Avenue—just as acres and acres of lowland in Bay City and Saginaw were built up with similar sawdust fill.

Lumber Barons

Many of the noted lumber barons in Michigan began their careers in the pine lands of St. Clair County. Frank W. Gilchrist, who made his fortune in Alpena, had his start in Newport (Marine City) when his father, Albert Gilchrist, bought the Henry Folger mill in 1848 and operated it until it was burned down eight years later.

George N. Fletcher, also of Alpena fame, operated his first mill for six years in St. Clair. This mill, which he bought from Grant P. Robinson in 1849 had two saws and an annual capacity of three million feet. Fletcher owned considerable pine land in the township of Kimball, and as a means of getting out the timber he built a wooden track logging road from St. Clair River to his pinery. After its abandonment as a log road it became a highway, generally referred to as the Wooden Track, and now known as Ravenswood Avenue, marking the south city limits of Port Huron.

Included in the big names in the Saginaw region was the firm of Avery, Eddy, and Murphy,[22] which bought, in 1853, the mill on St. Clair River belonging to Nathan Chase and John Miller (the same Miller who had been bookkeeper for the Black River Steam Mill) and operated it for many years. The Rusts—Amasa Rust[23] and his sons Aloney, David W., Ezra, and John—all had their start in Newport after moving there from Wells, Vermont in 1838. As early as 1842, Aloney and David W. Rust built a saw mill in partnership with their uncle, Samuel Ward. This mill was run alternate months by Ward to saw oak lumber for his ship-building, and by the Rusts to saw the pine logs brought to them down the Pine and St. Clair Rivers. The mill, with a capacity of three-

---

[22] Sewell Avery, C. K. Eddy, and Simon J. Murphy.
[23] Amasa Rust had married Samuel Ward's sister, Charlotte.

million feet, was operated until 1858 when the Rusts moved to Saginaw, and there they rapidly became wealthy.

The best known of all the lumber barons, however, the "Timber King" of Michigan, was David Ward. Ward, son of Samuel Ward's brother Nathan, and cousin of Eber Brock Ward, came to Marine City from Wells County, Vermont in 1836. The first money he earned was from the garden vegetables and melons he raised and sold aboard windbound vessels anchored in St. Clair River in front of his house—the same way young Tom Edison earned his first money in Port Huron before he became a "news butcher" on the Grand Trunk train running between Port Huron and Detroit.

David Ward as a young man taught school in Port Huron, Marine City, and Algonac, having attended for eight months O. C. Thompson's Academy in St. Clair. Ward also did considerable surveying (having learned the art from his father), platting White's addition to Port Huron as well as laying out the village plats of Lakeport, Ruby, and Brockway in St. Clair County, and when not otherwise engaged did pine land cruising with his father, an occupation in which he became an expert and which was his chief interest later on.

In the meantime, however, he had accepted an invitation from Dr. Amasa Hemenger in Marine City to "read medicine" in his office, an experience which prompted him to take a course of medical lectures [24] at the Cleveland Medical College (1847). He then took a final course of lectures and clinic work in the Medical Department of the University of Michigan, receiving his diploma from Dr. Zina Pitcher, then President of the Medical Department.

Immediately upon graduation, Dr. Ward married and bought a house in Port Huron, in which he lived for six years. Abandoning entirely any idea of practicing medicine, he spent his full time

---

[24] There was a life-long jealousy and bitter feud between David Ward and his cousins of the Eber Ward banch of the family—Emily and Eber Brock Ward. Because of a chronic bronchial ailment, David spent much of his time reading, and this gave him a reputation with his cousins of being a ne'er-do-well. To disprove the legend and to show Emily and her brother that he was not lazy, seemed to have been his only motivation in studying medicine and getting a degree. Certainly, he never practiced medicine.

timber cruising for himself[25] and for numerous patrons—among them the famed Maine lumbermen Charles Merrill and Royal V. Remick, the equally famed Rusts of the Saginaw region, Alfred D. Dwight of the Au Sable Boom Company, Dudley and Wheeler of Port Huron, and Francis Palms and Joseph Campau of Detroit.

Probably the one instance most indicative of Ward's industry and inevitable success was his race to the Ionia Land office in March of 1854 to register prize pine land selections before the "land looker" of another interested party reached there. The history of lumbering is rife with stories of rival land cruisers racing one another to land offices to register their findings, but Ward's is a classic one.

He had had his eye on large stands of cork pine near Otsego Lake and intended, in time, to acquire some of it, but on hearing that the St. Mary's Ship Canal Company was about to send cruisers into the same area, he planned to be there ahead of them. With only three thousand dollars of his own to invest, he chose the private banking firm of Dwight, Smith & Company and William K. Howard of Detroit to furnish the additional necessary money to purchase the pine land he would find and select.

Ward was still living in Port Huron at the time and immediately set out with John and James Bailey, and two packers to carry provisions and camp equipment. The men traveled first to Saginaw, and, leaving there on March 16, continued on through the woods in the deep snow to Houghton Lake—always camping twenty rods to one side of their trail so no one following could tell if any one had gone in ahead of them. They then crossed on the ice to Higgins Lake—where one of Ward's toes froze, causing added difficulty on the trip—and eventually reached Otsego Lake where they made camp and began their cruising.

By April 21, having selected sixteen thousand acres of the finest white pine, Ward started on the long trek with John Bailey to register his findings at the United States Land Office at Ionia, and

---

[25] Ward always insisted on receiving for himself one-fourth of the lands he chose for his patrons, a custom, it is said, he originated and which was eventually followed by land cruisers all over the United States. The land he acquired in this way, plus that which he bought outright for himself, soon made him the largest individual owner of timber lands in Michigan. One tract alone of his—that on the Manistee River in the northeast corner of Crawford County—contained ninety thousand acres of pine land.

on the first day out crossed the trail of the Soo Canal land cruisers. The second day, while traveling near Higgins Lake, they met two of the Soo Canal packers going in, and Ward, pretending that they had come from Grand Traverse Bay and were on their way to Saginaw, inquired of the men the route of the trail to the mouth of the Tobacco River. The men obligingly gave instructions on a pocket map and also generously informed Ward and his helper that they had provisions cached in the woods under their overturned canoe at the mouth of Tobacco River.

Two days later Ward and Bailey found the cache of provisions, from which they "ate heartily,"[26] and then taking the canoe[27]—the loss of which would delay the Soo Canal men at least a day—they started down the Tittabawassee, Bailey poling, and Ward paddling so fast and so continuously, a white "bone" was kept at the bow of the canoe. Seven hours later they reached Saginaw.

That same night they engaged a team and started for Flint, arriving in the morning, and Ward, wiring ahead to Detroit to have land warrants and money ready for him, reached there early the next morning. Bailey returned to Port Huron, and Ward in a light buggy with a strong, speedy horse left immediately for Lansing—a distance of 85 miles—traveling the rest of the day and all night over a plank road, and stopping only occassionally to water his horse at toll gates.

He reached Lansing at six o'clock the following morning, and took the stage to Ionia, and on reaching there in the late afternoon went directly to the Land Office where his money and list of land descriptions were locked in the safe. He worked all the next day with the Receiver and had just pocketed his perfected certificates of purchase when the Soo Canal agent was seen galloping up to the office, his over-riden horse covered with foam and steam.

David Ward's compensation for that coup was four thousand acres of some of the finest white pine in the Territory—a most substantial beginning for the great fortune he was to acquire as the "Pine King" of Michigan.

---

26 *Autobiography of David Ward,* privately printed in New York, 1912, p. 81.

27 In his *Autobiography* Ward is often given to lamenting other men's lack of principle, while emphasizing his own integrity. In this instance, he applied salve to his conscience by explaining that "to hook a canoe, pushed and driven as (he) was seemed then a merit." *Ibid.,* p. 85.

Chapter IX

FOREST FIRES AND THE BEGINNING OF THE AMERICAN RED CROSS AS A NATIONAL SOCIETY

Long before the pine and other timber trees of the St. Clair River region gave out, the lumber mills along the Saginaw, the Muskegon, and many other rivers, were reaching their peaks and fast depleting the dense and lofty forests of Michigan. But great forest fires also did their share in wiping out incredible swaths of valuable timber.

Although searing forest fires were numerous in the Thumb area of Michigan as early as 1862, probably the two greatest fires occurred in 1871 (at the same time as the great Chicago fire) and in 1881. The worst of these, as far as loss of life was concerned, was the latter, which took 125 lives and left thousands homeless and without food.

The Port Huron Relief Committee did a remarkable job in organizing and bringing help to the victims of that district, and it was mainly as a result of the appeals sent out by the Port Huron committee that Clara Barton began her efforts in behalf of Michigan's fire victims—the initial national functioning of the American Red Cross in a disaster.

When first reports of the disaster had reached Port Huron the Relief Committee was formed by the citizens and consisted of Omar D. Conger, U. S. Senator at the time, William L. Bancroft, and Ezra C. Carleton, who was then mayor. The committee requested Governor David H. Jerome to send out an official nation-wide appeal for help, and also sent appeals to newspapers in the larger cities and to a number of the leading magazines.

All sections of the country cooperated. Even the South, impoverished as it still was, sent donations varying in amounts from a fifty-dollar check from the people of Vicksburg, Mississippi, to fifteen hundred dollars from Memphis, Tennessee. And all kinds of groups were represented—for example, the Salem Society of Deaf Mutes of Salem, Massachusetts, and the Michigan State

Prison convicts—the latter having taken up a collection among themselves amounting to eighty-three dollars.

Probably one of the most unexpected contributions to come to the Relief Committee was $219 from P. T. Barnum, money donated by the circus personnel of that "Greatest Show on Earth"—men and women who had but a few weeks earlier performed under the big top in Port Huron.

The townspeople of Port Huron spent day after day down at the docks helping to unload the schooners and steamboats bringing in cargoes of supplies to be reallocated by the Relief Committee. Those cargoes of supplies ranged from food and lumber and household goods to smoking tobacco and medicines. And besides the boxes of medicine there were bandages, carbolic acid, olive oil, whiskey, and kegs of lime water sent to hospitals for the fire victims.

Hardly a facet of relief was overlooked, which can be attested to by the fact that L. B. Rice, Port Huron Nursery dealer, went from door to door soliciting money to provide for the replacing of fruit trees, and delivered, personally, over two hundred saplings to the burnt-over area in the Thumb.

Clara Barton, after receiving the appeal, wrote regularly to Senator Conger from her headquarters in Dansville, New York, advising him of the step-by-step relief activities of her group, which ultimately collected and sent three thousand dollars.

All in all, nearly half a million dollars in money and supplies were donated for the fire sufferers—a magnificent accomplishment of the Port Huron Relief Committee, and a great testimonial to the spontaneous generosity of our American people.

Chapter X

RAFTING ON THE ST. CLAIR RIVER

Great cribs of uncut logs being rafted to their destination down the St. Clair River provided one of the interesting sights of the by-gone lumbering era in Michigan. Although it posed a great problem to navigation, rafting was one of the St. Clair River district's important industries.

Rafting on the St. Clair River and its tributaries began at least as early as 1749 when planks and boards were sent down Black River (then Riviere Dulude) and into the St. Clair, on their way to Detroit.

Chaussegros de Léry, the French engineer in charge of construction work in early Detroit wrote (at Detroit) in his *Journal,* in July of 1749 —

> On the 27th I began to make plans and take the necessary observations for an exact account of the place, the quality of the soil, and everything that would give it value . . . . There is no cedar or pine. For these one must go 25 leagues to the River Dulude where there is a large pinery and a saw mill belonging to Mons. Gervais, habitant of Detroit, who brings boards and planks by raft. The current favors this method of transportation and the wood is not injured at all.[1]

We know, too, that after the British occupation, the enlargement of that part of the fort at Detroit called the Citadel was built in 1764 from timber floated down the St. Clair River in rafts from Patrick Sinclair's mill on Pine River. In the same way, the timber from the pine woods on the property of Louis St. Bernard, about a mile above Pine River in St. Clair, was brought to Detroit after the fire of 1805 to build St. Anne's Church.

Of course the rebuilding of Detroit after the fire gave impetus to the mills along the St. Clair River and its tributaries, and rafts became a common sight. The early rafts were guided by canoe or

---

[1] De Léry quote in letter of M. M. Quaife to W. L. Jenks, November 25, 1932. *Jenks Papers,* Jenks Collection, Port Huron Public Library.

bateau, or by men with boom poles who lived in little shanties built on the floating platforms that were cribs of timber. Daniel B. Harrington, one of Port Huron's earliest and best known pioneers, lived in such a shanty while rafting, as a young man, on the Black and St. Clair Rivers.

In the eighteen sixties tugs began to appear and took over the business of towing rafts and, later, the towing of lumber barges and schooners, as many as six and eight at a time, all piled high with the yellowish pine. James Moffat, in partnership with Elliott Brockway and John S. Botsford (all of Port Huron) built what was probably the first tug used especially for towing rafts on the St. Clair. This was the *Kate Moffat,* built in 1864, and the first of a long line of tugs built, or owned, by the Moffat interests—including the *Frank Moffat,* the *George E. Brockway,* the powerful *Mocking Bird* (famous for her screeching Modoc whistle), and the *Gladiator*—all built in Port Huron. And there were more—the *Masters,* the *Satellite,* the *Sweepstakes,* the *Stranger,* and the *Champion,* which was the most powerful tug on the Lakes. The well-known S. Arch Whipple painting shows how the *Champion,* with her tow of eight vessels, looked on her way down the St. Clair and Detroit rivers to Lake Erie.

With the appearance of tugs, log rafting became big business along the St. Clair River. Rafts became larger, looking like great, brown, barren islands floating downstream, often requiring the aid of two or more tugs.[2] Several of the larger rafts seen on the St. Clair have been mentioned in reminiscences and histories of the River district. Mrs. Crampton in her *History of the St. Clair River* wrote that the "largest raft that ever passed down the River" floated down in the year 1875 from Bay City and that it was in tow of the tugs, the *John Owen* (Captain Wesley C. Brown) and the *Merrick.*[3]

That raft had two million feet of oak, supported, or floated by one million feet of cork pine, and was about one thousand feet

[2] For a description of how rafts were made and of some of the tugs that towed them, see Emeline Jenks Crampton, *History of the St. Clair River* (St. Clair, 1921), pp. 10-11, and also Victor Lauriston, *Lambton's Hundred Years 1849-1949* (Sarnia: Haines, 1949), pp. 211-213.

[3] Crampton, *op. cit.,* pp. 10-11.

long and three hundred feet wide. It was eighteen hours passing through the St. Clair River, and sixteen days in all on the trip from Bay City to its destination at Buffalo.

Victor Lauriston in his *Lambton County's Hundred Years* writes that the largest raft ever towed down Lake Huron was probably one from Whitefish River, assembled at Wells Island. This raft of 97,860 logs "scaled 4,281,000 feet, log measure." [4] This was, presumably, in the eighteen nineties.

But in that same decade—in the summer of 1895—a large raft containing 6,500,000 feet passed down the St. Clair River in tow of three tugs—the *George H. Parker,* the *Protector,* and the *Boynton.* The reason that special mention was made of this raft at the time, was that it caused so much grief to navigation and expense to the owners. The raft was broken up in a collision with the steamer *Wade* at the southeast bend of the river, and the logs were scattered in all directions through the St. Clair Flats.

In trying to help the raft over the Flats the tug *Boynton* broke one bucket off her wheel, and the tug *Kittie Haight,* which was called in to aid after the *Protector* was held aground on the southeast bend, broke two of her buckets. Steamers coming up the river had trouble getting through the river at all, the Steamer *Tuscarora,* among them, and were held fast between the banks of the river and the broken up raft for some seven or eight hours.

But for all the complaints of vessel owners, rafting of logs on the St. Clair River continued to be big business, and even as late as the nineteen twenties large rafts were still towed from Georgian Bay into Sarnia Bay [5] across from Port Huron, Michigan.

---

[4] Lauriston, *op. cit.,* p. 213.

[5] Crampton, *op. cit.,* p. 11. See also Lauriston, *op. cit.,* pp. 211-213.

Chapter XI

BLACK RIVER RED SHIRTS BECOME THE BOYS IN BLUE

In the 1860–1880 decades, for its entire length from its main source in Sanilac County Black River was alive with rivermen hurrying the products of the pine forrests to the markets of the world. Their red shirts made colorful and handsome uniforms, and it was a royal sport for the crowds who gathered on the banks of the river to watch these men with their peavies in the spring drives breaking jams and riding the logs on the run to the mouth of the river, where men with pike poles would then distribute the logs to the individual booms of the owners.

Many of the "red shirts" became the "boys in blue" during the Civil War. In fact, Company "K" of the Second Michigan Cavalry was made up, to a great extent, of those hardy rivermen, and were recruited by Captain Archibald Campbell, a skilled "river-hog" himself, and later of Boonville and Chattanooga fame. The handsome monument on the Glass Mill Road in the Chattanooga and Chickamauga National Park attests to the regard in which Colonel Campbell and his hardy Black River boys of the Second Michigan Regiment of Cavalry [1] were held.

But Campbell figured materially, if indirectly, in another episode of the war—a circumstance which proved to have important effects as well as dramatic connotation. It had to do with the celebrated war horse, Rienzi, the black charger on which General Philip H. Sheridan (Campbell's commander) made his famous twenty mile ride on October 19, 1864 from Winchester to Cedar Creek to rally his demoralized army—a spectacular dash which helped immeasurably in the crushing defeat of General J. A. Early in the Shenandoah Valley, and which was memorialized by T. Buchanan Read in his poem "Sheridan's Ride."

The story of Sheridan's war horse has particular interest to the

---

[1] In this same National Park is a second monument on Snodgrass Hill, honoring another Port Huron man, Colonel William Sanborn, hero of the Battle of Chickamauga (in which he was critically wounded) and the Twenty-second Michigan Regiment of Infantry.

people of the St. Clair River district for he was raised in Burtchville Township, near Lakeport. When Captain Campbell recruited Company "K" of the Second Michigan Cavalry, principally from his Black River raftsmen, and prepared to leave for the front, the citizens of Port Huron purchased the jet-black colt[2] from William Leonard of Lakeport and presented him, fully equipped, to Campbell. He was called Rienzi by Campbell after the battle of that name in which the colt had shown such coolness and intelligence under fire.

Cambell continued to ride Rienzi until after the Boonville campaign and shortly afterwards gave him to his commander, General Sheridan, who had always admired the superb qualities of the "fiery colt." [3]

Sheridan was riding Rienzi when he was given the task of crushing the Confederate General Early, strongly entrenched in the Shenandoah Valley. His army had proceeded against Early, defeating him at Opequon Creek, Fischer's Hill, and Cedar Creek. But it was at Cedar Creek—where Sheridan rested his troops and then went on himself to Washington for a conference with Lincoln and Stanton—that success was almost turned into defeat.

On his way back from Washington to join his troops, Sheridan spent the night of October 18 in Winchester, and early the next morning he was awakened by the sound of artillery fire—

The terrible grumble and rumble and roar
Telling the battle was on once more,[4]

coming from the direction of Cedar Creek, twenty miles away.

Hurriedly breakfasting, he ordered his horse saddled, and, selecting two aides de camp and twenty men, he made preparations to proceed immediately to the front.

---

[2] Foaled in the spring of 1858, this celebrated colt was sold by A. P. Sexton, living near Lakeport, to Russell Leonard (for $90) who sold him to his son William, living in Burtchville on the Comstock Road. The latter broke him to harness and used him to haul cord wood the seventeen miles to Port Huron, where he was known as the Leonard Colt. He was three years old then, jet black except for three white feet, standing sixteen hands high, and of Morgan stock. It is said that the people of Port Huron paid $175.00 for him.

[3] Philip H. Sheridan, *Memoirs*.

[4] T. Buchanan Read, "Sheridan's Ride," in C. F. Bates' *Cambridge Book of Poetry and Song* (Crowell, 1882), p. 453.

He mounted his "beautiful Rienzi" and rode down the street to the Valley Turnpike.

And there through the flush of the morning light
A steed as black as the steeds of night
Was seen to pass, as with eagle flight,
As if he knew the terrible need,
He stretched away with the utmost speed.[5]

In the doorways of the houses in Winchester, Sheridan noticed, were a great number of women who kept shaking their skirts at him in a derogatory manner and making "other insolent gestures."[6] He knew then that the Confederate women had been told by the 'grapevine telegraph' that Early had surprised his troops at Cedar Creek, and that they were taunting him with that knowledge.

On reaching the edge of town Sheridan put his head down near the pommel of his saddle, listening intently for half a mile beyond Winchester. He was convinced that the travel of sound he heard was too rapid to be attributed to his own rate of progress —that it was his own army retreating toward him.

His conjecture was right. Beyond the high ground toward Mill Creek the first of the retreating fugitives came into view—an appalling spectacle of a panic-stricken army—hundreds of wounded men, throngs of others unhurt but utterly demoralized, and baggage wagons by the score, all pressing to the rear in hopeless confusion.

Striking his spurs he galloped toward Cedar Creek, calling encouragement to the scattered troops, coming now by squads and companies, even regiments, who on seeing Sheridan, began flinging up their caps with wild cheers and, turning back, followed him.

Sheridan dashed on, and as he advanced down the Valley and neared Middle Creek Brook a man from Lakeport, Michigan, Alexander McDonald, Sixth Michigan Cavalry, recognized the horse and rider. "It's Sheridan!" he cried. And McDonald led the cheers of the regiment as they, too, turned about in their flight and dashed along in the wake of "Gallant Phil" and the Leonard colt.

---

[5] *Ibid.*
[6] Sheridan, *op. cit.*, II, 81.

In his famous ride nothing seemed to daunt the general or his horse. He jumped Rienzi over rail fences and swept across streams, and when the retreating forces became impassable he circuited them and shouted encouragement until they faced around and returned with him to recover their camp.

And the wave of retreat checked its course there, because,
The sight of the master compelled it to pause.
With foam and with dust the black charger was gray;
By the flash of his eye and the red nostrils' play
He seemed to the whole great army to say:
'I have brought you Sheridan all the way
From Winchester down to save the day! [7]

Sheridan continued to ride the beautiful Rienzi in every campaign and battle in which he took part. After the war he provided him with all the care and comforts due his faithful service, and when Rienzi died at the age of twenty his stuffed remains were placed in the Smithsonian Institute in Washington, D. C.

Today, two of the most celebrated equestrian statues in the United States depict Sheridan and Rienzi on that ride—the heroic Sheridan statue on the capital grounds in Albany, New York, and the Gutzon Borglum one in Sheridan Circle in Washington, D. C. The saddle that General Sheridan used on that famous ride from Winchester to Cedar Creek is now one of the articles of living history in the Museum of the Port Huron Public Library.

---

[7] Read, *op. cit.*, p. 454.

Chapter XII

NO GHOST TOWNS IN WAKE OF VANISHING SAW MILLS

After the lumbering industry began to decline in the St. Clair River area, places affected by the industry were saved from becoming ghost towns—as had happened in some sections of Michigan —by the presence of additional interests, including shipbuilding and ship repair, the mining and manufacture of salt,[1] and innumerable other industries.

Port Huron is a good example of a surviving, one-time lumbering center. It was saved and kept vital by its fisheries, its tanneries, and its cooper shops, by its shipbuilding and dry docks, its ship chandleries and sail makers, its breweries and its boiler-works, by its carriage and wagon manufacturing and its automobile plants,[2] and by the manufacture of its nationally-known agricultural implements and road-making equipment.[3] The city was notably early in providing its inhabitants with electricity [4] and electric street cars,[5] and pioneered in the production of oil and natural gas—Port Huron being the first city in Michigan in the commercial production of both.

In the transition of Port Huron from a saw mill city to a still and even more vital industrial center, the high-pitched, discordant

---

[1] See PART EIGHT, Chapter XXXV, for salt mining and manufacture.

[2] See PART NINE, Chapter XXXVI (2) .

[3] See *ibid.*, (3).

[4] The Excelsior Electric Company of Port Huron was one of the earliest electric light companies in the United States.

[5] Port Huron was the third city in the United States to operate an electric street railway—Montgomery, Alabama was the first, in 1885 (the plant, however, was later destroyed by fire and the line returned to mule power, originally in use) , and Appleton, Wisconsin was the second, having its horse-car railroad electrified in August of 1886, just three months before Port Huron's line was electrified. The first electrified street railroad in America was in Windsor, Ontario, Canada, installed in June of that same year. The original installation on the lines was the Charles J. Van de Poole System.

Port Huron was the first city in the world to have electric cars cross a moveable bridge, and the first to have street cars lighted wih incandescent lamps.

whining and screeching in the planing mills mingled with the thud of the caulker's mallets on the hundreds of boats in Black and St. Clair Rivers, with the deafening clang and bang of the riveters in the boiler-works, and with the penetrating shrieks of the Modoc whistles on the impudent little tugs busily engaged in picking up business on the lake and river.

All made a cacophonous mechanical symphony, indicative of the vibrant, pulsating industries that gave the area continued life until the arrival of modern industries, and which gave the St. Clair River District the economic stability it needed in the transition from a lumbering center to the progressive community it is today.

PART FOUR

THE ERA OF SHIPBUILDING

Then came so many ships that I could fill
Three docks with their fair hulls remembered still,
Each with her special memory's special grace,
Riding the sea, making the waves give place
To delicate high beauty; man's best strength,
Noble in every line in all their length.

—John Masefield

Chapter XIII

MEN AND SHIPS THAT POINTED THE WAY

As once, long since, when all the docks were filled
With that sea beauty man has ceased to build.

—John Masefield

Geographically speaking, the great State of Michigan is an empire in itself, embraced by the long arms and vastness of great lakes, which in turn are surrounded by a continent of land rich in minerals and vegetation and scenic beauty. Their solitudes were unbroken until man learned to brave the loneliness of the seas and conquer the mysteries of the vast inland and its waterways.

And then, in what might be considered the twinkling of an eye in comparison to the aeons of time our land knows, these great lakes—these Seas of Sweet Water as the Jesuits called them—and their connecting waterways became the channels of a commerce that dwarfed even that of the Mediterranean in the proudest days of Tyre, or of Greece or Rome, and became one of the greatest trade routes of the World. They became, in fact, the world's most important unit of inland waterway transportation.

The men of the St. Clair River region led the way, both as shipbuilders and masters of ships, in that great commerce. They led the way in the development of water transportation—and water was the only highway in Territorial days—which was a factor of prime importance in the development of towns and settlements. They were aided in their progress by the presence in the area of large quantities of hardwood timber, especially oak, so valuable in the building of all the early ships—sloops, schooners, barques, brigs, and steamers.

These men who first chanced their fortunes and brought life and thriving business to the community can never be without interest —such men as Samuel Ward and Eber Brock Ward, Wesley Truesdail, Amos Hinckley, Edmund Fitzgerald, Thomas Dunford, H. E. Runnels, Thomas Alverson, Lars Jansen, Jacob L. Wolverton, Abram Smith, Archy Stewart, Archibald Muir, James Moffat, and Elliot T. Brockway. And the greatest of these were the Wards.

Sam Ward and His Floating Bazaar

In the spring of 1818 a tiny schooner made her way up the St. Clair River and stopped at a convenient dock of one of the "ribbon farms" [1] bordering its shores. This little craft, the Salem Packet, with her skipper Captain Samuel Ward of Salem (Conneaut), Ohio, piled at all the struggling ports between Buffalo, N. Y. and Green Bay, Wisconsin, and carried not only government supplies for military out-posts but also much needed merchandise to eagerly-waiting inhabitants of the thinly scattered settlements.

The tall, sparse, ruddy-cheeked captain, in his Salem Packet, brought such things to the farmers as powder and shot and fish-hooks, tobacco and axe-handles, and "ten rod whisky" [2] which he sold for a dollar a gallon. For their wives he supplied such items as calico at six shillings a yard, spices at about the same price per pound, and tea and sugar for "all he could get," [3] as one pioneer put it.

One can imagine what a welcome sight Captain Ward and his floating bazaar were to the isolated inhabitants of that frontier region on the St. Clair River. And not only did he bring them needed supplies from the shops in such cities as Buffalo and Detroit, but he also brought them news of happenings in the outside world and messages from far-off relatives and friends, for which those isolated settlers hungered.

Captain Samuel Ward was to do more than that, however, and probably few, if any, of those settlers suspected that this Yankee trader would in a few years point the way toward the tremendous future trade of the Great Lakes.

Born in Wells, Rutland County, Vermont in 1784, Ward was

---

[1] Long, narrow farms of the French settlers, stretching inland from the river and varying in width from two to five arpents and about eighty arpents in length—an arpent being a square, the side of which is about 192 feet.

[2] "Ten-rod whiskey" was high wine to which brown sugar was added, and also tobacco to give it color.

[3] William L. Bancroft, "Memoir of Capt. Samuel Ward," *Pioneer and Historical Coll., Mich.,* XXI, (1892), 339.

one of six sons and four daughters of a Baptist minister and part-time farmer, getting his usual three months of education in a district school in winter and working on the farm in summer. At nineteen he and his older brother Eber (father of Michigan's first steel magnate, Eber Brock Ward) sought employment in the salt industry in Syracuse, N. Y., remaining there or in the vicinity for fourteen years.

In the meantime, during the War of 1812, the brothers had a contract with the United States Government for transporting supplies for the American Army, their means of transportation being a small coaster, with headquarters at Sodus Bay, Lake Ontario. The coaster was eventually caught by the British and destroyed, but this business venture gave the brothers valuable experience and no doubt was instrumental in encouraging Samuel to move to Conneaut, Ohio (then called Salem) where he built his twenty seven-ton schooner, *Salem Packet,* for trading on the Lakes.

It was while on his trading trips that Captain Ward saw and appreciated the future value, as well as the perennial beauty of the land fronting on the St. Clair River; and in 1818, at the age of thirty-four, Ward purchased, in partnership with Father Gabriel Richard of Detroit, two sections of land at the junction of Belle River with the St. Clair.

It was never quite clear how Ward and Father Richard came about buying the land together. Perhaps the two had met and become friends on one of Ward's numerous trading stop-overs in Detroit. In any event, the land was soon divided, Father Richard taking the lower end of section 12 for the Catholics of the district, which became known as Catholic Point, and Captain Ward taking the upper part in section one, called Yankee Point, but which was later known by the various names of Belle River, Ward's Landing, Newport, Marine, and finally, Marine City.

By the spring of the following year (1819) Ward had a house, built of rounded logs, containing two rooms, and roofed with oak "shakes." And to this house he brought his family which consisted of his wife, whom he married in Salina, N. Y., and one son.

Here, after eventually buying additional land which lay on both sides of Belle River, Ward set up and operated a saw mill and grist mill, experimented with a tannery and a brick yard, and continued

113

to work his farm and to traffic with both the Indians and white families in the scattered settlements.

But Ward, the Yankee skipper, sailor, farmer, and merchant financier, was a trader at heart, and was not content with his land holdings and his one boat. So he set his energies to furthering that trading interest. To this end, when the Erie Canal was nearing completion, he built a 280-ton schooner which he named *"St. Clair."*[4] And that schooner—the first of the great fleet of ships Ward was to build in Marine City—was destined to make history.

The Schooner *St. Clair* Makes History

The completion of the Erie Canal in late October of 1825, which facilitated the settlement of Michigan and the shipping of farm products to the east, brought the expected increase of business to the Great Lakes, and Samuel Ward with foresight and industry had made preparations to get his share of that business.

The little schooner-rigged *St. Clair* had been modeled curiously like a canal boat, having full ends, with her rudder hanging over the stern and her masts so arranged that they could be lowered. William Gallegher, the husband of Mrs. Ward's sister, and one of the numerous relatives[5] Ward was to bring to Marine City, was the master builder of the schooner, and Mrs. Ward spun and wove the material for the sails and outfitted the cabin.

In the early summer of 1826, after making a successful trip to Green Bay with the *St. Clair,* Ward put on a cargo of potash, furs, and gun stocks at Mackinac—a cargo which tells something of the

---

4 Built on the St. Clair River at the foot of Broadway Street in Marine City. He also built one other boat the same year, the schooner *Sam Ward,* of 27 tons.

5 Jacob W. Wolverton, a nephew of Mrs. Ward, and Benjamin F. Owen, Eber Brock Ward's brother-in-law, were two of the many relatives brought here, and who, like Samuel Ward and Eber Brock Ward, proved to be geniuses in their professions. Wolverton, from the early Eighteen Forties, began building ships for the Wards (including the famed *Ocean,* the *Pacific,* and the *Gazelle*) and immediately became one of the leading American ship builders. "Not one of his boats was a failure; all of them were advances upon anything that had appeared before, and scarcely any improvement has been made since his day upon wooden craft for the lakes." B. F. Owen's skill and thoroughness in all the boats built by Wolverton were "sufficiently attested by the almost total exemption of accidents to the machinery of any vessel of his numerous fleet." Quotes are from William L. Bancroft, *op. cit.,* p. 345.

life in that frontier settlement north of Detroit—and started for New York City via the Erie Canal.

On the way down Captain Ward picked up barrels of whitefish—probably from the fisheries at Lower Lake Huron near Fort Gratiot—and at Detroit added to his cargo of potash, which was furnished to him by Thomas Palmer, and also put on board two horses to tow his schooner through the Canal.

On arriving at Buffalo, July 4th, Ward lowered the masts of the *St. Clair* and was towed through the Canal to Albany, where he reset her masts and sailed down the Hudson to New York City, arriving there July 26th. She was the first vessel to make a through voyage from the Lakes to the sea.[6]

Disposing of his goods, Ward took on merchandise for the firm of Buckingham & Sturges of Zanesville, Ohio, completed his cargo with salt at Syracuse (where he had earlier been employed) which he delivered to a firm in what is now Sandusky City, Ohio, and returned to the Lakes, reaching Detroit on the twenty-seventh of August.

Besides making history with the little schooner *St. Clair,* Ward made a profit in that one transaction, it is said, of six thousand dollars. Although his profit was phenomenal, however, for some reason Ward never repeated the trip.

The story is told by Ward's contemporaries that on returning through the Canal, Ward was annoyed, in fact deeply insulted, when he was required to pay the toll. The captain had expected not only to travel through the Canal free of toll, but also to receive a premium, since his was the first vessel freighted from the Lakes to the Atlantic Ocean. His disappointment on both counts may have been the reason for not repeating the trip.

Further Career of Sam Ward

Anticipating the influx of settlers, as he had the increase of commerce on the Great Lakes with the opening of the Erie Canal,

---

[6] George A. Cuthbertson, in his *Freshwater* (Macmillan, 1931), p. 298, in reference to this event makes the mistake of saying "schooner *St. Clair* of Detroit," and gives "Captain E. Ward" as master. He also, on page 19, refers to "Captain Samuel Ward of Detroit." Captain Ward's home was always in Marine City after he moved from Conneaut, Ohio. At his death in 1854 he was buried in Marine City, but later his nephew, E. B. Ward, had the body removed and interred in Elmwood Cemetery, Detroit.

Ward had acquired additional land and made plans to plat his village of Newport—a scheme accomplished by 1836. He had already established a general store on his original land and had secured a post office (Belle River), himself serving as postmaster.

But by 1830 he had also started vigorously on a career of boat building and ownership. In that year Ward built two more schooners, the 20-ton *Albatros,* in which Oliver Newberry of Detroit had a half-interest, and the the 73-ton *Marshall Ney.*[7] He now had four boats (he had built the historic *St. Clair* and the 27-ton schooner *Sam Ward* in 1829) carrying passengers and trading for him on the Lakes. These were followed in 1833 by the schooner *General Harrison,* his largest boat up to that time. This last schooner traded between Buffalo, Detroit, Green Bay, and Chicago, and the man who sailed her as mate was Ward's nephew, Eber Brock Ward—who, like his uncle, was destined to make history.

By 1838 Samuel Ward, with an eye for the increasing westward tide of immigration, began building the *Huron*—the first of a notable line of passenger steamers. It was a time of close economy for Ward. After the panic of 1837 money was scarce, and purchasers of Ward's lots in his Village of Newport were unable, after the down payment, to keep up the interest, to say nothing of their principal payments.

Ward's ready money ran out by the time the hull of the *Huron* was finished, and he was without funds to put in her engines. It was at this point that his nephew, Eber Brock Ward, who had been sailing for him for several years,[8] loaned him his savings of $775, and also secured additional loans for him from his father, Eber Ward, Samuel's brother. Soon afterwards the engines were

---

[7] The policy used by Captain Ward in paying his ship carpenters is worthy of notice. Wages paid by him, which averaged about $1.50 per day, were payable, half in goods, and half in cash in six months. However, if a man took flour or pork it was considered cash and deducted from his cash account. Because of this little ready cash was needed by Ward, as the carpenters would be obliged to get goods, especially provisions like flour and pork, before the cash was due.

[8] Eber B. Ward first began working for his uncle on the farm in 1833. In the winter of 1835 and 1836 he assisted him in getting out ship timber, and in the latter year made his first investment in his uncle's ship business, a quarter interest in a small schooner.

116

bought and installed. The *Huron* was completed (1839) and placed in the Lake Erie trade, with Eber B. Ward as captain.

So successful was the *Huron* that the United Passenger Lines (an established line operating between Buffalo, Lake Erie ports, and Detroit) considered her its chief competitor, and before the season was over (1840) induced Ward, for a valuable consideration, to withdraw her from that circuit with an agreement—which would "now be called illegal restraint of trade[9]"—not to reintroduce her.

Captain Ward kept to the letter of his agreement and operated the *Huron* on Lake Huron in 1842 and 1843 before running her for several years on the Port Huron-Detroit route. She was finally dismantled in 1848, her machinery being placed in another Ward boat, the *Franklin Moore.*[10]

In 1843, however, he completed the steamer *Champion,* more than twice the size of the Huron, and promptly put her in the Lake Erie trade. This competition was again so painful and so costly to the rival company that it soon offered Captain Ward ten thousand dollars to retire from the line permanently.[11]

With the *Huron* and the *Champion* the rapid growth of the Ward fortunes and ship holdings really began. These holdings were to make Ward and his nephew the largest ship owners on the Lakes. Samuel Ward had now reached the age when discretion often curtailed and delayed the zeal needed in new enterprises, and he wisely let his astute and capable nephew take over the weightier responsibilities in the rapidly expanding business.

With their profits they were able to build newer and bigger steamers, and from 1846 to 1854—the year of Samuel Ward's death—in quick succession twenty-two more steamers were built by the Wards, including the *Samuel Ward,* the *Ocean,* the tragic *Atlantic* and the *E. K. Collins,* the popular *Pearl,* the *Forester,* the second *Huron,* and the *Pacific.*

The Pacific deserves special mention. When the Michigan Central Railroad was finished as far as New Buffalo on Lake

9 W. L. Jenks, "Samuel Ward," *Jenks Papers,* Jenks Collection, Port Huron Public Library. Also printed in *St. Clair Republican,* Sept. 23, 1925, under the title: "Early History of Marine City and Samuel Ward."

10 E. J. Crampton, *op. cit.,* p. 34.

11 Jenks, "Samuel Ward."

Michigan, the Wards built the *Pacific* to put on the run from New Buffalo to the railroad's future terminal, Chicago. In one year she cleared for her owners five thousand dollars, more than the entire cost of the vessel.

Meanwhile, with the same foresight and enterprise which had prompted Ward to test the Erie Canal, and to capitalize on the completion of the Michigan Central Railroad, Samuel Ward and his nephew were able to profit from the great flow of iron ore from the Marquette country.

When iron and copper ore were found on Lake Superior, they took the steamer *Samuel Ward*,[12] up to the Sault, hauled her over the portage to Lake Superior and kept her there in profitable operation until the canal opened. During this time they operated another steamer from Detroit so as to offer merchants and travelers the benefit of a through line. In 1851 alone, the net profits from the Ward boats were over $240,000,[13] and a March 1852 inventory showed their steamer interests "valued at $475,000."[14]

In addition to his vessel interests, Samuel Ward had railroad and bank stock, and Michigan and Illinois land holdings amounting to over sixty thousand dollars; at his death in 1854, at the age of 69, his estate was valued, according to different sources,[15] at five hundred thousand to a million dollars. After providing for his wife and son (who was mentally incompetent) during their

---

[12] In 1854 a thousand tons of iron ore were taken out by the *Sam Ward,* the propeller *Peninsula* (built in Vicksburg by M. P. Lester), and the *Napoleon* (by now converted to a propeller), which was built on the St. Clair River just above Marine City by Andrew Westbrook, for Oliver Newberry of Detroit. And it might also be pointed out that when the brig *Columbia,* carried the first cargo of iron ore through the newly-completed Sault Ste Marie Canal, from Marquette to the lower lakes (for the Cleveland Iron Mining Co.), her master was Captain Justin Wells, who later settled in St. Clair Township and became a prominent and successful St. Clair County farmer.

[13] *Ward Papers.*

[14] *Ibid.*

[15] The will was duly admitted to probate, but no inventory of the property was ever filed, "probably a move on the part of Eber Brock Ward to avoid satisfying the curiosity of some of the Ward relatives who envied the successful nephew." Quote is from Jenks in paper on "Samuel Ward." By the "Ward relatives," Mr. Jenks probably had in mind David Ward (later, the "Pine King" of Michigan) who figured in a lifelong feud with his cousins, Eber Brock Ward, and his sister, Emily. David Ward's autobiography is full of invectives against his two cousins.

lifetimes, and after mentioning a few minor bequests, he gave the residue of his estate to his nephew, Eber Brock Ward.

The reason for his generosity to this one of his numerous relatives is revealed in a statement accompanying his will: it was "as a compensation for his long and faithful care over my interests, for his advice, assistance and good judgment in the general supervision of my affairs for a long term of years, during which time my credit has been unimpaired and my success in business has equalled my highest hopes."

One other interesting item in Samuel Ward's will is revealing of his character—that pioneer's own appraisal of his struggles and triumphs. In concluding the will he wrote that "success for his successors" was the "sincere desire of one whose early manhood was spent in discouraging efforts to subdue a wilderness, now teeming with population, and whose energy traversed the northwestern Lakes without a chart or pilot, accomplished every enterprise he undertook and attained against great obstacles and discouragements, a prosperity seldom equalled by an uneducated but self made man."[16]

Appraisals of Samuel Ward by some of his contemporaries show him to have been a man of kindly disposition but rather autocratic at times. He disliked opposition of any kind, whether in business or in politics; in fact, interference in any of his plans was anathema to him.

In politics Ward was not always a winner, but in matters of business he was usually successful, and there is one incident that typefies his handling of any opposition. It involves a feud with Wesley Truesdail over interference in his constant struggle to hold secure his control of lake shipping.

Wesley Truesdail was a St. Clair banker, lumberman, ship owner, and builder of the *Goliath,* the first steamboat built on the St. Clair River exclusively for freight purposes. At the time of this incident he was running the Bank of St. Clair—a county bank situated in St. Clair—and, as much of the business pertinent to the bank was at Detroit, Truesdail was required to make constant trips to that city.

Captain Ward had put his steamboat *Huron* (with his nephew

---

[16] *Ibid.*

in command) on the run from Port Huron to Detroit, the round trip requiring two days. One day Mr. Truesdail approached Ward, a director of the bank, and suggested to him that he (Truesdail) should be allowed free passage on the Huron, as long as he was required to go back and forth to Detroit so often on bank business. Captain Ward was quoted as having said that he "couldn't see it that way," and refused Truesdail free passage. Truesdail angrily told Ward that he would "try and make (him) see it."[17]

A week or so later Captain Ward and the inhabitants along the St. Clair River were surprised to see another steamer advertised to run from Port Huron to Detroit at the same time as Ward's boat. Ward immediately sought out the captain of the rival steamer and asked him why he did not run his boat up the river the day his (Ward's) boat came down, and in that way make a daily line. The captain informed him that Mr. Truesdail had chartered the boat and that Ward would have to ask him about it.

Without losing any time Ward called on Truesdail in his bank (then situated on the site of the Cadillac Hotel on North Riverside in St. Clair) and asked of him the same question he had asked the captain of the vessel—why he did not run his boat on alternate days with the *Huron* and thus make a most convenient daily line for the people. Thereupon, Truesdail bluntly told Ward that he intended to run him off the river.

Unfortunately, history does not record Captain Ward's exact reply to Truesdail, but it does record that he immediately arranged with his nephew to go from one merchant to another on his stops along the the rivers and in Detroit, asking that they lay aside for him any Bank of St. Clair bills that they received. On every trip up the river Captain Ward would collect the bills from his nephew, and thus armed would call at Truesdail's bank to demand specie for the bills that he presented.

It was not long before Truesdail, in turn, was calling on Captain Ward, demanding to know why he was making such a run on his bank. Captain Ward replied that he intended to run on his line just as long as Truesdail did on his, or words to that effect.

---

[17] Dr. E. D. Barr, "Navigation VS. Banking," *Pioneer and Hist. Coll., Mich.,* XXVIII (1897-1898), 652-653.

Needless to say, Truesdail soon abandoned steamboating. In fact, he let Ward have the charter of his vessel for the season, enabling Ward to run a daily line of steamers from Port Huron to Detroit, much to his own and to the general public's satisfaction.

The simple but eloquent epitaph, "A True Sailor," inscribed on the tombstone E. B. Ward erected for his uncle in Elmwood Cemetery, Detroit, was somewhat of a contradiction. True it is, he was a skilled navigator—in frail sailing craft or steamer, without benefit of beacons, harbors, charts, or pilots—and though he commanded numerous vessels, no disaster occurred while he laid their courses and directed their movements.

And yet, according to his intimates, from the days of his youth, when he was engaged in transporting troops for the U. S. Government on Lake Ontario during the War of 1812, until late in life when he was enjoying the title of Commodore of the Lakes, not one article of clothing, not one word or gesture, betrayed his calling. Instead, from his appearance, he might have been mistaken for a prosperous country merchant. What is more, he seldom, if ever, ate or slept on any of his vessels while in port, whether at Buffalo or Detroit, Mackinac or Green Bay.

This latter insight into the habits of Captain Sam Ward comes down to us from Capt. J. H. McQueen,[18] who had accompanied him on his historic passage through the Erie Canal and who later commanded several of the finest steamers in the Ward fleet. Ward was, in fact, a trader at heart, and his whole sailor-life was only a means of furthering his principal source of profit, trading.

A story of how Ward one time "cheated" his passengers out of their breakfast is—like the banking incident concerning Wesley Truesdail—another illustration of his shrewdness in business. The story is told by William L. Bancroft,[19] one of Port Huron's most illustrious pioneers, who, at the time the incident occurred, was Ward's guest on the *Ocean*. The steamer was running between Detroit and Buffalo, and she made a record run that morning to her dock at the latter port.

The *Ocean* was in the hey-day of her career and was crowded with passengers. The weather being fine, Bancroft went out on

---

18 Bancroft, *op. cit.,* p. 347.
19 *Ibid.,* p. 350.

deck early in the morning and found "Captain Sam" there ahead of him, gazing at the city looming in sight as the steamer, already ahead of schedule, pressed on steadily.

Bancroft's greeting was enthusiastically responded to by the captain, and Bancroft noted a certain gleam in Ward's eyes when he announced, "I'm afraid we shall cheat these passengers out of their breakfast."[20] Which is just what happened, for the *Ocean* reached her dock before the hour of breakfast, and, as was the custom, the passengers were obliged to seek that meal elsewhere.

As they were enjoying their own breakfast together, Ward explained to Bancroft with a chuckle that he never let his captains forget that "fuel was cheaper than provisions."[21] And Bancroft afterwards related that he always felt that the old skipper experienced more satisfaction in his savings at the expense of the passengers than he did in the great profits realized from the whole trip.

Before his death Samuel Ward, alone, and with his nephew, had built or owned at least seven sailing vessels and twenty-three steamers—the majority of them built in Marine City—and was second to none in control of the commerce of the Great Lakes. He had earned the title of Commodore of the Lakes, and when news of his death at Marine City reached Detroit, all the boats in the river hung their flags at half-mast in token of the respect in which he was held.

Eber Brock Ward

Samuel Ward's shrewdness and keen appraisal of character was never more apparent than in the confidence he placed in his nephew, Eber Brock Ward.[22] The younger Ward, even aside from his shipping achievements, proved unquestionably to be one of the most enterprising men of his day. And, like his uncle, he too made history.

---

[20] *Ibid.*

[21] *Ibid.*

[22] Eber Brock Ward was born on December 25, 1811, at Harmborough, Canada, where his family was visiting. In 1818 his family migrated to the Ohio Valley, where they lived before coming to Marine City (then known as Newport) in 1822. Ward moved to Detroit in 1846 although he continued to spend a large part of his time in Marine City looking after his interests there.

Eber Brock Ward continued to build ships both in Marine City and in Detroit where he moved in the eighteen fifties, but with the advance of railroads there was a noticeable encroachment on the passenger trade on the Lakes. Thus it was logical for Ward to give more and more attention to his other interests—lumbering, banking, plate glass making, steel making, and railroad building. In the latter field he beame president of both the Flint and Père Marquette, and the Burlington & Southwestern railway companies. (Some references list the company as Burlington & Iowa R. R. Company.)

Already interested in lumbering, Ward had increased his holdings in pine lands in Michigan and other north central states, as well as in the hardwoods of Ohio, and had built immense mills in Ludington, Michigan and in Toledo, Ohio.

When Ward heard of large deposits of sand on the Mississippi River below St. Louis, suitable for the manufacture of plate glass, he formed and headed the American Plate Glass Company and established at Crystal City, Missouri the first plate glass works in the United States.

And when silver deposits were discovered on the north shore of Lake Superior, Ward immediately promoted and became the largest stockholder of a company which bought a small island about a mile out in Lake Superior, off Thunder Cape. He called his island Silver Islet, and there he inaugurated extensive silver mining, later erecting a silver smelting works at Wyandotte, the Star Mineral Company.

One writer on the Lake Superior region recorded that this tiny island was for fifteen years the world's greatest silver mine and that men made their fortunes there quickly—the stock of the company going up in some instances from fifty to twenty-five thousand dollars. She also quoted a rumor that it was Silver Islet's ore "which won a titled husband for the daughter of one of the largest stockholders, a man of Detroit, Michigan."[23] This would, of course, have been Ward's daughter Clara, who married Prince Joseph de Caraman-Chimay of the royal family of Belgium.

With the discovery of iron in northern Michigan, he shipped eastward for scientific and practical testing the first five tons

[23] Grace Lee Nute, *Lake Superior* (Bobbs-Merrill, 1944), p. 169.

of ore taken from the Jackson mine; then he had the walking beam and shaft of one of the first large steamers he and his uncle built (the *Ocean*) wrought of this material. He was also one of the foresighted prime promoters, and shareholders, of the Sault Canal —then known as St. Mary's Falls Ship Canal—which opened the way to an immense traffic in grain as well as ore.

An ironmaster, William Kelly, experimenting in the woods of Eddyville, Kentucky, discovered a law of chemistry—that oxygen and cold air would unite with the silicon and manganese and other impurities in raw iron to produce steel—later to be known as Bessemer steel. After many manufacturers refused to have any part of it, Kelly found Eber Brock Ward willing to experiment with his "air convertor" process. In September of 1864, in his Wyandotte plant—the Eureka Iron and Steel Works—Ward produced the first ingots of the so-called Bessemer steel in the United States.[24] Less than a year later, in May of 1865, at his Chicago Rolling Mills, he rolled out the first steel rails.

An interesting sidelight concerning Ward's Wyandotte and Chicago plants is the fact that Ward had, at different times, considered both Port Huron and St. Clair as desirable sites for his operations. Before building his Wyandotte plant he studied sites from Port Huron as far south as Gilbraltar at the mouth of the Detroit River. He favored the property[25] of George Palmer in St. Clair (on the St. Clair River about a mile south of present-day St. Clair Inn), but after negotiations were begun Palmer kept raising his price until the exasperated Ward bought instead the John Biddle estate, on which the city of Wyandotte was built, and located his iron works there.

---

[24] Kelly was not to be accorded the honor of having his name applied to the invention for which his genius was responsible. Instead, the product is known as "Bessemer steel" after Sir Henry Bessemer of England who applied for a patent for the same process just ahead of Kelly. After an investigation it was found that Bessemer had been one of the two assistants working for Kelly and had disappeared the night of the successful experimental test. The commissioner of patents, on application for a renewal of the patent, gave it to Kelly in his name, ruling that he was the real inventor and that Bessemer should never have received a patent in the first place. The great steel manufacturers of America then paid their royalties not to Sir Henry Bessemer, but to William Kelly. The name of "Bessemer steel," however, had remained fixed in the mind of the public and so was retained for commercial purposes.

[25] The site of the Saluratus plant in St. Clair on the St. Clair River is a part of the old Palmer farm.

The St. Clair Flats, however, were a serious hindrance to the location of the iron works at Wyandotte because heavy, fully laden vessels had difficulty in getting over the Flats. The United States Government had made extensive improvements (due primarily to Ward's efforts) which greatly aided navigation—and made the advantages far superior than when Ward himself "was a sailor"[26]— yet the largest class of vessels still could not put on a full load when crossing the Flats. The delays were vexatious and expensive, and in the latter part of 1873 Ward attempted to buy the land known as the Lighthouse Reserve in Port Huron for a blast furnace and rolling mills, to be operated independent of his Wyandotte and Chicago plants. He gave as his other reasons for wanting the land in Port Huron the fact that there was plenty of ground for buildings and that there would be no towing bills to pay—that "vessels of the heaviest draft could come up to the docks."[27]

Just how far negotiations would have reached is hard to surmise, but before Congress could act on the considerations, and before he "received sanction from all authorities,"[28] Ward died of apoplexy (1875) on a Detroit street.

Ward's initiative, foresight, and steady hand were sorely missed after his death, and the Wyandotte plant fell behind in competition. After its final abandonment, Cleveland forged ahead, and Detroit did not become the steel city of the nation, as Ward had more or less prophesied. However, his prophecy that Detroit would become "one of the greatest industrial cities in the world" did come true, although it was in the utilization of steel rather than in its manufacture. It was used in the making of automobiles, and to such an extent that Detroit became the motor capital of the world, and the third largest manufacturing city in the United States.

This pioneer of the iron and steel industry and giant industrialist of the Northwest, had, before his death, the controlling interest in six of the greatest iron companies in the country—the Wyandotte Rolling Mill Company, the Eureka Iron & Steel Company of Wyandotte, the Chicago Mill Company (later, the Illinois Steel

26 Ward interview, *Sunday Commercial* (Port Huron), November 2, 1873.
27 *Ibid.*
28 *Ibid.*

Co.), the Milwaukee Iron Mill Company, the Wisconsin Iron Company, and the Leland Iron Furnace Company at Leland, Michigan. He had, in fact, become the first "Steel King" in America.

When Ward died at the age of 64, and forty-one years after he gave his Uncle Samuel his entire savings to help build the first steamboat launched on the St. Clair River (the *Huron*, 1839),[29] it is said that he had amassed a fortune of $5,300,000. He was successful because of hard work and a rare business acumen, and his ability to let no discouragement or disaster deter him in utilizing the resources he found at hand. The attributes he manifested in charting the course of his own life, both as a sailor and as an industrialist, are aptly described in the symbolic ships of the following verse:

> One ship drives east and another drives west
> With the self same winds that blow,
> 'Tis the set of the sails and not the gales
> Which tells us the way to go![30]

Other Shipbuilders and Shipbuilding Centers

Marine City continued to be a center of shipbuilding, having by 1910 produced at least 210 vessels. Of the more than a dozen other shipbuilders besides the Wards, perhaps the best known were the Lesters,[31] George King, W. B. Morley, John J. Hill, Robert Holland, and Alex Anderson.

Second to Marine City was Port Huron, with some 186 ships completed by 1907. Fourteen of them were built of steel by the Jenks Shipbuilding Company[32] (from 1900 to 1907), including

[29] It is of interest to point out here that with all his other interests Ward continued to build ships in Detroit—turning out some thirty boats from his shipyards on the Detroit River between the years 1871 and 1875. Among them was the tug *Sport*, the first steel ship on the Lakes. For the story of *Sport* see historical column "Where the Wild Goose Flies," Nov. 14, 1965, *Port Huron Times Herald*, also complete scrapbook of "Where the Wild Goose Flies" stories in Burton Hist. Coll., Detroit Public Library.

[30] From "Winds of Fate," by Ella Wheeler Wilcox.

[31] David, Philander, and M. P. Lester.

[32] Sidney G. Jenks and Angus M. Carpenter, officers.

the ill-fated passenger steamer *Eastland* that overturned at her dock in the Chicago River with a loss of 835 lives. James Moffat,[33] Edmund Fitzgerald, Archibald Muir, Ed Botsford, Thomas Dunford, Eliot Brockway, Thomas Alverson, and H. E. Runnels headed the list of early shipbuilders in Port Huron, along with Sidney G. Jenks, Angus M. Carpenter, and Frank D. Jenks.

Algonac was next with 82 ships, the last one built in 1897. Among these ships was the historic steamer *Philo Parsons,* built in 1861 by Algonac's leading shipbuilder, Abram Smith, and which figured in the only naval engagement of the Civil War on the Great Lakes.[34]

Later, of course, Algonac was the birthplace of American powerboat manufacturing, and was known throughout the country as the largest powerboat building city in the world. It became the home of the Chris-Craft company and the early *Miss Detroits,* and of the *Miss Americas* which helped their builder, Gar Wood,[35] the "International Speed King," win the Harmsworth Trophy year after year.

The Smith brothers, Christopher Columbus ("Chris") and Henry, who began building duck boats in the late eighteen eighties, were soon experimenting with motorboats, and from this industry emerged the speed craft that were to make them famous. As one reporter observed, "the Smith boys contributed as much pioneering effort to the present vast powerboat industry as did Henry Ford to automobiles."[36]

Besides speedboats, Chris-Craft built hydroplanes and troop carrying and coastal craft. A Chris-Craft landing boat, one of their war-time products, was used by the first American troop to storm ashore in Normandy, and later, wherever American boys made

---

[33] James Moffat, tug builder, also built the ferry boats, *Sarnia* and *Union.* As a member of the firm of James Moffat & Sons and John R. Gillett of Detroit, he also formed a wrecking company which was the most powerful of its kind on the Lakes, which owned seven tugs, including the famed *Champion* and *Sweepstakes.*

[34] See Chapter XIV for story of the *Philo Parsons.*

[35] In the early days Smith combined his hull building skill with the mechanical genius of Gar Wood. The two perfected powerboating and laid the groundwork for the town's great industry.

[36] Jack Manning, *Detroit Free Press,* March 26, 1961.

landings, this type of boat was used to carry the men to the beaches. Today the Algonac Chris-Craft plant is building cruisers and new fiberglass sailing yachts, and besides producing marine engines, of which a large quantity are shipped to Europe, the plant has a service parts department which supplies dealers throughout the world.

Following Algonac in shipbuilding is St. Clair, with a record of 62 (Simeon Langell being the chief builder) built on the St. Clair and Pine Rivers. Eleven of them were steel ships, built by the Columbia Iron Works[37] from 1905 to 1910.

There were also shipyards at Marysville, Fair Haven, Swan Creek, Harsen's Island, and Lakeport, and others in Fort Gratiot, Burtchville, China, Cottrellville, and Clay townships. In all, there were built in the St. Clair River region some 625 vessels up to the year 1910.[38] Without a doubt, there was not another area bordering on the Great Lakes as interested and as active in building and operating wooden boats. But with the coming of iron and steel to replace wood in shipbuilding, the supremacy of the St. Clair River region in shipbuilding began to disappear.

---

[37] Ed. Botsford and Frank D. Jenks of Port Huron.

[38] For a more complete listing of ships built in the St. Clair River region, with all available information, see *Alphabetical List of Ships Built in St. Clair County,* by Rev. Peter Van der Linden (1965), Typed. See also a chronological listing of ships built in St. Clair County, in Jenks, *op. cit.,* I, 405-416, and listings in *History of St. Clair County, Michigan* (Chicago: Andreas, 1883), pp. 432-433.

For some of the boats built or owned on the Canadian side of the St. Clair River, in Lambton Co., Ontario, see Lauriston, *op. cit.,* pp. 97, 208-213.

Chapter XIV

STARRING ROLE FOR AREA-BUILT VESSEL
IN CIVIL WAR INCIDENT

The *Philo Parsons* and the Rebel Raid on Lake Erie

A starring role in the well known Confederate raid on Lake Erie in September of 1864—the only naval engagement of the Civil War on the Great Lakes—was played by the steamer *Philo Parsons,* a sidewheeler built in Algonac by Abram Smith in 1861.

In the fall of 1864 there were three thousand Confederate prisoners said to be in camp on Johnson's Island in Sandusky Bay. Other Confederate prisoners, totaling some twenty-six thousand, were held in camps in Columbus, Chicago, and Indianapolis. It was estimated that the number of officers among the prisoners would be sufficient to command an army of eighty thousand, and, if freed, could cause enough trouble to divert some of the Union strength northward, relieving the wearied and hard pressed Southern forces. Elaborate plans by Confederate espionage agents in Canada, and masterminded by Col. Jacob Thompson with headquarters in Windsor, were made to free the prisoners.

Capt. Charles Cole, one of the agents under Thompson, wrote a note with invisible starch ink to a Major Trimble, a prisoner on the island, and by smearing a bit of iodine over the starch the Major was able to read the instructions. He was to organize a cell of the "Southern Cross" among the prisoners, pledge them to secrecy, and, at a given signal, overpower the guards and escape in boats that would be waiting for them. Cole would then seize the gunboat *USS Michigan* which was lying at anchor guarding the Island, by drugging the officers at a champagne dinner, and immediately give the signal to start the uprising.

In the meantime, a supporting operation was under way in which the passenger steamer *Philo Parsons,* running regularly between Detroit and Sandusky, would be seized and would join the *Michigan* in the rescue of the prisoners. This operation was under the direction of John Yates Beall, a young lieutenant in the Confederate Navy.

Advance agents were to take passage at Detroit on the *Parsons* for Sandusky, and their orders were to ask the captain, S. M. Atwood, to stop at Sandwich and pick up some friends who were going with them to Sandusky. This happened as planned, and the captain agreed. At Sandwich a dozen or more passengers came aboard, among them Beall. At Amherstburg another group of men embarked with baggage, which included a large leather-covered "pack-trunk" tied together with a stout rope.

The *Parsons* sailed on to Put-in-Bay and then on to Middle Bass Island, where Captain Atwood, feeling ill, and unaware that anything was amiss, went ashore to his home. The steamer was left in charge of the mate, his son-in-law, D. C. Nichols, and she continued on to Cedar Point. It was then that the passengers who had embarked at Sandwich and at Amherstburg joined with the other agents, under the command of Beall. They opened the pack-trunk, which was filled with guns, knives, and hatchets, and, arming themselves with these weapons, seized the ship.

Since it was too early for the expected rendezvous with Cole and the *Michigan,* Beall cruised around and was finally forced to return to Middle Bass Island for fuel. There another steamer, the *Island Queen* (George W. Orr, Captain) came alongside carrying about one hundred passengers, including some forty or more unarmed Union soldiers on their way to Toledo to be mustered out. Beall had his men board the *Island Queen* and order the crew of that ship to the hold of the *Parsons,* where they were to be put under guard. When one of the crew of the *Island Queen* refused to come out of the engine room he was promptly shot in the face, the bullet passing through his cheek. The women and children were allowed to go ashore after promising to say nothing of the affair for twenty-four hours.

Beall then had the *Island Queen* lashed to the *Parsons,* on which he had ordered Nichols to assist in raising a Confederate flag, and proceeded to Johnson's Island. But progress was too slow with such a burden so Beall had the *Island Queen* scuttled, by opening her feed pipe, and set her adrift.

Arriving near Johnson's Island, Beall scanned the Island anxiously. His part of the piracy had been carried out successfully, and now he was ready for the prearranged signal that was to be flashed from the bridge of the *Michigan*.

What Beall didn't know was that the plot against the *Michigan* had been revealed to the provost marshal at Detroit by a counterespionage agent and that the dinner party with the planned drugging of the ship's officers had been a fiasco. The eagerly looked for signal from the *Michigan* never came, and Beall finally gave up. He took the *Parsons* back up Lake Erie where some of his men went ashore at Amherstburg. Farther on, at Fighting Island, he put off Captain Orr and several of his crew in the marshes—from which they were later rescued—and then, near Sandwich, he set the Parsons adrift while he and his raiders escaped into Canada.

Captain Cole, who had been arrested on the *Michigan*, was taken to Johnson's Island where he was court-martialed and sentenced to death, but he eventually obtained a pardon through influential friends. Captain Beall, however, was not so fortunate. A few months later he was captured at Niagara Falls and hanged as a spy at Governor's Island, New York.

The drifting *Philo Parsons* had been picked up by a tug, and returned to passenger service. Later she was put on a passenger run between Detroit and Chicago, where she was burned at her harbor in the great Chicago fire of 1871.[39]

---

[39] She was evidently repaired after that, however, for Van der Linden says that, later, "She was lost on December 4, 1874. Last document surrendered 12-31-74 bearing notification 'total loss North Branch Chicago River,'" *Op. cit.*

Chapter XV

LAUNCHING THE *EASTLAND*—A COLORFUL PAGEANT

You should have seen, man cannot tell you
The beauty of the ships of that my city.
—John Masefield[1]

No industry in the St. Clair River region ever created more interest and fascination than did shipbuilding. No parent watched with more pride over the development of his offspring than did the townspeople over the progress of a ship evolving on the stocks. From the moment a skeleton ship began to take form, every step in her building was carefully observed, until, noble in mold and strength, the final and glorious moment of her launching arrived.

The colorful pageantry of a launching[2] was a familiar and always magnificent sight in the days when the tall, splendid spars of the ships helped to form the skyline of the city, when the atmosphere was permeated with the redolence of pitchy tar and the resinous sawdust from the lumber mills, and when the thud of the caulker's mallet mingled with the rumble of great loads of "sticks" for spars drawn by six span of horses down the roads to the waiting boats at the docks.

But the townspeople, even after the turn of the century, had not lost their great interest in the spectacle of a launching; and that day in May of 1903 in Port Huron, when the Jenks Shipbuilding Company on Black River[3] was launching a passenger ship with the name *Eastland* painted on her bow, was no exception.

This all-steel passenger steamer, the first four-deck ship on the

---

[1] From "Ships," in *Story of a Round-house.*

[2] Capt. Sam Ward in Marine City always insisted on having the launching of his ships take place on Sunday, believing as he did that Sunday was his "lucky day." Bancroft, *op. cit.,* p. 350.

[3] The shipyards were at the foot of Kearney Street on the north bank of Black River.

Lakes—and one which in time was to receive more notoriety in books, magazines, and newspapers throughout the country than any other ship of her day—was built for the Michigan Steamship Company and was intended for Lake Michigan excursion travel. She was 265 feet long, with a 38-foot beam, and could carry two thousand passengers and a crew of forty-five.

The day of her launching was a gala one. Schools were dismissed at noon, and most of the offices and stores closed their doors to allow clerks to attend the ceremonies. Homes and stores, especially along Black River, were decorated; flags waved, bands played, and a holiday spirit prevailed in the city.

Shortly after noon a crowd estimated at six thousand spectators began congregating. They lined the banks of Black River, the Grand Trunk railroad bridge, and even perched themselves thickly in trees and atop buildings, until every available point of vantage was occupied.

By two o'clock the passenger ship was ready for launching. At the bow of the ship a platform had been erected, and on this was a group of men and women associated with the Jenks Shipbuilding Company and the Michigan Steamship Company. As the Stars and Stripes were hoisted to the breeze, a great roar went up from the crowd, and at the same time whistles in the factories and on the steamboats and tugs in the rivers began shrieking and tooting, and church and school bells began ringing.

Promptly on the appointed hour of 2:15, two sharp blows were heard and the ship began to stir, and as she moved, Mrs. J. C. Peru, the wife of the captain who was to command her, struck a beribboned bottle of champagne against her steel bow. While the whistles continued to shriek and the bells to ring, the watching crowds saw the great steel ship glide sideways down the ways and strike the water. Huge waves caused by the plunging vessel overflowed the river banks, pushing back the crowds, and amid continued din and cheers, the newly christened *Eastland* righted herself and was ready to begin her life asea.

* * * * * * * * *

For twelve years the *Eastland* had a brilliant career, without a single mishap. In 1913 alone, she is said to have carried over two hundred thousand excursionists. Tall and painted white with gold trim, she made a handsome figure cutting through the waves at twenty-two miles an hour. She was called "The Speed Queen of the Lakes."

Her "moonlight" excursions were probably the most popular on the inland seas, and the famous steam calliope on her hurricane deck aft, playing the hit-tunes of the day, could be heard for miles over the water as the proud beauty sailed her course.

No one in the crowds along the banks of Black River the day the *Eastland* was launched imagined that the beautiful ship would ever figure in the worst disaster in Great Lakes history. But that fateful day arrived.

In the early morning of July 24, 1915, in Chicago, the *Eastland,* with some twenty-five hundred passengers aboard, was about to leave her dock near Clark Street on a gala excursion to Michigan City, Indiana, when she began to list. Within ten minutes, before the great crowd of passengers realized what was happening, the steamer lost her balance and toppled over on her port side in twenty-one feet of water. Hundreds were thrown into the water to drown, and hundreds of others were trapped and drowned inside the cabins. After many days of searching—and some bodies were not found until after the ship had been righted—the number of dead was estimated at 835.

After the furor created by the disaster had died down, the Navy took over the Eastland and converted her to a Naval Reserve training ship. She was ready in 1917 and renamed the *U. S. S. Wilmette,* and although she spent the rest of her life under that name—until she was scrapped in 1948[4]—those who had seen the launching of that proud ship, or who had enjoyed any of her excursion trips, thought of her always as the *Eastland.*

---

[4] Van der Linden, *op. cit.*

PART FIVE
WAR AND NEAR WAR ON THE ST. CLAIR

Chapter XVI

BRITISH SCHOONER *NANCY* DISABLED
ON THE ST. CLAIR RIVER

War on the St. Clair River has never been given much attention in state and local histories. In fact, one often reads that no naval battles have ever been fought on the St. Clair, and also that the district's Territorial Militia took no part in the War of 1812.

This is not so. The St. Clair River has more than once figured in serious skirmishes, which might well have had adverse effects of major importance on the well being of the United States had not local authorities and troops proved steadfast and victorious in certain contingencies.

Take for instance the affair of the British schooner *Nancy* in the War of 1812. Built in Detroit by the North West Company for the fur trade, the *Nancy* had been impressed by the British at Amherstburg and fitted out with armaments, to carry troops and supplies between such points as Detroit, Amherstburg, and Mackinac.

It was in early October of 1813, shortly after the Battle of Lake Erie, that she had started from Mackinac with gunpowder and ordnance stores on her voyage to Amherstburg to pick up much needed food supplies to take back to Mackinac, when she met with trouble on the St. Clair River. Times being dangerous, the canny commander of the *Nancy*, Captain Alexander Mackintosh, had decided to come to anchor in Lake Huron just above the rapids of the river, and send messengers[1] ashore to inquire in the vicinity as to the safety of having the vessel enter the river. Within half an hour the messengers reappeared, but high seas which were running now prevented the ship's boat from taking the men off the beach. The crew, returning to the schooner, informed Mackintosh that they had heard one of the messengers

---

[1] Capt. Charles Reaume, in the British service as an interpreter, and Dr. David Mitchell, army surgeon. Both were eventually taken prisoners.

shout that "the fort was taken." [2] Since it could not be understood what fort was meant, Mackintosh decided to run the *Nancy* to the foot of the rapids to try and learn the true state of affairs along the river, and especially at Amherstburg.

He dropped anchor approximately opposite the foot of present-day Grand River Avenue in Port Huron, and going ashore learned that Amherstburg and Detroit were again in the possession of the Americans and that General Proctor had been defeated on the River Thames. He also learned that "two large schooners & 2 Gun boats were in the river waiting the *Nancy* at the mouth of Thny Ecarto [3] & Point au Chene." [4]

The next afternoon a canoe flying a white flag approached the *Nancy,* and at the same time Mackintosh was hailed from the shore by a militiaman who ordered him to give up the ship. Mackintosh went ashore to see who the man was and found him to be Lt. Col. Beaubien,[5] in command of the militia companies then guarding the St. Clair River. Beaubien repeated his order to surrender the ship, and Mackintosh, telling him he would give him his answer within an hour, went back to the vessel to get ready to defend her. When he returned to shore he told Beaubien that he would defend his ship until necessity compelled him to give her up, and that if the wind proved strong enough he would attempt going back into the lake. Beaubien then replied, "We shall fire on you." [6]

Returning to his ship Mackintosh made sail, and was pulling in the anchor when the militiamen, some fifty in all, began firing. The vessel's guns returned the fire, but in the exchange of shots, which lasted for almost half an hour, the *Nancy's* main sail and cables were ripped to pieces, and when the *Nancy* finally made her way out into Lake Huron she had only her two top sails, her square sail and one cable. The crippled schooner eventually arrived at

---

[2] Mackintosh letter to Capt. Richard Bullock, October 16, 1813, *Pioneer and Hist. Coll., Mich.,* XV, 413.

[3] Chenil Ecarté (corrupted into Sny Cartey), a channel through the St. Clair Flats at Walpole Island. Point du Chene, now Algonac.

[4] Mackintosh letter cited.

[5] Jenks lists Lt. Jean Marie Beaubien as a member of the militia companies guarding the St. Clair River, and that he was appointed "aide-de-camp to the commander, to take rank as lieutenant-colonel." *Op. cit.,* I, 180. Mackintosh does not give Beaubien's first name.

[6] Mackintosh letter cited.

Mackinac, but without the much needed supplies she had hoped to bring back from Amherstburg.[7]

The next August (1814), the schooner *Nancy* was set on fire and sunk by Lieutenant Miller Worsley of the Royal Navy, to prevent her capture by the Americans on the Nottawasaga River.

Two sidelights on the affair of the *Nancy* are of added interest to the St. Clair River district. Among the fifty militiamen firing on the *Nancy* from the banks of the St. Clair River were many local and down river pioneers, including Pierre and Joseph Mini (Minnie), Francis Bonhomme, George Cottrell, and William Brown — all of whom, like Jean Marie Beaubien, were early land claimants in St. Clair County. And in that raiding party on the Nottawasaga River, which was instrumental in the destruction of the *Nancy*, was Capt. Charles Gratiot, the engineer who in that same summer of 1814 had built Fort Gratiot and given it his name.

---

[7] *Ibid.* Besides the failure to get the much needed supplies for the garrison at Fort Mackinac, the ship's crew were reduced to short rations, Mackintosh reporting that they had not "a single oz of Pork or meat of any kind on board, nothing but biscuit and very little of that."

Chapter XVII

THE SLOOP THAT MIGHT HAVE CAUSED
AN INTERNATIONAL CRISIS

The uprising in Canada known as the Patriot War, or, more familiarly, the MacKenzie Rebellion, had its reverberations on the American side of the St. Clair River. This was shown in the incident previously cited concerning Fort Gratiot and the attempted confiscation of its military stores by Patriot sympathizers.

Probably even more serious was the incident, in the summer of 1838, concerning a Canadian sloop carrying armed Patriots and stolen goods, which landed on the American side of the St. Clair River for refuge, and which might have caused an international crisis had it not been for the intervention of Captain John Clark of East China Township in St. Clair County.

Captain Clark, prominent in the St. Clair River district as farmer, legislator, and master of such popular steamboats as the *General Gratiot* and the *Lady of the Lake,* and a member of the Territorial Convention which framed the first constitution of the State of Michigan, was also noted for his diplomacy, his quick wit, and decisive action.[1] Those qualities were never more needed than when the Canadian sloop carrying the armed rebels crossed the river and came ashore near Captain Clark's farm.

On that summer day the small sloop, owned by a Canadian rebel, had landed an armed party near the general store in Moore Township, Lambton County, Ontario (opposite Marine City, Michigan) and looted not only the stock of goods but also some commissary supplies stored there under the charge of a Moore militiaman.

These were loaded into the sloop together with two prisoners, the militiaman and a customer who had witnessed the plundering, and the sloop headed across the river, evidently with the intention of taking the stolen goods to one of the Hunters' Lodges in the vicinity belonging to an American sympathizer.

---

[1] See also Part Ten, Chapter XXXVIII.

However, an alarm had been given and a party of Moore militia volunteers (on order of Capt. William E. Wright) and Chippewa Indians gave chase in log canoes — the Indians in the lead, shouting wildly, and the militiamen firing at the escaping pirate ship. The sloop effected a landing on the American side just above Marine City where her crew scurried up the banks of the river and, with muskets ready, hid behind the fence in front of the Clark farmhouse and waited for the militiamen and the Indians to come ashore. A battle on American soil seemed imminent.

In the meantime Captain Clark, in leather apron, was shingling the roof of his house when he heard the musket shots and wild yelling, and, peering out over the river he saw the sloop landing with the canoes, manned by Indians and militiamen, in close pursuit.

The Captain quit his hammering and, hurrying down from the roof, got his brace of pistols from the house, then with two of his farmhands ran down to meet the Patriots who had landed.

Some of the rebels had run through the brush toward the woods behind the farmhouse, but Clark stopped the others, told them who he was, and ordered them "in the name of the United States"[2] to lay down their arms. They were loath to obey, but the command was imperative. Captain Clark, who still held the rank of Colonel given to him in the Toledo War, and who was Justice of the Peace, was greatly respected, and his word was law in the district. The men stacked their muskets in the road and then fled to the woods as the Indians and militiamen, who had landed, started in pursuit.

Captain Clark met the pursuers and ordered them to go back to Canada. In answer, several guns were leveled at him, but the officer in charge, a Captain Gurd, shouted not to shoot "for God's sake [3] — that the man was Captain Clark — and the guns were lowered.

The Indians had been promised a part of the spoils of war and were determined to carry away the Patriots' guns, but Captain Clark informed them that the guns were now the property of the United States and that they were not to lay hands on them.

---

[2] Crampton, *op. cit.*, p. 25.

[3] *Ibid.*

He then told them that the sloop having been abandoned in American waters was also the property of the United States, as were any arms and ammunition on board, but that the stolen goods would be returned to the owners.

It seemed to be understood that this judgment on the part of Captain Clark was in accordance with maritime law, and the baffled Indians and the disappointed militiamen returned in their canoes to Canada, while the sloop was taken in tow by the steamboat *General Gratiot* to Detroit.

The abandoned muskets were gathered up and stacked in an old shed used for storing grain and wood, and one of Captain Clark's hired men was left to guard them. About midnight, however, the hired man became timid, or lonesome, and went to one of the neighbors to get some one to watch with him. In his absence a Patriot climbed in a window and handed out the guns to several of his accomplices, and all escaped to the sanctuary of one of the Hunters' Lodges.

No one cared very much, it seemed, that the muskets were taken away. The main thing was that no blood had been shed and that another international crisis had been avoided — thanks to the good sense and prompt action of a wise old pioneer.

PART SIX

UNUSUAL SIGHTS AND SOUNDS ON THE ST. CLAIR

Chapter XVIII

A UNIQUE CAR FERRY

The Great Lakes and their connecting waterways have seen many unusual ferries, from the days of the Indian canoe and the privately-owned rowboat to the powerful steam ferry of later years; but none has been as unique as the car ferry which once operated on the St. Clair River between Port Huron, Michigan and Point Edward, Ontario.

The rowboat ferries of the eighteen thirties on the St. Clair River were soon supplanted by scows rigged with sails, which were used especially for teams and heavy freight, but were subject to the wind.

Afterwards there were odd contraptions used for ferries. One was a startling innovation by Orrin Davenport of Sarnia, Ontario, which operated between Port Huron and Sarnia. It was a sort of catamaran made of two dugouts, and on its platform two ponies attached to a sweep furnished the power, while a large oar, hung on a pivot, did the steering. Another catamaran-like ferry, one with a broader platform laid on and attached to two canoes braced several yards apart had a paddlewheel in the center of the platform; the power to turn the paddle was furnished by a mule which tramped around and around on the platform.

The service of these ferries, unlike the scow with sails subject to the vagaries of the wind, was fairly trustworthy, and later a large scow propelled by four mules made the service quicker. But it was not long before sidewheel steamers made their appearance and closed the era of horse-powered ferries.[1]

---

[1] The first side wheeler ferry on the St. Clair River was the *United*, which Orin Davenport bought and brought up from Detroit in the 1840s and put into operation between Sarnia and Port Huron. In 1855 James Moffatt and George F. Brockway, both of Port Huron, built the *Union*, and in 1860 Moffatt put the *Sarnia* (also built in Port Huron) on the Sarnia to Port Huron run, the *Union* being sold to Saginaw. Some of the other early ferry boats were the *Hawkins*, the *Beckwith*, the *Grace Dormer*, the *James Beard* and the *Omar D. Conger*.

In the meantime, however, one other ferry was put in operation, a ferry which was run neither by horse power nor by motor power. When the Grand Trunk Railway of Canada completed its road, from the East to Point Edward, Ontario, it built, under the name of a Michigan corporation — the Chicago, Detroit & Canada Grand Trunk Junction Railway Company — the railroad from Port Huron to Detroit. This was in 1859, and that same year it put into operation a car ferry at the Rapids, at the head of the St. Clair River. Formerly, the transferring of passengers and packages of freight by ferry from railroad cars on one side of the river to cars on the other side, was a tedious, expensive and long-drawn out job. But now the new ferry carried over the cars themselves.

This unusual car ferry — the "Swing Ferry," as it was called — had no power of its own, but by means of a long cable, anchored on the American side, was swung back and forth through the force of the current.[2] The anchorage was just south of the Fort Gratiot Lighthouse, and the long cable allowed the ferry to swing from Port Huron to Point Edward, about where the piers of the Blue Water International Bridge now rest.

The Swing Ferry was in constant service until about 1867 when a mishap befell her. One day while making a crossing from the American side to Point Edward, the ferry collided with an up-bound steamer. The impact severed the cable, and the ferry floated downstream, whirling giddily around at the mercy of the eddies, until it was picked up near the mouth of Black River by the schooner *Reindeer*.

This unique car ferry — said to be the only one of its kind in the world until the Russians, more than twenty years later, built one similar to it for the Trans-Siberian Railroad — was replaced about 1870 by the iron car ferry *International*. The *International*, claimed to be the third car ferry in the world, was built in England at a cost of about $190,000 (reportedly paid for in gold) and was sent to this county in sections to be assembled here.

The famous Swing Ferry itself had a rather ignominious ending. It served as a floating dry dock for many years in Port Huron and was known under several names, the most familiar being the Wolverine Dry Dock.

[2] The Carleton Map of Port Huron, Fort Gratiot and Sarnia, shows the car ferry and cable. Map in *Map Collection*, Jenks Collection, Port Huron Public Library.

Chapter XIX

STORM CREATES FREAK LUMBER YARD

Probably one of the most surprising scenes along the St. Clair River and lower Lake Huron occurred on a Sunday morning in 1901, when the townspeople of Port Huron awoke to find that the sands of old Keewahdin Beach had become, virtually overnight, a vast lumber yard.

The shore, from above the site of present-day Gratiot Inn to Kraft Road, a distance of about a mile, was strewn with logs, bundles of lath, and pieces of lath — a large number of the bundles having been broken up in the surf. The lumber was tumbled and crowded up on the beach twenty feet back; and in the surf, as one eyewitness stated, "it looked for some distance as if the very waves were made of lath." [1]

Offshore, to make the scene even more exciting, were seven vessels aground — three steamers, their barges, and a tug. One, the barge *Amaranth,* was wrecked. *Whaleback 202* [2] was high on the shore, and the others — the steamers *John H. Pauly,* the *Wawatam,* [3] and the *Quilto,* the barge *Marian W. Page,* and the tug *Sarnia* — were all stuck hard in the sand.

A sudden gale had swept over Lake Huron the night before, causing a heavy sea, and these conditions were further complicated by clouds of smoke brought down by the northeast wind from burning brush in Canada, the smoke acting like a thick fog.

Residents had seen the Pittsburgh Steamship Company's steamer *Wawatam* with her consort *Whaleback 202* (both light) as they passed Port Huron and entered Lake Huron late in the afternoon on Saturday. The wind, which had freshened, became a gale as twilight came on, and the smoke was so thick the lightship could not be seen. To add to their plight the sound of the fog horn was blown away from them by the capricious wind.

---

[1] *Port Huron Weekly Times,* September 10, 1901.
[2] Owned by the Pittsburgh Steamship Company.
[3] *Ibid.*

After groping for some ten miles in the turbid darkness the *Wawatam* decided to turn around and head for the shelter of the river, but had not gone far when the whistle of another vessel was heard, a whistle which became more and more distinct as they came on, and then light appeared when the *John H. Pauly* hove in sight. Thinking the *Pauly* safe, the crew of the *Wawatam* decided to follow her, when they were startled by a megaphone message from the captain of the *Pauly* saying that they were aground. Too late, the *Wawatam* came on and was grounded also, and her consort would have collided with her had not the heavy seas lifted the *Whaleback* and put her up on the beach broadside in two feet of water, while the *Amaranth* and the *Pauly,* side by side, looked — as one observer stated — "as if they were about to make straight for the Ben Karrer cottage" [4] (the cottage being a little north of the site of Gratiot Inn).

Almost simultaneously the tug *Sarnia,* which had been out in the lake waiting for the tug *Champion,* with a raft of logs which was eventually broken up in the storm, was the next to go ashore in the wind.

It was not long before signals of distress were blowing and the Life Saving Station was notified — its first rescue work since the station was set up in 1898. The surf boat was quickly put on a wagon and hauled down to the beach where the men in their new white uniforms, rubber boots, and cork life preservers went first to the rescue of the seven crew members of the tug *Sarnia* which looked as if it were about to go to pieces any minute.

From the tug, the surf boat started for the *Pauly* and the *Amaranth,* and all nineteen people aboard those grounded vessels were safely removed, while at the same time the heavy seas were washing their cargoes of some 2,600,000 feet of lath off their decks and spewing it along the beach with hundreds of logs from the broken raft.

The rescue of the crews of the *Pauly* and the *Amaranth* was hardly accomplished when two more boats were blown ashore nearby, the steamer *Quilto* and the barge *Marian W. Page,* the latter loaded with iron ore. From these two boats ten more people

---

[4] *Port Huron Weekly Times,* September 10, 1901.

were rescued by the life saving crew. All in all, thirty-six people, including a woman and two children, were rescue that night.

During the night hundreds of the townspeople had gathered along the beach, watching the rescue work and helping those rescued to nearby cottages. But those crowds were nothing to the multitudes that began gathering on the beach the next day — people coming on foot, in carriages, and in street cars. In fact, one official of the electric street car company said that it was so difficult to handle the crowds that even the baggage cars were pressed into service. One estimate gave eight thousand as the number of visitors to Keewadhin Beach [5] that Sunday.

The *Pauly* and the *Amaranth* were the hardest hit of all seven vessels, but the grounding of the *Pauly* and the dumping of her cargo, and the wreck of the *Amaranth,* which was pounded to a total loss in the heavy seas, were not the only headaches for the owners of those vessels. The spectators, it seemed, were all anxious to have a memento of that spectacular marine disaster at the foot of Lake Huron, and the lath began to disappear by piece and by bundle. The owners in desperation demanded police protection, and got it, but an amazing amount of lath and logs had already been taken away — enough of both to start a small lumber yard — before the pilfering was finally stopped.

---

[5] Keewahdin Beach is now known as Gratiot Beach.

Chapter XX

THE CRYSTAL BARRIER
AND A BIT OF THE OLD SOUTH IN PORT HURON

In the late spring of 1877 there occurred in the St. Clair district an event, caused by atmospheric conditions, seldom seen on any of the connecting waterways of the Great Lakes. It was drama with an arctic-like setting, and, contrarily enough, it brought with it a bit of the Old South to the town of Port Huron.

The occasion was brought about by a great ice blockade which formed at the foot of Lake Huron. A long prevailing north wind had jammed the huge masses of ice coming down from the Straits of Mackinac into a solid barrier, a condition which in other seasons had been prevented by southerly and westerly winds blowing much of the ice back, to be melted in the broad expanse of the upper Lake and in Georgian Bay.

In the heavy run of ice, vessels had had great difficulty in reaching Port Huron. The steamer *Winslow,* for instance, was six days coming up from Detroit; and the propeller *Maine* took seven days to come down from Pointe Aux Barques, an ordinary run of twelve hours.

The north wind continued to pile up the great cakes of ice, and even the most powerful boats were unable to force a passage through the barrier. By the end of the first week in May some fifty vessels — propellers, sidewheelers, schooners, tugs, barges, and scows — were unable to move on up into the lake, and those caught in the lake were unable to gain passage into the river. Now and then there would be a day of south wind and sun, when parts of the ice jam would separate themselves and move down, but only to jam again near the St. Clair Flats, trapping more vessels, while the north winds, coming again, brought down more and more ice floes to pile up just north of the Rapids.

One pioneer who viewed the spectacle from the top of the Fort Gratiot Lighthouse said there was no sign of blue water as far as the eye could see — nothing but a gleaming field of ice. To the

150

north, the dark hulls of the vessels trapped in the ice looked like toy ships in the vast expanse. To the south, the spars and smokestacks of the ships reaching up above the ice floes brought to mind scenes in pictures of Arctic explorations.

Townspeople by the hundreds lined the shores of St. Clair River daily, watching the snow-white islets that glittered in the sun with all the radiance of the rainbow, as conflicting currents and eddies whirled among them, adding beauty to the scene. Equal numbers crowded on the shores of lower Lake Huron to view the mammoth ice blockade — the "Crystal Barrier," as it was called — many venturing out onto the closely jammed floes to mingle with the passengers and crews of the ships caught in the solid sea of ice. And in the evening, venturesome crowds, carrying flaming pitch torches, climbed over the ice floes to visit the vessels, the expeditions making weirdly-beautiful spectacles.

The ice-bound steamer *Winslow* had 140 passengers aboard, 70 of whom were Negroes from Virginia and Kentucky bound for Sault Ste. Marie to quarry stone for the canal, and night after night they could be heard playing and singing. Then on a Sunday afternoon, to the delight of the crowds, they came ashore with their banjos and tambourines and their bones and fiddles, and, perched in the sun atop the boxes and barrels of freight stacked on the old Butler Street [1] dock, proceeded to play jigs and reels, and to sing their ballads and folk songs.

One of the other passengers on the *Winslow* — a man purported to be a world traveler and familiar with the artistry of many of the great musicians of the day — was quoted as saying that he had "never listened to a finer concert" [2] than that provided by those ice-bound minstrels.

About the twentieth of May, ten steamers, owned in Port Huron and down river, working together made a concentrated effort to break the blockade. At first three, and sometimes four abreast would try to crush the ice. Finally a plan was worked out where two steamers were lashed together bow and stern and under a full head of steam rushed into the closely packed ice. Other vessels were then sent along side to cut away the ice so as to free them.

[1] Now Grand River Avenue.
[2] *Sunday Commercial* (Port Huron), May 6, 1877.

In the meantime the steamers were aided by south winds and warmer temperatures which helped to loosen the blockade and start the ice floes moving. Then it was that some of those pert, tough little tugs — the *Mocking Bird,* the *River Queen,* the *Kate Moffat,* and the *Sweepstakes* — busily picked up tows for themselves and soon cleared the lake and river of the "embargoed" fleet.

In connection with that great barrier of ice there was the matter of the colossal expense it caused. Most of the ships caught in the blockade had been ice-bound for approximately three weeks, and it was estimated that four thousand dollars a day did not begin to cover the expenses incurred by the owners of the fleet — one more facet which made the "Crystal Barrier" perhaps the most memorable ice blockade ever known on the Lakes.

Chapter XXI

WHEN THE TUG *GLADIATOR* TOOK THE PROPELLER *LOWELL* FOR A RIDE

Certainly shipwrecks, and especially collisions, were not unusual on the St. Clair River. It was not uncommon before the turn of the century that from fifteen to twenty-five or more vessels would figure in major and minor shipwrecks in a single season. But in the summer of 1876 the people of Port Huron witnessed the unusual sight of one vessel, after a collision, carrying another vessel on her bow upstream for almost two miles.

About noon on a June day in that year the tug *Gladiator* made a beautiful sight as she began to pass Port Huron upbound with four large sailing vessels in tow. But just as she was about to pass opposite the mouth of Black River, the propeller *Lowell,* steaming away at her dock in Black River for her passage up Lake Huron, suddenly moved out and attempted to cross the bow of the *Gladiator* rather than wait until the tow had passed.

The tug screeched its shrill, incisive whistle of warning, but the *Lowell* evidently thinking she could get by in time, kept coming on. Her reckoning was wrong. The *Gladiator,* as one witness stated, struck her "just abaft the beam," and, in a freak manner, carried her on her bow through the Rapids, out into the lake, and almost to the Fort Gratiot Lighthouse before she could be released. Had the tug been light, it was reported, or had a smaller tow, the *Lowell* would undoubtedly have been sunk.

When the *Gladiator* struck the *Lowell* the tow was immediately cut by one of the crew. Fortunately there was a strong wind blowing from the southwest which enabled the vessels to take care of themselves until the *Gladiator* could free herself of the *Lowell* and go back to pick them up.

The damage to the *Lowell,* surprisingly enough, was slight; her bulwarks were only marred, and she put into her dock in Black River to be repaired before going on with her trip.

The *Gladiator,* one of the famous fleet of tugs owned by the Moffat interests, was built in Port Huron by Frank Leighton (A. Stewart, master builder) in 1871. She was rebuilt in 1896 and saw long years of service — working for much of her life for the Dunbar & Sullivan Dredging Company — until she was dismantled at Stoney Island in the Detroit River in 1960.

The *Lowell* had a different fate. Just twenty years after her foolhardy and almost disastrous attempt to beat the tow into Lake Huron, that same *Lowell* burned to the water's edge in Port Huron, not far from the scene where she was picked up and taken for a ride on the bow of the tug *Gladiator.*

Chapter XXII

CHANTEYS OF THE SAILING MEN

The galleries of visitors on the river banks of the great highway that is the St. Clair River, who watch and enjoy the passing parade of "sea beauty" — the huge 730-foot streamlined freighters, the foreign boats, the pleasure craft — are following an age-old pastime in the district.

In earlier days, when the waters were filled with schooners and steamers, the galleries of watchers enjoyed the pleasures of sound as well as of sight. The sounds were the quaint chanteys, or lake ballads, sung by the sailors in rhythm with the motions of their work, and, later, the more lusty "gripe" songs of the men sailing the lumber barges and ore vessels.

The *voyageurs,* that colorful, courageous class of men of the French régime — impudently unafraid of their fellow man or the elements — were the original chanteymen. Seemingly forever gay, their *chansons* could be heard no matter what the predicament.

Almost as famous for their boat songs were the later French-Canadian canoemen, like those who brought Governor Lewis Cass and the Indian agents up the St. Clair River on their way to negotiate the Indian treaties which gave us the rights to these lands. Our pioneers of the early eighteen hundreds wrote in their memoirs of the canoemen's songs.

Thomas Moore's "A Canadian Boat Song" —

Faintly as tolls the evening chime
Our voices keep tune and our oars keep time.
. . . .

Row, brothers, row, the stream runs fast,
The Rapids are near and the daylight's past

written on a visit to the Lakes country in the summer of 1804—was inspired by the chansonnettes, or little folk songs of the *voyageurs,* and was as popular in its day as the Norman chanson, "Alouette," still is, even with landlubbers —

155

A-lou-et-te, gentille, a-lou-et-te,
A-lou-et-te, je t' y pleumerai . . . .

That famous, brightly-decorated birch canoe of Governor Cass with its red canopy, manned by French-Canadian canoemen, more than once plied the blue waters of the St. Clair River. Mrs. Peter Brakeman, the granddaughter of Captain William Thorn, wrote in her memoirs that she well remembered the time when Governor Cass, on a trip up the Lakes in the eighteen twenties, came ashore and visited her father, William Brown, when they were living in Cottrellville.[1]

The ten French-Canadians who manned the Governor's canoe came up the river, singing their French folk songs as they plied the oars, and landed at her father's place. And while her father entertained the Governor and his party in his home, the *voyageurs* sat on the shore and ate the corn soup which they had brought with them — a colorful group in their red wool caps, and blue capotes belted with gay sashes, making more of an impression on the young girl, it seemed, then did the more important personage, the Governor.

The visit over, the party reembarked in the great birch canoe. And the gayly-decorated craft, to the accompaniment of a merry chanson, streaked upstream with a surprising swiftness, and disappeared around the bend in the river as the last notes of a haunting melody lingered over the blue waters.

Soon, in place of the chansons of the *voyageurs,* the chanteys of the iron men were heard. They sailed the wooden ships and created little folk songs of their own as they plied the lakes and rivers. There were the halyard chanteys, and the capstan and the windlass, or pump chanteys, as the sailors heaved up the anchors or made sail. And many of them had a local flavor, like the one which provided a steady rhythm for the men working a capstan:

When the mate calls up all hands,
To man the capstan, walk 'er 'round!
We'll heave 'er up lads, with a will,
For we are homeward bound.

They were "rolling home to old Chicago" on a towline, when they

---

[1] *Brakeman Papers,* Jenks Collection, Port Huron Public Library.

passed the city "of Detrite" where the cinders fell upon the deck "all day and half the night!"

> When up the length of Old St. Clair
> And at Port Huron we let go;
> We'll hoist the canvas on the forestick,
> On the main and mizzen too.

There were many songs with pathos, narrating the loss of schooners and steamers, such as the lake ballad, or chantey, telling of the loss of the schooner *Antelope*. which could have been about the schooner of that name built in Vicksburg (Marysville) in 1853 which was lost in early winter some six years later, with only one survivor to tell the tale:

> On the eighteenth in the morning —
> And what I saw is true —
> The ice upon our riggin' froze,
> And the cold winds fiercely blew.

The cold had increased as the tempest raged, and the drifting, ice-encrusted *Antelope,* with canvas gone and masts broken, was driven ashore where she "struck stern on" and then "swung broadside" throwing three of the crew overboard.

> Our captain tried to swim ashore,
> Our precious lives to save,
> But by his bold endeavor
> He was lost beneath the waves.
> And only one of that gallant crew
> Was in life once more to stand;
> And for miles and miles the *Antelope*
> Lined the shores of Michigan.

The rollicking chorus from "The Old Mont Line" — a ballad describing the trip of the barges *Monticello,* the *Montgomery,* the *Montcalm,* the *Montpelier,* and the *Republic,* in tow of the tug *Niagara* from Detroit to Houghton for copper ore — is typical of the "gripe" songs of the men who sailed the lumber barges and the ore vessels

> Oh, maybe you don't believe me lads,
> And maybe you think I lie;
> But ship in this starvation tow
> And you'll see the same as I!

157

Some of the work songs with a local flavor were those telling about the tugs and their tows, and they mention not only the St. Clair River, but cities bordering on the river and area-built vessels, all in the same song. "The *Bigler's* Crew" was such a song, one of many stanzas and variations, according to the mood and versatility of the men singing it — and the men handing it down to the next generation.

One version of the song tells about the schooner *Bigler* on her way from Milwaukee to Buffalo with a cargo of grain, and of a typical incident at the St. Clair Flats. After being towed out into Lake Michigan by the *Robert Emmett*, the *Bigler* reached the Manitous, and later "made Skilagelee and Wabbleshanks," cleared out into Lake Huron through the Straits and boomed for Thunder Bay when —

> The wind it shifted to a close haul, all on her sta 'b 'rd tack,
> With a good lookout ahead we made for Point aux Barques.
>
> We made the light and kept in sight of Michigan's east shore,
> A'booming for the river as we'd often done before.
> And when abreast Port Huron Light, our small anchor we
>   let go:
> The tug *Kate Moffat* came along and took the *Bigler* in tow.

But the ambitious *Kate Moffat* took other sailing vessels under her wing, too, and there was trouble ahead:

> The *Moffat* took six schooners in tow, and all of us fore-
>   and aft,
> She took us down to Lake St. Clair and stuck us on the Flats.
> She parted the *Hunter's towline* in trying to give relief,
> And stem to stern went the *Bigler* smash into the *Mapleleaf*.

However, the *Moffat* finally got them to the Detroit River and then into Lake Erie, where they boomed "hell-bent for Buffalo" and where they could drink a "social glass."

According to some authorities there were no finer chanteymen than the Negroes — often referred to as "lake minstrels." Constance Fenimore Woolson, telling of a Lakes trip in the summer of 1872, relates that on one Saturday night after the evening meal, the tables were rolled away and the Negro waiters, with their banjos and guitars, formed a vocal and instrumental band for dancing,

158

and which they all enjoyed "until close upon Sunday morning." [2]
Miss Woolson recorded one of the stanzas sung by those lake-min-
strels, in what she termed "their melodious voices," while dancing
a contre-dance:

Old Huron's long, old Huron's wide,
   De engine keep de time;
Leabe de ladies on de side,
   And balance in a line.

But the Negroes, especially those men who worked aboard Captain Eber Brock Ward's fleet of ore vessels, had their "gripe" songs
too, which like many others had an unending number and variety
of couplets. In "Red Iron Ore," deck hands who looked "like red
devils" and whose "fingers were sore," told their tale of grievances:

De Capt'n's in de pilot house a 'ringin' de bell,
An' de mate's down a'tween decks givin' de niggahs hell!

Oh, ah'd rather be dead, an' a'lyin' on de san'
Than make another trip on de Ole *Black Sam!*

Her smokestack's black and her whistle's brown;
An' ah wish de Lord ah'd a stayed in town!

It's wo'k all night an' wo'k all day,
An' all we get am not half pay!

Dey's tons o' copper down in dat hol'
Step along dah, niggah, dam' yo' soul!

De *Ward's* boun up, de *Moran's* boun' down,
An' de *John M. Nichol* am ha'd agroun'!

An' de *Wm. H. Stevens'* a'lyin' roun' de ben'!
An' all she's a'don' is a'killin' good men!

Chanteying practically disappeared in the middle or late eighteen eighties, but the "gripe" songs — also called "amusement
songs" — lasted much longer, and there are still elderly residents
living along the waterfronts who claim to remember hearing frag-
ments of the songs sung by the sailors on the lumber and ore
vessels as they worked their way up and down the St. Clair River.

---

[2] J. H. Beers, *History of the Great Lakes* (Chicago, 1899), I, 480. The
episode first appeared in *Harper's Magazine* under the title, "In the Cabin
of a Liner."

Chapter XXIII

EXCURSION BOATS RECALLED

Nostalgic memories for many in the Blue Water district are awakened by seeing the SS *South American* [1] pass up and down on her regular weekly cruise running between Buffalo and Duluth — just as did the attempted resumption of lake and river cruises by the *Aquarama* a few years ago. They are memories of serene passage over scenic routes, good meals, excellent orchestral music, "Moonlights," picnic excursions, and, most of all, that wonderful relaxation that comes only with boat travel.

Of fond memory to many are the points along the route the *Aquarama* took on its first cruise from Detroit to Lake Huron and back — Stag Island, the St. Clair Flats, Tashmoo Park (now a marina), and the narrow, winding Sny Cartey that leads to Wallaceburg. And the same may be said for trips on the D & C boats to Buffalo and to Cleveland, to Put-in-Bay, Mackinac Island and Georgian Bay.

Pleasant memories are also evoked of the excursion boats — themselves the "nautical beauties" that carried the gay throngs to those places and were familiar at one time or another on the St. Clair River. They bore such names as the *Northland* and *Northwest,* the *Juniata,* the *Octorara* and the *Tionesta,* the *North American* and the *South American,* the *City of Mackinac II,* *City of Alpena II* and *City of St. Ignace,* the *Darius C. Cole,* the *Idlewild,* the *Mary* and the *Unique,* the *Huronic, Noronic* and *Hamonic,* and the *Put-in-Bay* — the latter having docked at the Waterworks wharf in Port Huron as late as 1951, when she was put back into excursion service between Detroit and Port Huron in an unsuccessful attempt to revive that ship's popularity.

But foremost in the reminiscences of area residents are the White Star Line steamers — the *Tashmoo,* named for an Indian prince noted for his fine physique, the *Owana* and *Wauketa,* carrying the names of the twin Indian princesses of the Iroquois tribe

---

[1] The *South American* has since been sold to the Seafarers International Union and taken to Piney Point, Maryland to be converted into a Merchant Marine training ship.

who figured in a dual romance in the days of Indian navigation on the Great Lakes; the *Greyhound,* so named because of its speed, and famous for its pair of gilded, wooden-carved hounds; and the *City of Toledo,* named for its port of departure.

Of all these the *Tashmoo* was probably the most popular and the most beautiful. Described as "slender as a gazelle," and claimed by many to have been the fastest excursion boat running, even though she was beaten in her famous race with the *City of Erie* by forty-five seconds (her backers claiming she developed engine trouble), the *Tashmoo* was affectionately called "The White Flyer" and was the pride of her owners, the White Star Line. As one enthusiast wrote of her, "she was the prettiest girl on the Great Lakes."

Then, after nearly 40 years of reigning as queen of the rivers and lakes, the *Tashmoo* was punctured by a submerged rock in a channel of the Detroit River. With fourteen hundred passengers aboard, she hurried on to an Amherstburg dock and after successfully discharging her passengers, sank in eighteen feet of water.

For almost a quarter of a century her proud skipper was Captain Burton S. Baker, who was born on the St. Clair River in China township and who began sailing at the age of seventeen. In 1922 Captain Baker (still master of the *Tashmoo*) was eulogized for his more than sixty-five thousand landings between Detroit and Port Huron without a single mishap in the years he had been sailing her. At the time of the *Tashmoo's* death blow her skipper was Captain Donald McAlpine, who, oddly enough, was master of the *City of Erie* when that steamer raced and beat the *Tashmoo,* with Baker as master.

The era of river excursion boats continued happily in the Blue Water district until the coming of the Interurban Railroad, which ran between Port Huron and Detroit, taking in all the river ports and making the trip in two hours. The fickle public deserted their old standbys, the steamers, which took from five to six hours to cover the same route, and the steamboat interests discontinued their local service and sought other, more profitable, commercial lines.

But perhaps the "nautical beauties," eventually consigned to the scrap heap, had the last laugh after all, for the Interurban, in its turn also disappeared, the victim of the coming of the automobile and the development of good roads.

Chapter XXIV

FIGHTING THE RAPIDS OF THE ST. CLAIR

Boat watchers, observing the tug *Aburg* (owned by McQueen Marine Ltd. of Amherstburg, Ont.) assisting ocean-going boats in and out of port at the Sarnia Government Dock, are reminded of the stories told of how the early and diminutive steamboats helped the schooners fight their way up through the Rapids of the St. Clair River to gain admittance to Lake Huron.

Much has been written about the early vessels — schooners, barques, windjammers, and the like — wind-bound at the Rapids and filling the river with the beauty of their lines and sails. Sometimes a dozen or more of these vessels at a time would have to lay to and wait for a fair wind to take them through the rapids and into the lake. And stories have been told, of the struggles of steamboats themselves with those same Rapids, when the little steamers had to chug and puff and fight their way through to the lake, leaving in their wake the dense, gray smoke pouring from their wood-filled furnaces.

Passengers on some of the early steamers often told of a stump on the Canadian shore, just opposite Pine Grove Park in Port Huron. It was an exciting race, in the strong current, between stump and steamboat before the boat would finally win. The steamboat on those occasions would push boldly forward and get well ahead of the stump when, through a slight deviation from a straight course, the force of the current would cause her to fall back and the stump would again be ahead. However, by repeated trials and perseverence the boat would eventually steam victoriously into the lake.

A good story concerning schooners and steamboats fighting the Rapids relates to the steamboat *Governor Marcy*, one of the earliest steamboats on the Lakes and the first to enter the Saginaw River, after which she made regular trips between Saginaw and Detroit. This was the same *Governor Marcy* which on another occasion had had to put back into the St. Clair River for several

162

days after meeting rough weather near Saginaw Bay, during which time the capacity crowd of passengers enjoyed a "ramble about the beautiful region," as William A. Clark of Saginaw reported, and were afterwards entertained at Fort Gratiot where Lt. Silas Casey, later Major General Casey of Civil War fame, played host to them.[1]

This story tells of the time when several schooners were becalmed at the foot of the Rapids, and the *Governor Marcy*, steaming in sight, was hailed by one of the schooners for a tow. Evidently the schooner's captain was anxious to make time for he went aboard the *Marcy* and offered her captain one hundred dollars for a tow into Lake Huron. The captain accepted the offer and also allowed several of the passengers to come aboard for the ride.

The towline had just been made fast, however, when a fresh breeze sprang up. The vessel hoisted sail, cast off from the steamboat, and proudly sailed into Lake Huron leaving the *Governor Marcy* to struggle with the current and race the old stump on the Canadian side.

After the schooner got fairly into the lake she lay to and waited for the steamboat to chug and puff and fight her way through into the lake. At last the *Governor Mercy* came along side and allowed the vessel's passengers to get back on board.

The *Governor Marcy* continued to be a familiar sight on the St. Clair River until the late eighteen forties, when, on a trip up Lake Erie, she was wrecked off Dunkirk and never recovered.

It was not long after this (1851) that the four famous sidewheelers — the *Arctic*, the *Ruby* (from which the village of Ruby took its name), the *Pearl*, and the *Caspian*, all built in Marine City by Wolverton for the Wards — began to make their regular trips on the St. Clair River; the powerful little tugs were appearing on the scene to do the work of towing that the early steamboats tried so hard to do.[2]

---

[1] William A. Clark, Memorial Report, *Pioneer and Hist. Coll., Mich.,* III (1881), 606.

[2] The Indian, too, did his share of towing the early schooners through the Rapids, and received his pay in whiskey (*netass*), the Indian having to dive into the water to retrieve the bottles of whiskey thrown to him.

Chapter XXV

THE MYSTERY SHIP

Perhaps the most unusual sight of the century in the St. Clair River region was caused by the "King of Storms" in November of 1913, a storm which left a tragic toll of some 235 seamen drowned — 178 on Lake Huron alone — and twelve ships sent to the bottom, and more than twenty others driven ashore. The unusual sight was that of a steamer which had capsized in the storm and was floating, bottom side up, out in lower Lake Huron about eight miles northeast from the Fort Gratiot Light in Port Huron.

The weather report of Saturday, November 8, 1913, issued by U. S. Weather Observer A. L. Wismer from his office atop the Federal Building on Water Street, certainly was foreboding.

> Lower Lakes: High southwest to west winds. Rain or snow and colder tonight and Sunday. Severe storm centered over eastern Superior covers entire lake region. Northwesterly winds in rear of storm center have attained gale proportions on northern Lake Michigan and western Superior. Wind to shift to northwest on Lake Huron Saturday afternoon or early evening on open lake. Falling temperatures generally.

This weather report in itself was warning enough that the "King of Storms" was building up a strength — a storm later described as having had a cyclonic character with the 65-mile wind frequently blowing one way and the sea running in the opposite direction.

In fact, what was happening on land in Port Huron was enough to give the townspeople an inkling of what could and did happen on the open lake. Carrying blinding snow, the wind in its fury whipped across the countryside stalling automobiles, street cars, and Interurbans; swept from its moorings the temporary pontoon bridge across Black River at Military Street; crushed in store windows; tore roofs off stores and homes; destroyed bathhouses and boathouses along the river and lake fronts, and otherwise did more than one hundred thousand dollars in damage to the city of Port Huron alone. When the steamer *W. H. Smith* limped

164

into port in Port Huron on Monday sheathed in ice, her upper-works broken and battered, and her crew in a state of exhaustion, it was an ominous forerunner of news of the eventual tragic toll of lives and ships that followed in the wake of that storm.

It was on Monday afternoon, November the tenth, that Captain George W. Plough of the Lakeview Life Saving Station, sighted through his glass what seemed in the hazy weather to be "a whale-back barge at anchor"[1] far out in the lake. He called Captain Tom Reid of the Reid Wrecking Company (who earlier in the day had offered his assistance, if necessary), telling him of what he saw. Captain Reid immediately sent out a tug, and when it returned it was reported that what Plough had seen was "a steamer bottom up."[2]

The tug returned for a diver to try and ascertain the steamer's name, but the water was too rough for a descent. On November 15, however, Captain Robert P. Thompson of the Thompson Wrecking Company, also of Port Huron, sent out the tug *Sport*[3] with a diver from Detroit, William Baker, who located the name plate and identified the mystery ship as the 524-foot *Charles S. Price,* which had passed Port Huron, upbound, Sunday morning. She was upside down with her stern on the bottom in ten fathoms of water, and with only the bottom of her bow projecting out of the water. Two days later, on November 17, the huge steel steamer sank from sight.

In the meantime the storm was carrying the bodies of the crew members of the vessels wrecked on Lake Huron—vessels including the *Price,* the *Hyrus,* the *Argus,* the *James Carruthers,* the *Regina,* the *John A. McGean,* and the *Isaac M. Scott*—up onto the Lake Huron beaches on the Canadian side. The bodies were carried on wagons to Zurich, Goderich, Thedford and other Ontario towns, where inquests were held. Two of the crewmen lost with the *Price* were from St. Clair—Arz McIntosh and Howard Mackley. The

---

[1] Official Report, Nov. 9 through 15, 1913, of Capt. G. W. Plough, Lake View Life Saving Station, District No. 11.

[2] *Ibid.*

[3] This same tug *Sport* was designed and built by Frank E. Kirby for E. B. Ward in his shipyards in Wyandotte, and was launched in 1873. It was the first steel ship on the Great Lakes, and was built of the first so-called Bessemer steel manufactured (by Ward) in America.

body of Mackley was never found. Another member of the crew, Assistant Engineer Milton Smith of Port Huron, not liking the weather forecast had quit his job and had walked off the *Price* in Cleveland on Saturday, the day before the storm broke.

One of the mysteries of the storm relating to the *Price* was disclosed at Thedford, where the bodies of some of the crew members of the *Price* were discovered wearing life preservers marked *Regina*. This gave speculation that there may have been a collision between the vessels—the two having been seen earlier on Sunday, struggling close together—and that life preservers may have been thrown by the *Regina* crew to those who had been knocked in the water. However, the diver who identified the name of the *Price,* had carefully investigated the hull of the ship and found no other ship under the bow and no sign of any collision damage. What happened to the *Price* and the *Regina* will always be one of the secrets of the Great Lakes.

PART SEVEN

STORIED ISLANDS OF THE ST. CLAIR

Chapter XXVI

THE ST. CLAIR FLATS, PARADISE OF SPORTSMEN

Hello! my friends. An' how you find yourself?

. . . .

Come on de Flats an' stay all night wid me.
You hear de bull frog croak, de mud hen sing,
You bring home plenty feesh. Come up an' see.

—Hollands[1]

As the St. Clair River flows southward to Algonac it sends off a channel, Chenal Ecarté (corrupted into Sny Cartey), east to the Canadian shore, forming Walpole Island. A little farther south and west of Algonac, where the river enters Lake St. Clair, is the delta known as the Flats, created by silt washed down from the Upper Lakes.

Here the river divides into two channels, North Channel and South Channel, and about five miles farther down another, Middle Channel, branches off from North Channel, turning to the south; between these two lies Harsen's Island.[2] Middle Channel, as it progresses, again branches off to the south into Chenal à Bout Ronde, and between this and Middle Channel lies Dickinson Island.[3]

On North Channel, and along the shore of Anchor Bay, are the communities of Fair Haven, Anchorville, and New Baltimore. Anchor Bay is noted for its winter fishing. When the ice is thick enough it becomes a veritable city of shacks belonging to fishermen who haul them far off shore with their automobiles.

---

[1] Mrs. Hulda T. Hollands, from "Joe Bedore's Invitation."

[2] On the southern shore of Harsen's Island, three miles from Algonac, is Sans Souci, and a mile farther, on the north side of North Channel is Pearl Beach, a small fishing center and meeting place for duck hunters.

[3] Also known as Stromness Island.

The St. Clair Flats[4] (the property of the State of Michigan and held in trust for the people of Michigan to whom they are leased for resort purposes) are famous for fishing and for the hunting of wild fowl. They have been the paradise for sportsmen as far back as the seventeenth century, and have also been the subject of writers since that time. Explorers, missionaries, sportsmen, novelists, poets, short-story writers, essayists—all have recorded their impressions of this unusual gateway to the Blue Water district.

Lahontan, the ardent sportsman, enjoyed deer hunting on the "little Islands" as early as 1687 when he came up the river to take over command of Fort St. Joseph, and wrote about it in his *New Voyages to North America.* Here it was that Lahontan and his "huntsmen" flushed out the deer and as they attempted to swim over to the mainland were knocked on the head by the "Canow-men who were planted all around the Islands."[5]

And nine years before, when LaSalle and Hennepin had sailed up the same river in the Griffin, Father Hennepin, recording the story of that historic voyage in his *New Discoveries,* marvelled at the beauty, the vegetation, and the wild game of the country, and at the unusual formations in the Strait in particular.

Map makers, too, even before these explorers, had made special mention of this unusual natural feature we call the Flats. In 1670 Father Gallinée, who was also an engineer, noted on his map of the route he traveled from the Upper St. Lawrence, through Lakes Ontario, Erie, St. Clair, and Huron, all the chief characteristics of the country, including the Flats; and opposite the Flats are printed the French words for "great meadows" (or "prairies").

In later years the Flats drew equal attention from sportsmen, travelers, and writers. When Perry Hannah, founder of the Grand Traverse region, rafted lumber in his youth down the St. Clair River for John Wells of Port Huron, he would often run a boat in among the lagoons and bayous of "Little Venice," as he called the Flats, and gather a bushel of ducks' eggs in an hour's time, to sell in Detroit.

---

[4] See Jenks, *op. cit.,* I, 27-29 and 84-86, for a more lengthy discussion on the natural features of the Flats and title to the land.

[5] Lahontan, *op. cit.,* I, 139.

Writers like Constance Fenimore Woolson, whose stories and novels were second in popularity only to Bret Harte's tales of the West, did her share in publicizing the Flats region to the public at large in her *Lake Country Sketches,* which included the story, "The St. Clair Flats."[6]

And local characters and color did the rest. Joe Bedore, the inimitable and popular French-Canadian inn keeper; the Old Club, made up of wealthy Detroiters (since 1872) and soon to celebrate its one-hundredth anniversary of organization; the great variety of fishes and wild fowl; and the excursion passenger steamers *Tashmoo, Greyhound, City of Toledo* and *Idlewild*—all helped to make the St. Clair Flats a famous vacation resort.

The fish are still attracting the fishermen, and the wild fowl, the hunters. From time immemorial the St. Clair Flats have been a stopping place for wild fowl on their annual migrations, and they are still among the finest hunting grounds in Michigan for ducks.

---

[6] Her impressions of the St. Clair Flats—her "beautiful grass-water"—were made on a visit in 1855. But fifteen years later on a return visit Miss Woolson was lamenting the "unmitigated ugliness" of the ship canal cut through the "enchanted land," making its loveliness . . . but a legend of the past." Clare Benedict, *Constance Fenimore Woolson* (London: Ellis, n.d.), pp. 456-457.

Chapter XXVII

HARSEN'S ISLAND, LAND OF LEGEND

The Declaration of Independence was hardly a reality and the Continental Army of General George Washington was still at Valley Forge when the first settlement by white man was made on the piece of land at the mouth of the St. Clair River we now know as Harsen's Island.[1]

The original settler, the man who gave the island its name, was Jacob Harsen, a Hollander, and a gunsmith by trade, who came on horseback to Michigan Territory from New York State where he was associated for awhile with John Jacob Astor in the fur trade.

Already on the island was a settlement of Mississaugas and Chippewas, who had first come to the district at the invitation of Cadillac after he founded Detroit in 1701, and Harsen continuing in the fur trade, bought skins from the Indians and shipped them east on the backs of Indian ponies. Later, when he was joined on the island by Isaac Graveraet, a silversmith, they combined their skills in producing guns and silver ornaments to be traded to the Indians.

Harsen, who had five sons and two daughters, had settled on the island in 1769, but when the Indians became hostile he moved his family to Windmill Pointe on the Detroit River. However, he was an avid hunter, and since the wild game were plentiful on the island he had left, he was determined to make peace with the Indians. His efforts were successful, and Jacob Harsen returned to the island sometime prior to 1778. He received from the Indians a grant of three thousand acres of land, and for more than 170 years—until the death of Benjamin Harsen in 1949—descendants of his, bearing the Harsen name, had resided on the island.

Many dramatic incidents took place on the island in the early days of its settlement, and more than once tragedy struck at the

[1] Largest of the American group of Islands. Tashmoo Park is on its south shore.

Harsen family. One such incident, probably considered a retribution by Jacob Harsen, involved his oldest son William and occurred on a Sunday, a day on which the father forbade the use of firearms.

On that particular Sunday a large and inviting flock of ducks alighted on the water near the house and the son, forgetting the admonitions of his father, grabbed his gun and left the house to go for them. He attempted to fire but the priming flashed in the pan of the old flintlock and he rushed back into the house to reprime it. As he entered, the butt of the gun struck the door and the gun was discharged, the charge entering the arm of his seven year old niece, badly mangling it. The little girl was taken to Detroit where her arm was amputated.[2]

Another brother, James, was accidentally shot in the eye by the half-breed, John Riley, and died some months later, and still another brother, Bernard, and his sister, Mrs. Isaac Graveraet, were killed instantly by the explosion of a twenty-pound keg of gun powder. It was accidentally set off by a pipe-smoking Moravian missionary whose pipe ashes had fallen into the keg, where they had smoldered and finally set off the powder—which also destroyed the house.

Of the prehistoric Indians who may have inhabited Harsen's Island we have little or no knowledge except perhaps of traces of mounds found there. These were, however, probably only burial mounds, for the island has been known as a favorite burial ground for roving tribes as well as the Mississaugas and Chippewas.

From that island the warrior braves in all their paraphernalia of savage splendor went out in their birchbark canoes to do battle with their foe. And to that spot, too, they returned amid wild whoops and chantings with their hideous trophies—strings of stained and reeking scalps waving from long poles, and groups of shackled prisoners who might well have furnished the food for the war feast.

One of the most frightening experiences of the settlers along the

[2] Mary Graveraet. Much of her childhood was spent in the home of Judge James May of Detroit. In spite of her handicap she learned to cook and sew and perform other household tasks. She became the second wife of Harvey Stewart, and the stepmother of the first Aura P. Stewart, one of the St. Clair River district's earliest pioneers.

St. Clair River near Harsen's Island, and especially of the Harsen family, occurred at the time of the War of 1812. After the rout of Proctor's army and his Indian allies at Fort Stephenson by Colonel George Croghan and his men, the general hastily withdrew to Malden (Amherstburg), while the Indians, fleeing in panic, eventually escaped out onto Lake Erie, some continuing on up the Detroit River, Lake St. Clair, and the St. Clair River.

One night two large canoes full of Indians, still in flight, were seen paddling up the St. Clair River when a severe summer thunderstorm struck the district. One blinding, deafening crash of thunder followed another, accompanied by driving rain and high winds, and as the Indians tried desperately to reach shore across from Harsen's Island, one of the canoes overturned throwing some twenty Indians into the water. The night was very dark except for the sporadic lightning, and those who reached shore kept shouting encouragement to their struggling brothers.

Mrs. Graveraet, with her brother, Bernard Harsen,[2] was living in the Harsen homestead at the time, and she later said that she had never heard anything so terrible as the howling and shouting of the savages. They spent the night in terror, not knowing what was happening, or what might later happen to them.

At dawn the next morning the watching Harsens saw two canoes filled with Indians leave the opposite shore and approach the island. Some twenty or thirty warriors landed, and the Harsens waited in trepidation. But as the warriors came toward the house they looked extremely grave, and their faces were painted with charcoal. Greeting the Harsens, the leader solemnly told them that they were in mourning for the loss of two of their friends who were drowned when the storm broke. They also, almost apologetically, tried to explain how they had been induced to go to war by the British, who told them that the Kit-che-mocomans ("Long Knives") were great cowards and easily defeated. They had found the opposite to be true, however—that the American Long Knives had killed a great many of the British at Lower Sandusky and that they themselves had just returned from there. And then,

---

[2] These were the same two who were later killed in their home by an explosion.

contrary to what the Harsens had fearfully expected—plunder by the Indians, and perhaps death—the warriors warned them that the Long Knives were coming, and sympathetically advised them to leave immediately.

As it happened, Mrs. Graveraet and her brother did move to Detroit, but only for a short while, for in those trying times the transition of fealty was quickly taking place, and those of former British allegiance soon became United States citizens. In fact, at the outbreak of the War of 1812, a brother-in-law of Mrs. Graveraet, Henry Graveraet, was already acting as an Indian interpreter for the United States Government and as a messenger between General Harrison and Commodore Perry in that war.

Chapter XXVIII

WALPOLE ISLAND, BURIAL PLACE OF TECUMSEH

Walpole Island,[1] the largest of all the islands in the St. Clair River, and Canadian owned, is a reservation for some twelve hundred Chippewa and Potawatomi Indians. It is not known exactly what tribes occupied the island for any length of time in earlier days, however, it is believed that the Attiwandarons (Neutrals) in the sixteen hundreds, perhaps the Mascoutins, and later the Mississaugas, a nation closely allied to the Chippewas, frequented the island. We know that Walpole's history can be traced back to the seventeen hundreds when the Chippewas spread their empire from the Upper Peninsula onto the island.

Like Harsen's Island, Walpole Island was probably used as a council spot and rallying point before wars, and may have been a place for celebration after a victory. Perhaps it was the scene of such ghastly feasts as that of 1763 when on the heights overlooking the Rapids at the foot of Lake Huron an English surveying party was ambushed by the Saginaw Chippewas, murdered, their bodies cut up and broiled, and eaten the following night.

But there were feasts of a more friendly and civilized nature later on—feasts to which the pioneers were invited, who, though they did not anticipate enjoying themselves, were sometimes pleasantly surprised. There was the time, in particular, when Mr. and Mrs. Peter Brakeman, then living at Point du Chien, were invited by the Indians to a kind of dinner party. Peter Brakeman carried on an extensive business with the Indians in those days, especially buying up grain and white flint corn grown on Walpole and Harsen Islands and shipping it to Mackinac, and he was a great favorite with them.

One day an Indian arrived at the Brakeman home with an invitation for them to visit on the island, bringing with him the chief's "card"—a small piece of birchbark. The invitation was also

[1] For a short history of Indian Reservations in Lambton County, Ontario, see Lauriston, *op. cit.*, pp. 3-7.

extended to any other friend they wished to bring. The Brakemans asked John K. Smith (one of the first three St. Clair County Commissioners and the first postmaster of Algonac) to accompany them, and he accepted.

When the time arrived for the visit, an Indian, O-gau ("Pickerel") by name, came for them in a large canoe in the bottom of which he had placed a clean rush mat and on which he had the guests sit while he did the paddling. Half way across the river the Indian gave several loud whoops—as much as to say "we are coming"— and the Indians on the island answered in the same style. As they landed the chief and other important Indians met the party and shook hands with them. Mr. Brakeman had brought with him presents of pipes and tobacco, which the Indians received with enthusiastic grunts of approval.

A large tent had been erected for the occasion, and rush mats were spread over the dirt floor for the guests' convenience. As they entered the tent an Indian kept beating on a drum made of a section of hollow log over the top of which a piece of tanned deer skin was tightly drawn and brought down around the sides, where it was held with strings of deer sinews.

Across two sides of the interior of the tent, near the top, long poles had been hung, and strung on these poles, from one end to the other, were pigeons, nicely dressed and boiled whole. After much time spent in drumming and visiting, several of the squaws— probably the "table committee"—busied themselves taking down the pigeons and passing them to the guests, each guest having two of the pigeons placed in his hands.

There were no plates, or cutlery of any kind; the guests sat crosslegged on the rush mats and picked the meat from the bones with their fingers. The fowl were surprisingly palatable, and quite satisfying as a meal even without the little squares of maple sugar later passed to them for "dessert."[2]

Visiting was again resumed and continued until quite late in the evening, when O-gau reappeared, and after much handshaking O-gau solicitously helped the guests into the canoe and then took them back across the river to their homes on the mainland.

---

[2] Mrs. Peter Brakeman, *Brakeman Papers,* Jenks Collection, Port Huron Public Library.

Walpole Island is now noted as the final burial place of the Shawnee chieftain Tecumseh. On August 23, 1941, the pages of history were turned back 128 years when the bones of that famous warrior were lowered in the monument, or cairn, erected on the island for their interment.

For approximately nine years, the bones had been concealed at diverse places on the island, their whereabouts sometimes known only to a single resident. Tradition says that the bones were originally unearthed on the mainland, not far from the island, many years after Tecumseh's death; and there is a legend that for a great number of years Shawanoe, his aide-de-camp, had daily raised and lowered a flag over his grave.

Hundreds of Canadians and Americans, including religious, civic, military, and political dignitaries lined the beach for the ceremonies that summer afternoon. The colorful pageantry of Indian men and women in tribal costumes depicting incidents in the warrior's life—from the time he came to Canada, allied with the British crown, through his death at Moraviantown—highlighted the ceremonies. And while a full military guard and the Second Kent Division of Chatham added solemnity to the occasion, Tecumseh's bones, reposing in a mahogany casket, were lowered in the shaft of the concrete and brick cairn.[3]

Manitowaube, Tecumseh's first lieutenant, who for his devotion and faithfulness to the Imperial crown was given a silver medal by the Prince of Wales (later Edward VII) when he visited Sarnia in 1860; Shawanoe; and other Indian chiefs who fought with Tecumseh—Keyoshka, Minomener, Miskokomon, Thceahyaba, Nadhee, Shageemah, and Paccoos—are all buried on the island. And many grandchildren and great-grandchildren of these Indian warriors and their tribesmen, including Potawatomis, Chippewas and Ottawas, are now dwelling there.

---

[3] The mahogany casket was the gift of Chris C. Smith, pioneer speedboat builder of Algonac. The cairn was the gift of Lambton County, the Bureau of Indian Affairs at Ottawa, and of Gar Wood, the international speedboat champion.

PART EIGHT

PIONEERS! O PIONEERS

For we cannot tarry here,
We must march, my darlings, we must
  bear the brunt of danger
We, the youthful sinewy races, all
  the rest on us depend
Pioneers! O Pioneers.

—Walt Whitman

Chapter XXIX

ANCIENT MARINERS AND HEROINES OF THE LAKES

William Thorn, Pilot of Pre-Revolution Days

At the time General Anthony Wayne was routing the Indians in the Battle of Fallen Timbers of 1794, Captain William Thorn was already a veteran pilot of the little sloops and schooners active in the fur trade running between Detroit and Mackinac, and later in the transporting of men, guns, and supplies between Detroit and other British posts after the outbreak of the War of 1812.

Captain Thorn, born in Providence, R. I. in 1743, came west before 1770, and after living in Detroit for some time, settled on the St. Clair River at Cottrellville, about 1780. He was the father of John Thorn, who platted the land on the north side of Black River known as the Village of Gratiot (one of the Plats that formed the town of Port Huron in 1837), and the father-in-law of James Fulton, who bought and platted the first land in the City of St. Clair.

It is said of Captain Thorn that he took the first ship through the St. Mary's River and into Lake Superior (he was in the employ of Michael Dousman, the fur trader at the time). And it is also said of him that when on one occasion his vessel was windbound near an island at the mouth of the St. Mary's River, he went ashore and found there a frying pan left by the Indians, and so named the place "Frying Pan Island."[1]

From the same source, Thorn's great-granddaughter, Anna Brakeman, comes an account of another incident. His vessel lay at anchor in a bay in Lake Erie, and Thorn and his crew were entirely out of provisions except for the flour which they stirred into a pot of boiling water and called pudding. He then named the place "Pudding Bay"—the name by which it was known for many years, before being changed to Put-in-Bay. The word was

---

[1] Brakeman Papers, Jenks Collection, Port Huron Public Library.

181

probably slurred in pronunciation to "Putin'," and the name then fixed at Put-in-Bay.[2]

On one of his trips to Sandwich, at the time of the Battle of the Thames when the British General Proctor and his Indians were routed, Captain Thorn was arrested as a spy by a British officer and imprisoned. This was in spite of the fact that for more than twenty years before the transfer of posts he had been engaged in sailing British vessels on the Lakes and had therefore deemed himself a British subject.

In the end the charges against the captain were not sustained, and after nearly a year as a prisoner—during most of which time he was a captive of the Indians—Thorn was released and started for his home in Detroit, traveling on foot through the woods. There on a lonely trail he met a woman in flight from the Indians, who was about to give birth to a child.[3] He helped her through her confinement and after finding her shelter proceeded on foot to the home of a daughter in Monguagon (now Trenton). There, as he later reported, his daughter "helped to rid him of lice" he had acquired in prison, and then drove him in a French cart to his family in Detroit, to which place he had removed from the St. Clair River at the beginning of hostilities. After the war he moved back to his farm at Cottrellville and continued to live in St. Clair County until his death in 1842, at the age of ninety-nine.

Probably one of the most dramatic incidents of Captain Thorn's life was the time he piloted the Croghan-Sinclair expedition on its unsuccessful attempt to retake Fort Mackinac from the British. At that time Thorn was living at his farm and was lame because of a dislocated hip, so he was taken aboard in a chair just above Roberts Landing at Cottrellville. Later, as a low fog settled over the district, Thorn, who was unable to climb a ladder, had himself strapped in his chair and hoisted with pulleys to the masthead and from there piloted the fleet safely on its way to Mackinac.

---

[2] This may be true, for in a letter from Brig. Gen. Henry A. Proctor to Sir George Provost, in 1813, Proctor refers to Put-in-Bay as "Putin' Bay." *Pioneer and Hist. Coll., Mich.,* XV, 354.

[3] Marginal note by W. L. Jenks in Lanman's *History of Michigan* (New York: French, 1839), p. 236, as told to him by John W. Brakeman. Copy in Jenks Collection, Port Huron Public Library.

But lake navigation was old and familiar business to Captain Thorn. He said himself that he began sailing to Mackinac seven or eight years before Fort Mackinac was moved from the mainland to the Island, and in that case he must have been sailing along the shores of the St. Clair River long before the Declaration of Independence was signed. It is interesting to note some facts about the St. Clair River, as reported by Captain Thorn—that the river was much wider than it is now, that what is now Point Edward was then an island, and that he had sailed through the east channel as early as 1770, the main channel to the east of it having been gradually filled in and the present channel deepened and widened.

Evidences of that old east channel, according to Judge William T. Mitchell in an address to the St. Clair County Pioneer Society in 1883, were then still to be seen in Sarnia Bay and the depressed surface between it and Lake Huron.

Alexander Harrow, British Pilot

Living on the St. Clair River at the time of the British occupation, and a contemporary of William Thorn, was another noted Lakes captain, Alexander Harrow.

One cannot read about the important posts of Detroit and Mackinac during the British occupation, of Fort Sinclair on the St. Clair River, or of such important personages as Patrick Sinclair, Major A. S. De Peyster, Commodore Alexander Grant, or Sir Frederick Haldiman, Governor General of Canada, without constantly finding references to the services and activities of Alexander Harrow, one of the earliest of the settlers on the St. Clair River.

When De Peyster was relieved at Fort Mackinac by Patrick Sinclair, it was Harrow, then in the British service and commissioned a lieutenant and commander in the Naval Armament of the Lakes, who brought Major De Peyster and "his lady" to Detroit. Another time, while in charge of the sloops *Wellcome* and *Angelica,* Harrow got out timber and lumber from Sinclair's Pinery on Pine River for use in the King's Shipyard at Detroit; he also helped Sinclair make the transfer of Fort Mackinac from the mainland to the Island.

It was also Captain Harrow who, by order of Sinclair, took Francis Belcour, the unsatisfactory manager of Sinclair's Pinery on Pine River, to Mackinac in 1780 and returned with Jean Baptiste Point de Sable, who replaced Belcour.

In command of an armed vessel, he aided in the defense of Quebec when the Americans began their unsuccessful conquest of Canada, and it was Harrow who was superintendent of the gunboats at the Battle of Fallen Timbers and a close observer of the action near Fort Miami between General Anthony Wayne and the Indians.

Captain Harrow was born in Aberdenshire, Scotland in 1755, came to America in 1775, and was sent two years later to the Upper Lakes and placed in command of the sloop *Wellcome,* one of the fleet of British vessels on the Upper Lakes.

During most of the time of Harrow's services the British fleet consisted of some ten vessels of varying sizes, from eighteen to one hundred and fourteen tons. In the fleet were the sloops *Wellcome, Angelica, Adventure* and *Felicity;* five schooners, *Gage, Hope, Dunmore, Faith,* and *Wyandot;* and the scow *Ottawa.* Harrow commanded at least four of these vessels, the *Wellcome,* the *Felicity,* the *Gage* and the *Dunmore,* as well as the *Chippewa,* and the largest schooner then on the Lakes, the *Rebecca.*

It was in 1794, the year Harrow was in command of the gunboats near Miami at the Battle of Fallen Timbers, that he decided on settling permanently on a tract of land comprising 14,400 acres, which he had purchased on the American shore of the St. Clair River just north of Algonac. The Americans took possession of Detroit in 1796, and Harrow came under the jurisdiction of American courts. In that year he settled on his farm on the St. Clair River, where he continued to live until his death in 1811, and where today, more than a century and a half later, some of his lineal descendants are living on a part of that land.

During all of the time of his service on the Lakes Captain Harrow made daily entries in his Log Books—not only reports of matters on shipboard, and notes on the weather, but interesting observations on people and events. Those Log Books have been preserved and are now valuable documents of Americana.[4]

---

[4] The complete collection of all the known Harrow Log Books are now in the Burton Historical Collection, Detroit Public Library.

Alexander St. Bernard, and the
Assassination of King Strang

The fascinating history of the Great Lakes and their connecting waterways is full of incidents in which St. Clair River area captains were central figures. One such skipper was the prominent and adventurous Captain Alexander St. Bernard of St. Clair—a son of Louis St. Bernard, who cut much of the timber on his holdings and rafted it to Detroit to be used in rebuilding that city after the disastrous fire of 1805.

Captain St. Bernard, as a boy, piloted the *Grand Turk* (the first boat built at St. Clair) which carried or towed much of his father's timber to Detroit, and he was one of the crew of the *Marshal Ney* (built in Marine City), which was chartered by the Government to take supplies to old Fort Dearborn, and was one of the earliest boats to enter at Chicago.

But Captain St. Bernard could boast of being a pioneer in other ways, one of which was that he piloted the *U. S. S. Michigan* (later the *Wolverine*), the first iron warship in America, if not in the world.

Begun in Pittsburgh in 1842, the *Michigan* was built in sections which were transported overland to Erie, where they were assembled. To St. Bernard was assigned the great honor of taking her out of the harbor, and for the next quarter of a century he remained with her in the Government's service.

It was while Captain St. Bernard was pilot of the *Michigan* that the bizarre character, James J. Strang, came into prominence. The saga of Beaver Island and the Mormons is well known history: After the murder of Prophet Joseph Smith in Illinois, Strang, vying for the honor of becoming his successor, led a band of his followers first to Voree, Wisconsin and then to Beaver Island, had himself crowned king, and after some years was in turn eventually murdered by two of his enemies.

Not so well known, however, is the innocent part played by Captain St. Bernard in the dramatic moments of the assassination of King Strang and how close he, too, came to being killed.

All part of a scheme to do away with Strang after some dozen years of autocratic rule, Strang's enemies, headed by Dr. H. D. McCulloch (who also owned a store on Beaver Island), were instrumental in having the *U. S. S. Michigan* put in at the dock

185

in front of McCulloch's store, then on some pretext or other had the master of the ship, a Captain McClair, summon Strang on board. The officer sent to fetch Strang was the pilot, Alexander St. Bernard.

The "king" was no stranger to St. Bernard. He had piloted the *Michigan* when Strang and his co-defendants were taken aboard her some years earlier to stand trial at the U. S. District Court in Detroit on 14 bills of indictment—a trial at which Strang ably defended himself, claiming persecution because of his religious beliefs, and was acquitted. St. Bernard described Strang as a fine looking, "sociable sort of man," but not popular "among the Gentiles" (non-Morman fishermen) and on hostile terms with many of his own sect.[5]

St. Bernard found Strang at home with several of his wives, and was received cordially. Accepting the summons, Strang willingly accompanied St. Bernard back to the boat. As they stepped on the dock, two assailants came from behind a woodpile and fired at Strang, two shots hitting him in the head and one in the back. He grabbed hold of St. Bernard's arm for support—the blood from his wounds spattering on St. Bernard—and then slumped to the ground.

Loyal Saints carried their leader to a nearby house and the ship's doctor, hurriedly summoned, declared Strang's wounds fatal. He died some weeks later (July 9, 1856) at his old home in Voree, Indiana.

After the shooting the murderers sought sanctuary on the *Michigan.* The sheriff demanded their release to him, but Captain McBlair refused, saying that the prisoners would be taken to Mackinac and surrendered there. The sheriff, although a surging mob of loyal Saints egged him on, was powerless to enforce his will upon the master of the *U. S. Gunboat Michigan,* and the *Michigan* steamed away from Mackinac with the prisoners.

There seems to be no record of the murderers ever having been prosecuted, or even arraigned. In fact, they soon returned to Beaver Island, and, joining the avenging crowd of disgruntled Saints and non-Mormon fishermen, succeeded in driving from the island the

5 Alexander St. Bernard, "The Murder of King Strang," *Pioneer and Historical Coll., Mich.,* XVIII (1891), 626-627. The account was furnished by O. Poppleton and was first published in the *Detroit Free Press,* June 30, 1889.

other leaderless Mormons and their families. They were taken by boat and put ashore at Green Bay, Milwaukee, and Chicago, some of them later joining the Utah settlement; according to Captain St. Bernard, however, after the Mormons were evicted from Beaver Island, some of them evidently "returned to their homes west of Marine City."[6]

John W. Little—Stamina and Courage Win Battle of the Sea

Limitless are the stories of heroic deeds performed by Lakes captains and their crews, by fishermen, and by members of the Coast Guard. But one story stands out. It tells of the courage and stamina of the skipper of the steamer *George Dunbar*, foundered in Lake Erie in 1902, and of three valiant fishermen, all typical of the brave men—and women—who have fought the elements and misfortunes at sea. The skipper was Captain John W. Little of Port Huron, and the fishermen were Frank Dischinger, his son Frederick, and James Hamilton, all of Kelleys Island.

On the morning of June 29, 1902, the *George Dunbar* cleared from Cleveland with coal for Alpena, and on board, besides the captain, were his wife and daughter and seven members of the crew. About ten miles off Middle Island the *Dunbar* was caught in a fierce gale and was fatally wrecked and foundered. Five of the crew took to a life-raft—which was eventually lost, some bodies later being washed ashore, still lashed to parts of the wreckage—while Captain Little, together with his wife and daughter and two members of the crew, escaped in the yawl boat. A few miles from shore, however, the yawl capsized and soon disappeared in a trough of the sea.

Captain Little kept close to his wife and daughter as they drifted, supported by life preservers, toward Kelleys Island, and with great presence of mind constantly shouted encouragement to them. For hours he kept them treading water with their hands and feet and at frequent intervals even had them put their fingers down their throats and throw up the water they were swallowing. At the same time he encouraged them to persevere by repeatedly telling them they would soon drift close enough to Kelleys Island to be seen and that then they would all be rescued.

---

[6] *Ibid.*

187

As the hours passed and they kept on treading water—rising on top of the seas like gulls one moment and then lost to sight as the waves receded—Captain Little, with all his pretense at confidence, soon realized, hopelessly, that in spite of all their efforts they were unable in the worsening gale to keep themselves in a course for Kelleys Island.

Miraculously, however, they were seen bobbing up and down in the choppy water, and there were those among the growing crowds on shore watching the valiant fight, who, with courage to match that of the shipwrecked victims, made preparations to set out to the rescue. The surf was breaking nearly a mile from shore, the foam of the on-coming breakers being thrown up over a twenty-foot bank along the beach. But three fishermen, with almost superhuman effort, managed to get a small boat afloat, while several others in the crowd, who waded to their waists in the surf, held the boat until the oarsmen could square away and pull into the sea—all of them conscious, no doubt, that there was but one chance in a hundred of reaching the drifting figures, or, for that matter, of the rescuers themselves coming back alive.

Two of the fishermen pulled at the oars, while the third kept bailing out the skiff and watching for sight of the bobbing figures. On and on the determined fishermen pulled until they finally reached the shipwrecked castaways, only to find it would be impossible to take three persons into the boat, which already had ten inches of water in the bottom. One of the fishermen threw out a life line which Captain Little managed to make fast to his exhausted wife and daughter and then hung on as best he could himself while the fishermen with great skill brought the boat about in a wide trough of the sea and began the long hard pull for shore, the boat constantly filling with water from the high waves.

To those watching from shore it appeared time and time again that the boat would be swamped, but fortune was with the fishermen and they at last made the surf near the shore. Here the men jumped out of the boat and despite a terrific undertow carried the half-drowned castaways farther up on the bank where other willing hands relieved the exhausted men of their burdens.

The Littles were taken to a nearby cottage to recover from their ordeal, and were later returned to their home in Port Huron; the three fishermen, whose self-sacrifice and bravery had imperiled their own lives, were each awarded the gold life-saving medal provided by an Act of Congress for "heroic deeds in saving life from the perils of the sea."[7]

Lewis R. Boynton, Commodore
of the Mackinac Ferry Fleet

The celebration in connection with the dedication of the Mackinac Bridge in November of 1957 brought to light many bits of historical information, among which were the references to Captain Lewis R. Boynton in the book *Before the Bridge*,[8] a history of St. Ignace, Michigan, commemorating the opening of the bridge.

There is in the book the story of the original ice crusher of the Straits, the ferry *City of St. Ignace,* with special reference to Captain Boynton, who was not only her master from the time she was built in 1888 but a chief collaborator (among the practical navigators) with Frank E. Kirby, the naval architect, in her design and building.

The source of this story of Captain Boynton and his car ferry is actually an account (reprinted in *Before the Bridge*) in *The St. Ignace Republican,* April 4, 1888, of a civic celebration held in his honor when he brought the *City of St. Ignace* on her maiden trip from Detroit, and when Honorable J. J. Brown (father of Senator Prentiss M. Brown, then Chairman of the Mackinac Bridge Authority) presented a set of colors to that steamer and lauded her skipper.

Captain Lewis R. Boynton was born in Port Huron, Michigan in 1833 and during his residence there was familiarly called "Tod" Boynton. At the age of thirteen he was printer's devil for William L. Bancroft, editor of *The Lake Huron Observer*. This was Port Huron's first newspaper and was originally edited by Ebenezer B. Harrington, brother of Daniel B. Harrington, and a one-time law partner of Stevens Thomas Mason, the "Boy" Governor of Michigan.

---

[7] *Weekly Herald* (Port Huron) , July 4, 1902.

[8] *Before the Bridge, A History and a Directory of St. Ignace and Nearby Localities.* Published by the Kiwanis Club of St. Ignace, Mich., Inc., 1957, commemorating the opening of the Mackinac Bridge.

According to Mr. Bancroft, Tod was an excellent office boy but full of pranks. For instance, he periodically played hooky. Business would go along on an even tenor for some time in the little *Observer* office, and then Tod would suddenly disappear for a week or two, sometimes for a month. But just as suddenly he would reappear, and Bancroft was never surprised to open the office on a morning to find Tod setting up type just as if he had never been away.

Naturally, each desertion would be more aggravating for Editor Bancroft, but Tod's accounts of his adventures while away were always so interesting and hilarious that they "silenced reproof," as Bancroft himself said in his *Memoirs*.[9]

But eventually, on one of his disappearances, young Boynton found the life he really wanted and did not go back. It was a life on the inland seas. He was soon sailing as second mate on the steamer *Huron* of the Ward line, and before he was twenty-one he was master of the propeller *David Stoutman*.

For fifty-seven years Boynton saw continuous service as a marine captain. For almost half of those years — from the time (1881) he was master of the steamer *Algomah*, the first ferry to tow a barge carrying railroad cars from St. Ignace to Mackinaw City — his interest was with the Straits ferries, his headquarters being at St. Ignace, where he made his home and where he became known as "Commodore of the Mackinaw Railroad Ferry Fleet."

It was Captain Boynton who entertained Admiral Makaroff of the Russian Navy when he came to this country in 1900-1901 to study the design and handling of the Mackinac ferries. Later, Russian icebreakers modeled after the Mackinac boats were used on Lake Baikal in Siberia.

In 1945, another delegation of Russian engineers came, this time to study the U. S. Coast Guard Cutter *Mackinaw*. It is of interest to note that this same *Mackinaw*, considered the most efficient craft of its kind in the world, followed the original principles of design as worked out by Captain Boynton and the builders of the ferry, *City of St. Ignace*.

---

[9] Letter from Bancroft to Judge William T. Mitchell, from Hot Springs, Ark., Nov. 30, 1897, published as part of his *Memoirs* in the anniversary edition of *The Sunday Herald* (Port Huron), December, 1897, under caption, "Graphic Pen Pictures."

Captain Lewis R. Boynton was one more of the enterprising men hailing from the St. Clair River district, who contributed so vitally to the development of the great State of Michigan.

Mrs. Charles Flugal, Heroine of the Lakes

Numerous, no doubt, were the heroines among the pioneers who travelled on the Lakes, and fascinating and dramatic the incidents must have been that proved them so. Unfortunately, very few of these incidents have been recorded.

Now and then, however, a story comes to light that gives us an inkling into the courageous manner in which pioneer women have met with terrifying experiences at sea. One of these stories concerns an early resident of Port Huron, Mrs. Charles Flugal, and of the time she discovered fire aboard ship on the open lake. Acting courageously and wisely, she prevented almost certain disaster.

Mrs. Flugal had accompanied her husband to Fort Gratiot in 1834 when he came there with the troops as a baker. Flugal was stationed at Fort Gratiot until he was mustered out of service in 1837, after which he continued in the bakery business in Port Huron for many years.

The Flugals, whose home was in New York state, were married at Sackets Harbor in 1822. Mrs. Flugal later accompanied her husband to many of the forts where he was stationed, and it was while on her way with her baby to Green Bay, Wisconsin to join her husband (a short time before they came to Fort Gratiot) that the incident which proved her a heroine occurred.

Mrs. Flugal was sailing for Green Bay aboard the steamer *Ontario* — the first United States-built steamer on the Lakes — and besides the crew, Mrs. Flugal and her baby, there were eight hundred other passengers, many of them immigrants. A short time after midnight, when they were still well out on the open lake, Mrs. Flugal's baby became ill, and she decided to go to the galley for a cup in which to mix some medicine. On the way she smelled smoke, and when she opened the door into the galley, heat and smoke struck her in the face, and she saw flames eating along the cupboards in the pantry.

Stifling a cry of horror she quickly shut the door and cautiously but swiftly made her way to the captain's quarters. The captain

191

was asleep but the mate having heard her roused himself and asked her, sharply, what it was that she wanted. She told him that the ship was on fire — that the pantries in the cookroom were already a mass of flames.

Between them and without undue noise they roused the captain and the rest of the crew and succeeded in getting the fire under control before the passengers were hardly aware of what was going on. The boat was so heavily loaded with passengers that had Mrs. Flugal become hysterical and sounded the cry of "Fire" panic would most certainly have ensued — the fighting of the fire would have been hindered, and many, if not all of the eight hundred passengers would have perished.

In recognition of her courage and her presence of mind, Mrs. Flugal was given one of the most prized possessions on shipboard. The report of the incident stated simply that the captain, in recognition of her services, presented Mrs. Flugal with a lemon. But only the pioneer, sailing the seas in those early days when scurvy was so prevalent — due to the scarcity of fresh fruits and vegetables — could appreciate just how precious that gift was considered.[10]

The Flugals were among a great number of pioneers who settled in Port Huron via Fort Gratiot, and they continued to live there for over fifty years. Mrs. Flugal died in 1887 at the age of eighty-five.

The Warm-Hearted Amazon

The story is often told in books on shipwrecks, of the heroic deed of one Abigail Becker, the "warm-hearted Amazon" wife of a Canadian farmer. She single-handedly saved the lives of three sailors from drowning, when the schooner *Conductor*, loaded with grain for Buffalo and driving through a blinding snowstorm, crashed aground on Lake Erie off Long Point Light.

---

[10] In those days when there was a deficiency of fresh vegetables and fruits and the diet on board ships consisted mostly of bread, salt pork and salt fish, lemon and lime juices were for many years the most important food materials used on shipboard as a preventive of scurvy. It is interesting to note that by the Shipping Act of 1867, every British ship going to countries where lemon or lime juice could not be obtained was required to take enough to give one ounce daily to every member of the crew.

A similar incident took place on the shores of Lake Erie, involving the almost superhuman deed of an unnamed heroine who might also be called a "warm-hearted Amazon." Although the heroine was not from the St. Clair River district, it was to her that a St. Clair County lakes captain owed his life when he went aground in a scow off Fairport, Ohio.

It was in November of 1906, while Captain George W. McElroy of Port Huron, was piloting a sand scow from Port Huron to a Lake Erie port in tow of the tug *Bangs* that a storm struck on the second day out. The wind worsened into a sixty-mile gale, accompanied by snow, and when off Fairport the scow broke away from the *Bangs,* and was carried far out to sea by the gale blowing from the shore. The captain was not too worried or frightened, for "she was a sturdy old raft," as he later explained.

All day long the scow drifted around, lost to view in the blowing snow, but toward evening when the storm shifted its course the scow was again brought to land — about two thousand feet from the breakwater, the captain figured, for he could see the lights of Fairport and could hear the sea dashing against the breakwater.

Captain McElroy began swinging his lanterns from the time he first sighted the city's lights until he passed beyond view of them, expecting every minute that someone would see his lights and that a boat would be put out, yet he drifted past without seeing anyone or even any movement — nothing but the receding lights of Fairport.

Finally the scow hit the sand, but in the high-breaking surf it began making one revolution after another along the beach, and it was seven o'clock in the morning before it was finally grounded for good. Fortunately he was in sight of a farmhouse, so Captain McElroy sat himself down in sight of the farmhouse and hopefully waited. It was three long hours, however, before he saw any signs of life about the place. Finally the door of the farmhouse opened and a woman appeared, shading her eyes with one hand as she gazed out to sea.

Captain McElroy shouted to her for help and the woman shouted back — something he was unable to make out — and then she went back into the house. In a few minutes she reappeared,

193

wrapped in a long cloak and hood, and, with a large coil of rope on her arm, made her way down the incline of the lane toward the beach.

Down on the beach she shouted to him that her husband was away but that she could help him if he would throw her his line. The captain saw that she was "quite an old lady" and doubted if she could be of much help, but he threw out his line and then let down his yawl and got aboard. In the meantime the woman had fastened her rope to the line he had thrown her, and walking back up the hill with it, took her stance.

"She was quite an old lady," the captain repeated afterwards, "but she was hefty, and maybe she couldn't pull! She stood on the top of that hill and I thought she'd yank the yawl out through the air! I don't know yet how she ever did it!" [11]

Finally, after many heroic pullings and haulings, the woman got the yawl far enough in so that the captain was able to safely disembark and make his way out of the breaking waves onto the beach. His rescuer then made her way down to the beach again, and, supporting him, led him back to the farmhouse, where she gave him hot tea and food and cared for him until he was able to contact the skipper of the tug.

Captain McElroy was never to forget his own particular "warmhearted Amazon" of Lake Erie.

Emily Ward, The Pioneer Woman With Yankee "Faculty"

It was not unusual, of course, for pioneer women to perform heroic acts in their encounters with the Indians, or during the severe storms that ravished the virtual wilderness that was Michigan. But sometimes even the acts of ordinary living in the frontier settlements of the Territory required extraordinary ingenuity, resourcefulness, and courage. Take for instance the time when, still in her teens, Emily Ward (a sister of Eber B. Ward) and her party were marooned on the Canadian shore near Sombra, Ontario. Emily with courage and ingenuity, rescued them.[12]

---

[11] Interview in *Port Huron Weekly Times,* Nov. 2, 1906, "Story of a Strong Old Lady."

[12] The story of the incident is told in *Grandmother's Stories,* by Frances Hurlbut. Privately printed in Cambridge, by the Riverside Press, 1889.

One June day Emily, together with her sister Sallie, her five-year old cousin Harrison Ward, and a neighbor girl named Margaret, set out from Marine City in a rowboat for the Canadian side of the St. Clair River to gather wild strawberries. When they reached the shore they were careful to pull the boat high enough up on the beach so that the waves would not carry it away.

After gathering the berries in a patch near a thicket which was a considerable distance inland, the party began a leisurely trip back to the beach, the young boy running ahead of the rest. When they reached the beach Emily discovered that the boy had managed to push the boat out into the water and that it was floating away with the current, too far out to be retrieved. There were the four, stranded miles away from any habitation, with the prospect of spending the night in the woods where wolves and an occasional bear were known to roam.

Emily knew that there was an island below, on the Canadian shore, and she believed — or rather hoped — that the current would carry the boat to that island and ground it. But the problem was, how to get to the island.

She looked around the beach while the rest sat huddled together, frightened, and crying over their plight. She finally found some driftwood of logs and a few long poles, the kind pioneers used in building mud chimneys.

In those days every girl wore a long undergarment called a chemise, which hung to the ankles. Using these and the girls' skirts and aprons and sunbonnets as rope, Emily tide the logs together for a raft. A very flimsy affair at its best, the raft was only large enough for two, so Emily and Margaret set out, leaving Sallie to take care of the boy. Both staying and going required great courage — the occasional howl of a wolf warned clearly of the dangers of the woods, while on the frail raft which could easily fall apart at any time, the danger was the deep, rushing water of the river.

The arrangment was that both girls should stand up and pole the raft, but as soon as they got away from the shore Margaret was afraid to stand up so Emily had to do all the work. The current helped considerably, however, and after awhile they could see the head of the island.

The girls knew that there was an encampment of Indians on the island at the time, but they were not especially afraid for the tribe had always seemed friendly, and by the time the raft reached the island the full moon was up and the girls could see all of the Indians down on the shore, gazing out at them. She could also see in the distance the outline of their rowboat, stranded about where she thought it would be.

It was evident that at first the Indians could not make out what it was that was coming toward them, and when they finally did see the crazy-looking raft with the two girls, they shrieked and shouted with laughter. But they were very kind to the girls. The men untied the raft and fetched their rowboat, and the women wrung out their wet clothes and took the girls to a wigwam and helped them dress. After that the Indians assisted the girls into the boat, and with many friendly grunts and exclamations they pushed the boat out into the stream. Emily and Margaret went back for Sally and the boy to take them across the river and home.

Many years later, while living in Detroit, Emily passed the island on a trip up the St. Clair River on one of her brother's excursion steamers [13] and told the story of that strawberry-picking incident to a fellow passenger, H. M. Stanley, the noted painter of Indians. He remarked to her that the incident "would make a pretty picture." [14] Some time afterwards, on her sixtieth birthday, Stanley presented her with a painting depicting the incident.[15]

It was also Emily Ward who saved the light and other objects of value when a storm destroyed the lighthouse on Bois Blanc Island. Her father, Eber Ward was keeper of the lighthouse at the time and was away on one of his periodic trips to Mackinac for provisions. Emily, watching from a window in the residence during the storm, discovered the masonry of the lighthouse tower

[13] Probably the *Milton D. Ward,* named for one of Eber B. Ward's sons.

[14] Hurlbut, *op. cit.,* p. 109.

[15] The painting is now in the private collection of a descendant of the Ward family, Mr. David Sutter, Grosse Pointe, Mich. Stanley's painting depicting Major Gladwin and Catherine, the Indian woman who, according to legend, warned the British commandant of Pontiac's plan to capture the fort at Detroit, hangs in the entrance hall of the Burton Collection of the Detroit Public Library; and his "Indian Telegraph" is in the permanent collection of the Detroit Institute of Arts.

being undermined. Still watching, she saw a break appear in the wall, and then another, until seams stretched the entire length of the lighthouse.

One thought possessed her — she must save the precious light. She braved the fierce, cyclonic-like winds, and crossing the yard, went inside the lighthouse. In spite of the fact that she felt the building sway she climbed the spiral stairs to the top of the tower, removed the light and other instruments, and brought them down to safety. Within minutes later the lighthouse toppled over, fortunately falling clear of the residence which Emily had reached.

What set Emilly Ward apart from her contemporary sisters, however, was not so much her courage as her superabundance of "faculty," which was a Yankee way of referring to her great business ability.

This ability was manifest in the management of both her household and her school,[16] and especially in the advice given to her brother, Eber Brock Ward, and in the management of many of his business enterprises. She had an innate grasp of business principles and an "intuitive perception" [17] of the causes which brought prosperous times or financial depressions; her brother gave her the credit for much of his phenomenal business success.

Ward is quoted as saying that he once lost twenty thousand dollars on land speculation, a transaction he insisted on carrying

---

[16] Emily Ward, with the assistance of her brother, established a school in Marine City about 1850, called Newport Academy, or "Aunt Emily's" Academy, and conducted it for many years. Much like Rev. O. C. Thompson's Academy in St. Clair, which was noted for the later prominence of some of its pupils (Governor David H. Jerome, U. S. Senator Thomas W. Palmer, and David Ward, the "Pine King of Michigan"), Emily Ward's Academy was also noted for the quality of its pupils, producing such well-known men as Don M. Dickinson, Postmaster General in the first Cleveland Administration, and J. P. Hagerman, for whom one of the best known passes in the Rocky Mountains is named. After Emily Ward moved to Detroit in 1867, the academy property was given for a high school (the present Marine City High School stands on the site). The building itself was moved to South Main Street, after which it had a varied career, serving as the Village Hall (with the jail located in the basement) and as a Presbyterian church. Today, the same building is the Marine City Library.

[17] William L. Bancroft, "Memoir of Captain Samuel Ward," *Pioneer and Historical Coll., Mich.* XXI (1892) , 369.

out against Emily's advice and better judgment.[18] Thus he learned to depend in a good measure on her counsel and her business acumen. When she had charge of the cabin furnishing of the Ward boats, it is recorded that she saved her brother five thousand dollars on every boat he built in Marine City.[19]

For the last twenty-four years of her life Emily Ward lived in Detroit, in a house on Fort Street West. The house was built for her by her brother across the street from his own palatial residence,[20] which was a show place in the city for many years. She died there in 1891 at the age of eighty-two. In her great courage, her kindness and generosity, and her unusual business acumen, Emily Ward was one of the most notable and forceful pioneer characters of the St. Clair River district.

---

[18] *Ibid.*

[19] *Ibid.*

[20] Later, the home of the House of Good Shepherd.

Chapter XXX

THE ST. CLAIR RIVER DISTRICT'S MOST CELEBRATED PIONEER: THOMAS ALVA EDISON

The furor in the academic world over the intelligence tests propounded by Thomas Edison for I. Q. ratings of prospective employees and scholarship aspirants, was created by what many professors and other prominent men in the country considered the unfairness of the difficult questions. In fact, Albert Einstein, at the height of the controversy, admitted that he was unable to answer one of the questions — "What is the speed of sound?" — without reference to a textbook. Arthur Brisbane, the sensational Hearst journalist, declared that Edison himself could not have answered one-quarter of the questions when he was a boy.

But Edison had, some sixty years before, at the age of sixteen and in Port Huron, answered in a most substantial way one of the more difficult of the "practical" questions of his intelligence test of 1929. The question was: *If you were in a town where a catastrophe occurred, how would you communicate with another town across a river a mile wide if all ordinary means of communication had broken down?*

Shortly before the Edisons moved to Port Huron (1854) the Grand Trunk Railway Company of Canada had completed its road to Point Edward, Ontario from the eastern seaboard, and in 1859 had built the railroad from Port Huron to Detroit under the name of a Michigan corporation, The Chicago, Detroit & Canada Grand Trunk Junction Railway Company. A depot and switching yard were built along the banks of the St. Clair River at Fort Gratiot, and connection between the two roads was made by means of a car ferry (the "Swing Ferry") across St. Clair River.

The depot and the switching yard were just north of the Edison home, and the queer, brass-trimmed locomotives with their tall, diamond-shaped smokestacks and long, pointed cow catchers intrigued young "Al" — as Edison was more familiarly known in his boyhood. Frequently engineers would let him ride in the cab and toot the whistle, or even pilot the locomotive for a short distance.

The experience had a practical sequel some time later. At the close of the unusually severe winter of 1863-64, large ice floes in the St. Clair River severed the submarine cable between Port Huron and the Canadian side. A continuation of the drifting ice made repair impossible and all telegraph communication remained cut off.

Edison, who by that time had had experience in telegraphy, offered to attempt communication across the river if the railroad authorities would furnish a locomotive and an engineer to help him — his idea being that the blasts of the whistle might be broken into long and short sounds corresponding to the dots and dashes of telegraphy.

The railroad company after considerable deliberation consented, and ran a locomotive along a siding near the car ferry dock and had the engineer get up steam. Al jumped into the engineer's seat, and, seizing the valve controlling the whistle, began to toot the whistle to the rhythmic cadence of the Morse code and sent his "Hello!" message over the ice-bound waters.

Time and time again the short and long toots sounded in the attempt to contact the Canadian side. In the meantime curious crowds had gathered on both sides of the river, and the towns-people milling around on the American side, near Fort Gratiot, were asking what "Sam Edison's boy" — who was always getting into scrapes — was "up to now?"

The persistant boy kept sending out the incisive whistle until a Canadian telegraph operator, finally catching on, sent back clear and welcoming toots from the railroad yard on the opposite shore, and, thanks to Al, communication between the towns was resumed.

That incident was long remembered by the people of Port Huron and certainly by Edison himself — an incident which was to have nation-wide echoes some sixty years later in Edison's controversial "egnoramometer" system of questionnaires.

* * *

In Milan, Ohio, where Samuel Edison had moved his family from Vienna, Ontario, and where Thomas Alva was born in 1849, the senior Edison had been fairly prosperous during the town's boom days as a grain port. But when Milan was deprived of its flourishing grain trade by the coming of the railroads — with which the Milan canal authorities at first refused to cooperate — Samuel Edison realized that he must look elsewhere to provide for his family, and they moved to Port Huron, Michigan. He had remembered the beautifully-situated little lumber town at the confluence of Black River with the St. Clair when, some eighteen years earlier on his flight from Canada at the beginning of the so-called Mackenzie Rebellion, his long legs had carried him safely from the pursuing Tories, all the way from Vienna to Sarnia and then across the ice of the St. Clair River to the American side.

The Edisons arrived in Port Huron in the spring of 1854, coming up the St. Clair River from Detroit on the Ward steamer *Ruby,* on the last leg of their journey, and disembarked at the Butler Street dock. Carrying their bulging satchels and wicker hampers, Samuel Edison and his family,[1] including seven-year old Thomas Alva,[2] trudged up the sandy hill that was old Butler Street (now Grand River Avenue) and then took the Fort trail to their new home in the pine grove on the Fort Gratiot Military Reservation — a two-story colonial style house,[3] situated at the north end of what is now Pine Grove Park, and which Samuel Edison had previously purchased.

It was in that house that Thomas Edison spent his boyhood years, between the ages of seven and 17. It was in the cellar of that house that he assembled his first laboratory, and it was there that

---

[1] The family consisted of Edison and his wife, Nancy Elliott Edison, William Pitt, the eldest son, Harriet Ann, and Thomas Alva. Marian Edison, the eldest daughter, had married while the Edisons were living in Milan, and two sons, Carlisle and Samuel Ogden, and a daughter, Eliza, had died.

[2] It was just before Thomas Edison left Port Huron that he began to use the name Thomas, instead of Alva.

[3] The "House in the Grove" was erected in 1840 by Chancellor Walworth of New York State for his daughter, Mrs. Edgar Jenkins, whose husband was sutler, or post storekeeper at the fort. The house passed into the ownership of L. M. Mason, who subsequently sold it to Bethuel C. Farrand, and he in turn sold it to Samuel Edison. The Edisons occupied it until 1864, when it was requisitioned by the Government. The house burned down in 1867. Its approximate site is now marked by a large boulder in Pine Grove Park, erected by the Rotary Club of Port Huron in 1929. Memory sketch of the house was made in 1920 by Mrs. Caroline L. Ballentine, daughter of B. C. Farrand.

he reconstructed his "laboratory on wheels"[4] after his well known ejection from the Grand Trunk train when one of his sticks of phosphorus set fire to the baggage car. There in the cellar, amid the accumulation of crocks of butter, great earthenware jars of eggs preserved in layers of coarse salt, barrels of potatoes, and kegs of carrots kept firm in sand brought up from the Lake Huron beach — there was his experimental workshop.

Snarled loops of wire, scrap lead, and batteries were scattered about. Some two hundred bottles, gathered with the help of his friends, Michael Oates and James Clancy, from the townspeoples' trash piles, and labeled POISON, had crowded out much of his mother's canned goods. And in those bottles were the chemicals bought at the local drug store with money he earned as a newsboy and truck gardener — chemicals that were often the source of offensive odors which penetrated into the upper part of the house much to the annoyance of the rest of his family.

There it was that Edison — after his printing press and his laboratory were tossed from the train — continued to print the *Weekly Herald,* the $12'' \times 16''$ news sheet which created so much comment (being noted even by the *London Times*) as being the first and only newspaper printed on a train. The *Weekly Herald* was soon converted to a "society" journal, called *Paul Pry,* but some of the gossip that was printed so irritated the townspeople — one to the point where he gave young Edison a ducking in the river — the newspaper was soon abandoned.

---

[4] Of especial interest in Edison's laboratory in the baggage car was the set of shelves on which he kept his chemicals. In Detroit during the long layovers of some ten hours between trains, young Edison was left to his own devices, and besides spending much time in the Public Library he wandered about the city, talking with men in machine shops and dickering for equipment to use in his laboratory. It was on one of his wanderings about town that he came upon the cabinet shop of a young man named George Pullman—another budding inventor—who along with his job-contracting duties was working on a new idea—a sleeping car. It wasn't long before Pullman was making for young Edison some wooden equipment for his chemicals, including shelving, with a railing across the shelves to keep bottles and jars intact. This same George Pullman was organizing the Pullman Palace Car Company (1867) about the time Edison's "wandering years" took him to Boston, where he perfected his Electrographic Vote Recorder—the first of his more than twelve hundred inventions.

It was also in the cellar that young Edison hid when one of his more serious pranks involved him with the soldiers at the fort. Often times at night, he and Michael Oates,[5] on returning home after selling their papers in town, would hear the sentry calling the corporal of the guard for some help. This would be repeated from sentry to sentry until the corporal would come to see what was wanted.

One dark night Tom and Michael hid themselves in the grove near the post walk and when the opportunity came, Tom, in as stentorian a voice as he could muster, shouted out for the corporal of the guard no. 1. The second sentry, thinking it was the terminal sentry who had shouted, repeated it to the third. This brought the corporal on the run along the half mile only to find he had been fooled. For three nights Tom and his chum tried this prank, but by the third night the sentries had discovered the trick and were watching for them.

In the chase that followed Michael Oates was caught and shut up in the guardhouse for the night, but Tom got home and escaped to the cellar. Here, in one small compartment, were two barrels of potatoes and a third one, almost empty. He poured the remnants of the latter into a basket and then sat on the dirt floor and pulled the empty barrel over him.

He heard the soldiers rousing the family and soon his father, carrying a candle, and the sentries with their square lanterns, came down into the cellar. Tom, cramped and almost suffocated with the offensive odor of long-rotted potatoes, could hear them talking. The corporal was sure "the boy" had gone into the cellar and thought it most unlikely that he could have gotten out.

But Tom was not detected, and, with the assurance from his father that there were no secret hiding places, the baffled soldiers left. After awhile Tom succeeded in sneaking off to bed, but the next morning his father gave him "a good switching on the legs" in punishment.

---

5 The boy to whom Tom Edison once fed Seidlitz powders, the gases generated from which were supposed to make the little Dutch boy "fly," but which, instead, almost killed him.

Edison's First Underground Electric Wiring System

Edison is called the "Father of the underground wires in America," [6] and reference in this connection is always made to the account of his first electrical wiring system in a city — that of the Pearl Street Central Station in New York City.[7] But the idea for that famous system, built in the eighteen eighties, had its inception in a system of underground wiring conceived and put into practice by Edison some twenty years earlier in Port Huron, Michigan, when he was little more than twelve years old. It had to do with his homemade telegraph system.

Edison at the time was still a newsboy on the Grand Trunk railway between Detroit and Port Huron. But he had numerous other projects. In addition to what he sold on the train, he had two stores in town where he sold the same candy, peanuts, newspapers, etc., as well as produce which he raised in his truckgarden. In these projects, he had an assistant, James Clancy, who with his mother and step-father, a man named Ward, also lived on the Military Reservation.

After Tom had built his telegraph set and learned the Morse code, it was to the home of this chum, almost a mile away, that he strung the equipment in his first attempt at telegraphy. Discarded stove-pipe wire was attached to houses, trees, and flimsy poles, and insulated with old bottlenecks tacked up with tenpenny nails. Castaway instruments were found and repaired, and with a few bottles containing a little blue vitriol which completed his battery, Tom managed to produce a weak but sufficient current.

James helped Tom with his paper route and, like Tom, would take home any remaining papers. Tom taught him to relay news from these papers over the homemade telegraph wire, while he practiced receiving and copying it as James tapped it out to him.

Every moment of Tom's day was crowded with his many business interests, and his only chance to practice telegraphy was at

---

[6] Frank L. Dyer & Thomas C. Martin, *Edison, His Life and Inventions* (New York: Harper, 1910), II, 988.

[7] Edison, shortly before, laid out such an underground wiring system for some 425 lamps, but the system, somewhat crude, was limited to the immediate vicinity and constructed with no idea of permanency.

night. But his father insisted on bed at an early hour. Not too sympathetic with his son's numerous activities, the stern parent no doubt felt the young boy was dissipating his energies over too many surfaces, although the father had his own many interests — one of which was a passion for the day's news. Each day he waited anxiously for the newspapers Tom brought home and then sat up, late into the night, reading them.

This gave the boy an idea. If, on some day, no newspapers were forthcoming for his father, and if James Clancy were contacted by the homemade telegraph and could provide current headlines satisfying his father's interest in the day's happenings, he might permit his son the privilege of late hours at his telegraph key.

The boy's idea worked. As the news came line by line over the wire and was passed on by Tom to his father, the man realized that his son was serious and that this facet of his imagination was indeed practical. After this he permitted Tom to work as late as he chose in his experimental laboratory.

But further obstacles arose. Rival south-side gangs of boys [8] tore down his wires, and much of the delicate work was ruined. To outwit them, Tom with the help of James made an excavation deep enough to accommodate them (standing upright) and their "power plant." This they roofed with boards, and to confuse the pranksters still further they also strung their wires underground — using a long piece of discarded submarine cable, supplemented with old sewer tile through which they passed the wires from the plant. It was a project of sizable proportions considering that the underground wiring system ran some 160 rods and crossed underneath a section of the fort parade grounds.

All went well until the family cow wandered out of an enclosure and stepped on the not-too-sturdy planking which covered the excavation, crashing through to the bottom and ruining the power plant.

Although the incident resulted in great trouble and expense to the senior Edison, it was the deciding factor in his change of

---

8 In Tom Edison's day in Port Huron the part of town north of Black River was called Frenchtown, and that part south of the river was called Dutchtown—a misnomer since many of the residents were German and not Dutch. There was always great rivalry at that time beteween the north and south side gangs of boys.

heart. From that time he gave substantial help and encouragement to the boy, who in his devotion to his dream, had refused to recognize adversity. It was then that the father built a room and helped his son equip a laboratory on the ground floor of his own famous Observatory Tower; but in the meantime the inventive genius of the boy, his sense of practicality, and his ability to overcome difficulties were all shown in that underground cable —connotations of which were apparent more than twenty years later in his plan of an electric underground wiring system in New York City.

The Edison Observatory Tower

One of the more whimsical of the numerous projects that Samuel Edison, father of the inventor, engaged in to make his fortune, was the erection of the one hundred-foot Observatory Tower,[9] situated on the bank of the St. Clair River, south of his home and slightly north of the site of the present filtration plant in Pine Grove Park.

This was at the time when the geodetic survey of the Great Lakes was being made with Captain George G. Meade of the U. S. Corps of Engineers (later General Meade of Civil War fame) in charge (1857–1861). It is said, in fact, that Meade was engaged in his survey work up in Huron County when a courier reached him with orders to assume command of a Union regiment at the outbreak of the War.

It was during his numerous stopovers in Port Huron, traveling to and from his headquarters in Detroit, that Meade had become acquainted with Samuel Edison. In their memoirs and reminiscences some pioneers have implied that it was Meade who supervised the construction of Edison's wooden tower.

For the price of twenty-five cents, one could climb up winding stairs to the top of the tower, which was equipped with a telescope on its breezy platform, and enjoy the beautiful view of Lake Huron to the north and of St. Clair River to the south, together with the surrounding landscape. In the promotion of the Observatory Tower such phrases as "a pleasing prospect" and "the pros-

[9] Mrs. C. L. Ballentine's memory pen picture of the Edison house shows a portion of the top of the Tower.

pect is a charming one," were used in the advertising pamphlets — hence the origin, no doubt, of the name of the street, Prospect Place, which was cut through from Pine Grove Avenue to a point near the site of the former tower.

The Edison Observatory Tower enjoyed rather a varied career and made money only spasmodically. At first very few sightseers toiled up the long flight of steps. In fact, the senior Edison took in only three dollars the first two months and was somewhat discouraged with his investment. It seemed that the tower was destined to be but an intriguing lookout for young Tom and his friends when Tom was not working in his laboratory on the ground floor, or at his job in Miciah Walker's jewelry and book store as telegraph operator — Walker having the local telegraph office.[10]

But then one day, in August of 1860, the Canada Great Western Railway ran an excursion at reduced rates from Oxford County, Ontario to Port Huron, to enable its passengers to enjoy Lake Huron and to picnic in the "Grove" (now Pine Grove Park). The excursion proved immensely popular, with eager travelers from Oxford-On-The-Thames, Ingersoll, Woodstock, London, Forest City, and Norwichville crowding into twenty-three coaches, drawn by two locomotives — more than one thousand people in all, not counting those who came by regular train.

The crowds were met at Sarnia by the steamer *Kaloolak* and the ferryboats *Lion, Islander,* and *Union,* and were carried across to Port Huron, where they spilled over from the picnic grounds in the pine grove to the site of what is now Gratiot Park in north Port Huron.

More than six hundred of the picnickers on that August afternoon paid twenty-five cents apiece to climb the hundred-foot tower to see the "pleasing prospect" of the Lake Huron–St. Clair River district, bringing to Sam Edison a fairly good day's revenue. Other excursions followed, from inland towns both in Michigan and Ontario, but except for those times revenue from the Tower was practically nil, and in time, although the admission charge was

---

10 Some biographers of Edison, including Simonds and Josephson, erroneously refer to the jewelry store proprietor as Thomas Walker. His name was Miciah Walker, called by his contemporaries, "Mac" Walker. See Chapter XXXIII for sketch of Miciah Walker.

gradually reduced to five cents, the tower was left mainly to Tom and his friends.

Then came the Civil War, and while it was in progress a controversy arose between Edison and President Lincoln's Secretary of War, Edwin M. Stanton, over the Tower. Whether it was alleged that the Tower was a hiding place for Confederate spies or a way station and haven for runners in the Underground Railroad, or what, was never quite clear. In any event, it is said that Stanton in 1864 ordered the destruction of the Tower. Edison, half-heartedly, "put the ax to it,"[11] but in spite of both Edison and Stanton the Tower continued to stand until the early summer of 1865 when an electric storm struck the district with winds of cyclonic force and toppled the Tower over into the Rapids of the St. Clair River.

Tom Edison's Shock Therapy

Many of the stories concerning Tom Edison's boyhood in Port Huron had to do with what the townspeople called his "crazy pranks." They were considered mischievous and often times destructive in their results even though there was always a constructive, practical idea motivating the episode. These included the well known fire episode on the Grand Trunk train, when a stick of phosphorus from Tom's chemical laboratory was dislodged and fell to the floor of the baggage car, setting fire to it, and also to the not so well known episode concerning the time he inadvertently caused what could have been a very serious fire in a village of frame houses protected only by a volunteer fire department and the bucket brigade.

The incident occurred in the year 1859, when a group of boys including Edison, Edwin Petit, and Edward Minnie — all about eleven or twelve years of age — had in their possession a small circular saw for cutting the firewood they sold around town. Young Tom, already showing his propensity for inventing devices to take the drudgery out of work, decided he would build a steam engine to run the saw.

The experiment took place on the Minnie property on the southeast corner of Military and Court Streets, in a shed which

---

[11] Bancroft, "Graphic Pen Pictures," *Sunday Herald* (Port Huron), Dec. 20, 1897.

stood back of the house along Court Street and which was partially obscured by a high board fence. Out of an old boiler and pieces of stove pipe Edison constructed a cylinder and a "steam chest," and, as the story goes, the contrivance worked fine. But one day something went wrong. The steam engine blew up, wrecking the shed, and to make matters worse the shed and fence caught on fire.

The townspeople, especially nearby property owners, hurriedly formed a bucket brigade that reached to the town pump a block away, and the fire eating away at the shed and fence was fortunately put out before it got too much headway.

Despite the fact that, according to one of the numerous versions of the story, one of the boys was "blown clean through the fence," none was seriously hurt, and the spread of the fire was averted. Although Edison was severely criticized for another of his "crazy pranks," in later years, on one of the great inventor's visits to his home town, those same critics would recall to him with amusement, and almost pride, that early experiment of his in the old shed on Court Street.

One of the least publicized of Tom Edison's boyhood activities in Port Huron, however, was, oddly enough, one without unfortunate results. It had to do with the time Tom and his old electro-magnetic battery aided a local doctor immeasurably in saving the life of one of his patients.

One winter evening while walking along Commercial Street near the water front, the daughter of Duncan McKellar, proprietor of the Albion House, slipped on the ice and fell, striking her head. She was picked up, unconscious, and carried into her father's hotel, situated on the corner of Commercial and Butler Streets. A physician, Dr. J. T. Travers, was called but despite his administrations she remained in a coma.

Late that evening the distraught mother and father, and a nephew, Arthur Conkey (who later told the story),[12] hovered nearby watching the girl anxiously for some sign of a return to consciousness, or, for some reassuring word from the doctor that she would eventually recover. But Dr. Travers' efforts were of no avail, and the watchers sensed that he, too, was beginning to fear for her life.

---

[12] Interview with Arthur Conkey (then a Lakes captain) printed in *Times Herald* (Port Huron), October 18, 1931.

Then as he continued to study the patient, Dr. Travers made a quick decision. Late as it was he told McKellar's nephew to go to the Edison home and "tell Young Al," to bring his galvanic battery to the hotel immediately, explaining that the battery might possibly revive her.

There was a look of incredulity on the faces around the bed. But this was no time to question; something — anything — must be done. The nephew was told to hurry.

The boy started out on the long trek up Commercial Street and took short cuts to the Grove. Sleet, wind-borne from across Lake Huron cut into his face and encrusted the deep snow, slowing his progress, but he finally reached the Edison home, and, rousing the family, reported his errand.

Tom was not in sight when he entered the house but was soon found tapping away at his telegraph key, no doubt sending some message to his chum, James Clancy. He was obviously reluctant to leave his telegraph instrument and go out into the stormy night, but Duncan McKellar was a friend of his father, and Tom was told to hurry and take the battery to the hotel as the doctor had requested.

Tom put on his reefer and his shiny-peaked cap, wrapped his thick, woolen muffler around his neck, looped it under his chin, and was ready. Between the two they carried the heavy battery over the icy trail to Commercial Street and the Albion Hotel.

Dr. Travers was waiting for them, ready with his instructions. There were two handles to the battery, and Tom was told to take hold of one, Arthur the other. As they did so a current of electricity passed through their bodies. Dr. Travers then told them how and where to rub their free hands on the unconscious girl.

After a considerable length of time—and at a point when Tom was gently rubbing the patient's forehead—the girl groaned slightly and, opening her eyes, looked with recognition at her mother. Tom's galvanic battery had revived her.[13]

After the McKellar incident, Arthur Conkey reported that he accompanied Tom and his battery many times to homes "to relieve

---

[13] Almost forty years after the accident of the McKellar girl, Conkey wrote to Edison about the affair and Edison wrote back and said he remembered the incident "very well."

210

some sufferer,"[14] and the money received for the services—usually a dollar a trip—was spent by Tom for chemicals and apparatus in his experiments.

How Port Huron and the District
Learned About the Battle of Shiloh

Probably the one episode in Edison's boyhood in Port Huron, prophetically illustrative of the great ingenuity and resourcefulness for which Edison the man was to be noted, was his newspaper selling on the Grand Trunk railroad during the time of the Civil War.

On a Sunday morning in early April of 1862 began the fierce and costly battle in the Civil War known as Shiloh—a battle which lasted for two long days. The news of those two fearful days at Shiloh was astounding to the American people. Never before on the continent had there been anything approaching it in magnitude or horror; the Battle of Bull Run had been but a skirmish in comparison. The losses in men killed, wounded, and missing totaled over twenty-three thousand, and General Grant reported that after the second day he saw an open field so covered with the dead and wounded that it would have been impossible to walk across it in any direction without stepping on bodies.

News was still slow in coming to the frontier towns in the early eighteen sixties, and the people had to rely on the weekly newspaper, three-fourths of which was printed from sheets of type metal made up of stock or timeless material secured from Detroit or Chicago, with little news of immediate interest other than local items.

True, the progressive editor of the Port Huron Press, James J. Scarrett, had attempted a daily edition of his paper at the outbreak of the war, carrying some spotty news, but shortly afterwards he enlisted at the call of President Lincoln (eventually giving his life for his country, dying from a disease contracted in camp after the battle of Antioch Station) and the daily survived only a few months.

Tom, as a rule, negotiated for two hundred papers daily, of which he usually managed to dispose. On one particular day shortly after the Battle of Shiloh, when he arrived at the Detroit

---

[14] Conkey, *ibid.*

Free Press office, the astounding reports of that terrible battle, with its appalling number of casualties, were coming in over the wires and appearing in great headlines in the paper.

Looking at those headlines it occurred to young Edison what enormous sales his papers would have if the people along the line and in Port Huron could know beforehand in general what was happening, and an idea came to him. He hurried to the telegraph operator and offered him, free for six months, a copy of Harper's Weekly and a daily evening paper, if he would wire ahead to all the principal stations where they stopped—Utica, Mt. Clemens, New Haven, and Port Huron—asking the stationmaster to chalk up on the bulletin boards used to announce the hours of arrival and departure of trains the news of the great battle and the appalling casualties. The operator agreed.

His next step was to get, on credit, the one thousand papers he figured he could sell. As he rather expected, the superintendent of the delivery department refused his request, but he then went directly to the editor's office. The man[15] in charge there, evidently intrigued by the boy's ingenuity, wrote a few words on a slip of paper and told him to take it back to the superintendent and he would get what he wanted.

Tom hired a boy to help him fold the papers, and in the meantime the telegraph operator had kept his word and had wired the news ahead. At the first stop, which was Utica, and where as a rule Tom sold only a few papers, he saw a crowd around the station as the train pulled in. His first thought was that there had been an accident, but as he jumped off the train the crowd made a rush toward him, and he knew that his scheme had worked. He sold over one hundred papers at five cents a copy. At Mt. Clemens there was another crowd. He decided to "raise the ante"—to use a phrase the inventor himself is said to have used in telling of the incident in later years—and he sold nearly three hundred copies at ten cents a copy.

It was the same at every station and by the time he reached Port Huron he was crying "Paper! Twenty-five cents apiece! Paper! All about the great battle! Paper! Twenty-five cents apiece!" and

---

15 Said to have been the editor himself, Wilbur F. Storey, although this has been disputed.

he sold every copy he had, the people surging around him, bidding against each other, and many paying much more than a quarter for a precious copy.

The financial results of that phenomenal business coup far exceeded the boy's expectations, but, more than anything else—as Edison was to point out many years later—the incident proved to him the great value of telegraphy, and he decided from that moment to become a good telegrapher and to learn all he could about electrical science.

Visit to Home Town Marks Historic Event: Edison Demonstrates His Phonograph

It was shortly after the cable-breaking incident in the St. Clair River—when Edison succeeded in making communication between Port Huron and Sarnia with toots of the locomotive whistle in the rhythm of the Morse code—that the budding inventive genius began the "wandering years" that took him to Stratford, Ontario, to Fort Wayne, Indianapolis, Cincinnati, Nashville, Louisville, Boston, to New Jersey and Menlo Park, and, eventually, to ever-lasting fame.

In the meantime he made several visits to his boyhood home town. One visit in particular occurred in 1890[16] when he came

---

[16] Other visits were when Edison, in 1896, brought the body of his father home from Norwalk, Ohio for burial in Port Huron, and in 1914 when he and Mrs. Edison came in the company of Mr. and Mrs. Henry Ford.

Perhaps the most memorable celebration held in Port Huron, and one which drew nation-wide publicity, took place on February 10, 1940 in conjunction with the world premiere in Port Huron of Metro-Goldwyn-Mayer's motion picture, *Young Tom Edison.* Much of the city was transformed in appearance into the village it was in Edison's day, and the townspeople dressed in the style of that era. Some 55,000 people from Michigan and western Ontario milled about the city's streets, and among the dignitaries present were Edison's widow, Mrs. Mina M. Edison Hughes; Mickey Rooney, star of *Young Tom Edison;* Louis B. Mayer, president of M-G-M studios; John Considine, producer of the picture; Premier Mitchell F. Hepburn of Ontario, Canada; Rt. Rev. Msgr. Edward J. Flanagan, founder of Boys Town, Nebraska; James E. Davidson, president of the Nebraska Power Company (and a former local resident); Edsel B. Ford, president of Ford Motor Company; Harvey J. Firestone, president of Firestone Tire & Rubber Company, Akron, Ohio; and J. A. Clancy, general manager of the Grand Trunk Railway.

(*Continued on page 214*)

to see his older brother, William Pitt Edison, who was gravely ill, and when he brought him a facsimile of his latest invention, the phonograph.

The year before, Edison, with his family, had made a triumphal tour of Europe, the most striking phase of which transpired while he was in Paris, where the great Exposition was in progress and where his inventions were displayed.

On the opening day of the Exposition, when the importance of Edison's contributions to the world was manifest, two of his inventions received singular attention. The first was his incandescent bulb, when a great, forty-foot high lamp was lighted; the second was his phonograph, two of which were arranged on a stand in front of President Carnot of France when he officially opened the Exposition, and which were exact duplicates of the one related to this story. One of the phonographs on that occasion engraved the remarks of the president, for preservation in France, while the other was afterwards shipped back to the United States to be presented to President Benjamin Harrison.

It was on his return from Europe that Edison received word of his brother's severe illness, and he came on to Port Huron to see him. Pitt Edison, at the time, was living in the Henry Cline boarding house, then on the site of the Elks Temple, on the southwest corner of Military and Pine Streets.

When it became known that the renowned inventor was coming to visit his brother, a number of prominent citizens,[17] remembering a previous desire of Edison's—to see the "world's greatest engineering feat," which was the St. Clair Railroad Tunnel under the

---

(Continued from page 213)

A message from Charles Edison, son of the inventor, and then Secretary of the Navy in the second Franklin D. Roosevelt Administration, was read and highlighted the official luncheon at the Hotel Harrington. But probably the most dramatic moment of the day came at twilight when Mrs. Hughes pressed a button which lit a 50,000-watt lamp, the largest incandescent lamp in the world, which had been set up on a wooden stand in front of the Chamber of Commerce offices, then on the southwest corner of Military and Wall Streets. Today that lamp is an item of living history in the Museum of the Port Huron Public Library.

[17] The men were Henry Howard, I. D. Carleton, H. G. Barnum, N. E. Thomas, and Thomas Southerland.

St. Clair River, then nearing completion—had secured a pass, signed by the chief engineer, Joseph Hobson, and had prepared a tour for him through the tunnel, from the Tenth Street construction entrance in Port Huron to Sarnia, Ontario.

The party, which also included Charles Batchelor, Edison's chief mechanical assistant, who had accompanied him to Port Huron, was guided by one of the assistant engineers as they climbed down the stairs and ladders to the entrance of the tunnel, where a narrow plank served as the bridge across the excavations made for the mason work of the tunnel portal. Upon entering, a line of electric lamps could be seen lighting the great circular iron bore, and one can imagine the remarks of the members of the party to the man who had made those lights possible.

The trip through the tunnel was somewhat hazardous for the men because of the work going on. Two narrow gauge tracks for work carts had been laid some distance from the entrance, and in one of them was a narrow plank walk for the accommodation of the men as well as for the mules which pulled the carts up the grade toward the entrance. Several times during the progress of their trip the men heard the rattle of the carts and were obliged to seek refuge on any foothold they could find while the carts passed up or down. Although there was no considerable depth below the tracks at any point, there were long gaps between the planks which had to be jumped, and in several places where there were no planks at all the men had to pick their way along the rails, jump from tie to tie, several feet apart, or cling to the concave sides of the great tube.

When the tour was over and the carriages brought the party back to the Cline boarding house from the ferry dock, Edison invited the men in to see a present he had brought his brother. There in Pitt Edison's room, on a table near the bed, was a phonograph which Edison had brought with him from his laboratory in West Orange, New Jersey, exactly like the two phonographs which had been on the speaker's table in front of President Carnot when he opened the Paris Exposition. And there in that old boarding house the men relaxed after their arduous walking-tour through the long tunnel, while the indefatigable Edison demonstrated the

215

working of his invention—a model which had to be continuously wound to produce sound—and entertained them with the marvel of its voice and music.

That phonograph was probably the first one seen outside of demonstration rooms, for it was to be several years before a cheaper model was manufactured for sale to the public. One cannot help but wonder whatever became of that phonograph. What a precious relic, with all its associations, it would be for a museum today.

Chapter XXXI

ANDREW WESTBROOK,
THE BOLD AND FEARLESS PIONEER

When the schooner *Ghent,* carrying the Cass-McKenney expedition from Detroit to Fond du Lac to negotiate the Indian Treaty of 1826, was becalmed in the St. Clair River near Marine City, it was a mile or so above the farmhouse of Andrew Westbrook.

This was the same Captain Andrew Westbrook of the Michigan Rangers who had served with distinction in the War of 1812, and Colonel George Croghan, one of the becalmed expedition party, had commanded Westbrook in the late war. After entertaining the ship's company with numerous stories of the episodes of that "bold and hazardous pioneer,"[1] Colonel Croghan decided to pay Westbrook a visit while they were detained in the river.

Always a controversial figure, Westbrook was dubbed by the British, "the Traitor Westbrook," because he had left Canada and had joined the American cause; by some Americans he was called "the Pirate Westbrook," because he was said to have been a captain of a privateer in the early part of the war. At home, he was often called "Baron Steuben" by his friends and neighbors because of certain amiable eccentricities, and his house was referred to as Baronial Hall.

Westbrook, after the war, had settled on the St. Clair River above Marine City,[2] where he became one of the district's most prosperous farmers, having acquired additional land, built and owned ships, and managed in the meantime to hold important

---

[1] Thomas L. McKenney. *Sketches of a Tour to the Lakes* (Baltimore: Lucas, 1827) , p. 147.

[2] He lived there until his death in 1835 at the age of sixty-four. Westbrook, described by his contemporaries as a fine looking man, over six feet tall and well proportioned, was married four times and had fourteen children. His second wife was Nancy Thorn, daughter of Captain William Thorn, and sister of John Thorn. For a story about two of Westbrook's sons, see PART TEN, Chapter XXXVIII.

offices. Governor Cass appointed him, in 1817, the first supervisor of highways, and also appointed him one of the first three county commissioners[3] after the proclamation of May 12, 1821, organizing St. Clair County.[4]

Born in Massachusetts five years before the Declaration of Independence was signed, Westbrook, when eleven years old, was brought to Delaware, on the Thames in Upper Canada. He lived there until the age of forty-one, a man of considerable wealth with several thousand acres of land, a fine house and barn, and several other buildings including a distillery.

When the war broke out Westbrook's sympathies were with the States, and he was virtually driven out of Canada. Going to Detroit he offered his services to Governor Hull, who commissioned him a captain in a company of scouts, called the Rangers, and Westbrook performed many valuable services for the American cause—services costing him his home and property, which were confiscated by the British.[5]

In regard to this property, he then decided to destroy it rather than let the British have the advantage of it, and on his first trip back to Delaware with his marauding Rangers—some seventy in number—he gathered them around his former home and pointed out his property. Dramatically swinging a fire-brand, he invited the men to take anything they wanted from his premises and then set fire to his house, his barns, and his distillery.

This was only the beginning of his numerous raids to annoy the enemy—raids into Delaware, Port Talbot, Moravian Town, and other settlements, where they took many British officers prisoner, plundered and paroled the inhabitants, burned mills and destroyed wheat and flour, and took cattle and horses worth thousands of dollars.

---

[3] Andrew Westbrook, George Cottrell, and John K. Smith.

[4] Originally, the County of St. Clair, created by Governor Cass, March 28, 1820, had an area four times as large as the present county and included not only the present county but a large part of Sanilac, Lapeer, Tuscola, Genesee, Saginaw, and Huron counties. For a detailed account of reductions and boundaries of St. Clair County see Jenks, *op. cit.,* I, 16-20.

[5] Congress later passed an act granting to Westbrook two sections of land in the township of Clay, amounting to some three hundred acres, to indemnify him for his Canadian losses during the war.

One of his more daring exploits occurred the time he attempted to intercept the enemy's mail in its passage from Burlington to Long Point. On this trip Westbrook had taken with him only two soldiers, and, entering deep into the enemy's country, endeavored to intercept the mail carrier at several places but each time was unsuccessful.

It was not in Westbrook's nature, however, to return without some spoils of war, and since he could not intercept the mail he decided to capture the officer commanding between Amherstburg and York—a Major Tawsby, who was an old enemy of Westbrook's —and take him back as a prisoner of war. In the town where the major had his headquarters Westbrook ascertained the location of his residence and entered it at night. He approached the bed on which the major was sleeping, and with one hand he gently roused the major, while with the other he pressed his pistol to the officer's chest and told him he was his prisoner.

The commotion awakened the major's wife, who was about to cry out, but Westbrook cautioned the woman to be quiet. "Madam," he warned her, "your husband's life is in your hands— if you are quiet he lives as my prisoner; if you create an alarm I will kill him!"[6] As terrifying as the situation must have been, she suppressed her desire to scream.

Westbrook procured horses from the major's stables and started back with his bound prisoner, but they had not gone far when he discovered that the party was being hotly pursued. Westbrook, however, knew the country well, having lived in the vicinity at one time—in fact he still had a small house some distance in from one of the bypaths. The fleeing abductors now took possession of the house, a refuge of which the pursuing British soldiers would not be aware.

In the meantime the major had complained of pain in his wrists, caused by the cord which bound them so tightly, and he proposed to Westbrook that if released he would, on his honor, go on as a prisoner, without resistance. Westbrook, on the major's pledge had untied him, and the party had continued on to Westbrook's cabin. Westbrook also wanted to pick up some threshed wheat he thought was there. The wheat, as it turned out, was still in the

6 McKenney, *op. cit.*, p. 147.

chaff, and had to be threshed, so Westbrook told one of the soldiers to turn the handle of the fan while he fed the hopper.

The major was seated not too far from the corner of the room where the muskets were stacked, with bayonets fixed. At one moment, when the soldier was bent over turning the fan, and Westbrook was filling the hopper, the major sprang to the corner of the room, and, seizing a musket, charged upon Westbrook, demanding his release.

Westbrook threw down the basket of wheat he was holding, and, parrying the thrust of the bayonet at his breast, received it in his thigh. He shouted to the soldier for his pistols, "with the full determination to blow out the major's brains,"[7] but then decided to take the prisoner alive to Detroit.

Westbrook again bound the major's wrists together, got him on a horse, and, "after tying his feet under his horse's belly,"[8] rode on without further delay. He eventually succeeded in delivering the major at Detroit, having made his extraordinary capture one hundred and twenty miles into the enemy's territory.

With the story of this incident, and many others concerning Westbrook, Colonel Croghan had entertained the members of the expedition party; and now on that summer day in 1826, while the schooner *Ghent* was becalmed in the St. Clair River, the Colonel, accompanied by Thomas McKenney, U. S. Indian Agent, and George F. Porter, assistant to Colonel Croghan and on his first tour of inspection as inspector-general of the army, went ashore to make that colorful pioneer a visit and renew acquaintance, and to hear from Westbrook himself the account of the Tawsby affair.

The ship's boat was put down and the colonel and his party went ashore to call on Westbrook. During that visit, when the one-time Ranger—still erect and forcible in appearance, but with the "fierceness of the reddish cast (of his hair) now softened by an intermixture of grey"[9]—entertained his guests with baronial hospitality and "paraded his decanters and tumblers,"[10] he also retold at their request the story of the major's capture and even showed them the hole in his thigh made by the thrust of the bayonet.

[7] *Ibid.*, p. 148.
[8] *Ibid.*
[9] *Ibid.*, p. 150.
[10] *Ibid.*

220

Chapter XXXII

PORT HURON'S MOST IMPORTANT PIONEERS: DANIEL B. HARRINGTON AND WILLIAM L. BANCROFT

There is a popular tendency to label some one pioneer the founder, or "father" of a city. In a sense, the label in Port Huron could be shared by a number of men, such as the proprietors of the plats that made up the future city—John Thorn, Charles Butler, Daniel B. Harrington, and Edward Petit—as well as many others, including lumbermen, bankers, and merchants, all of whose accomplishments furnished the stimuli that provided its early, stable growth.

But often the title "father" is synonymous with "greatest" pioneer, and if this is true one must consider two men in Port Huron for that category—Daniel B. Harrington and William L. Bancroft. The two were leaders, with the executive energy that could promote and carry civic projects to success. Both, among other activities, were newspapermen, lumbermen, bankers, and railroad promoters.

Daniel Harrington was a boy of twelve when, in the spring of 1819, he arrived in the St. Clair River district, from Ohio, in an open bateau with his father Jeremiah Harrington.[1] They were on their way to Saginaw Bay with a small group of men on a fur trading expedition, but in Detroit Governor Cass had advised them to wait until the fall, due to Indian trouble, so they stopped near the mouth of Black River and set to work planting and cultivating some Indian fields they found along the river in present-day Port Huron.

Twelve years before, when Daniel was born in Sodus, N. Y. (1807), his father had decided to move to Ohio,[2] eventually settling in Fremont, where he built a log house and prepared to farm. Shortly afterwards, however, the War of 1812 broke out,

---

[1] A brother of Jeremiah Harrington was the last survivor of the Battle of Lexington.

[2] The Harringtons, in 1816, lived in Delaware, Ohio, in a double house, one half of which was occupied by the family of Rutherford B. Hayes, the future president.

and it was there, on the present site of Fremont, that General Harrison erected Fort Stephenson, less than half a mile from the Harrington farm. It was there, too, that Major George Croghan performed the feat which brought him to fame—the cunning bit of maneuvering of his one six-pounder cannon, calculated to fool the enemy into thinking his ordnance much greater than it was, and which so confused the enemy that they broke and fled, causing the British General Porctor to withdraw to Fort Malden.

An incident some years after the war was indicative of the executive energy which Daniel Harrington was later to show in promoting the future city of Port Huron.

It was the habit of Daniel and the other boys in the neighborhood to hunt in the ditch below the encampment of the fort for the leaden balls shot from Croghan's one cannon. The boys used this lead for shot and slugs with which to shoot ducks—the wild game greatly supplementing their families' meager provisions.

But Daniel also used that lead for another purpose. He fashioned it into short, thin sticks and inserted the sticks into narrow pieces of wood, whittled into shape, making adequate pencils. These he sold, realizing a small but appreciable income, and when his father led the little company of venturesome men north to the Saginaw Bay region on the fur trading expedition, part of the money Daniel had earned went to purchase the supplies with which their open bateau, the *Saginaw Hunter*, was built.

Shortly after their stay in the Saginaw Bay country, where Daniel was a favorite with the Indians and where he learned to speak in the Chippewa language, the Harringtons returned to the St. Clair River district and settled near the mouth of Black River.

There in the immediate years to follow, while managing to receive the average pioneer youth's education in the district schools, Daniel clerked in Judge Zephaniah Bunce's store at Fort Gratiot, and helped his father raft logs to Detroit and other points, living in a shanty built on the raft during the trips.

Eventually he would own his own timber lands, build and operate saw mills, plat the Village of Desmond[3]—one of the plats that made up the town of Port Huron in 1837—and found the town's first newspaper. In addition, Harrington served as representative in the state legislature (1847) and as a state senator

3 See PART NINE, Chapter XXXVI.

(1852), was postmaster of Port Huron (1834-1841), and was one of the town's foremost bankers and railroad executives.

Daniel and his brother, Ebenezer Burke Harrington,[4] were the motivating forces (as well as part owners) behind *The Lake Huron Observer*—"a Democratic Journal"—first published in 1837, and the second newspaper in the St. Clair River district.[5] Ebenezer, a lawyer by profession, was the paper's first editor, a position he held until late in 1838 when he moved to Detroit to practice law and where he was for a time a law partner of Governor Stevens Thomson Mason.

Daniel Harrington was one of the organizers and the first president of both the First National Bank and the Port Huron Savings Bank. In 1874 he erected the Opera House Block[6] (on the west side of Military Street between Water and Pine Streets) which was, at the time, the largest and finest business block in the city. The Opera House brought to the citizens all of the great actors and musicians and singers of the day, Port Huron being a convenient stopover for artists traveling between Chicago and Detroit.

It was due to Harrington's efforts, while state senator, that the Port Huron and Lapeer Plank Road was completed to Brockway, 80 miles into the western wilderness of the county. This did more to open up and develop the country than any enterprise of later years except the railroads.

But here, too, Harrington took an active part. He was one of the projectors and the first president of the Port Huron and Northwestern Railway, a railroad built from Port Huron through Sanilac and Huron counties, and which was of the greatest value to the early growth and economy of Port Huron. Unfortunately, Harrington died[7] before the enterprise was completed, but it was to his

---

[4] The name is often, and erroneously, given in local histories as Edmund. Ebenezer B. Harrington was elected to the state senate in 1839. He was one of the commissioners appointed to oversee the publication of the Revised Statutes of 1838, and published a volume of the decisions of the court of chancery, known as Harrington's Reports. He continued to practice law in Detroit until his untimely death in 1844 at the age of 36.

[5] The first newspaper in St. Clair County was *The Whig,* published in the village of Palmer (St. Clair) in 1834. See Jenks, *op. cit.,* I, Chapter 18, for an account of the press in St. Clair County.

[6] The Opera House burned down in 1914.

[7] Mr. Harrington died at Port Huron, July 7, 1878.

energy and public spirit that much of the success of the railroad was credited. In his multitude of interests, and in his accomplishments, Daniel B. Harrington might well be considered Port Huron's greatest pioneer.

A close second for the title would be William L. Bancroft. Born in Martinsburg, N. Y. in 1825, Bancroft, with his family, arrived in the little village of Port Huron in 1844 aboard the steamer *Red Jacket.*

One of the first activities of the nineteen-year-old boy on his arrival in Port Huron was to buy *The Lake Huron Observer,* which he edited, and he continued its Democratic principles. After five years he sold the paper and went to New York State to study law, returning to Port Huron in 1851 to practice with Omar D. Conger, and in 1854 again went into the newspaper business as owner and editor of the *Port Huron Commercial.*

The town's chief industry was lumber, with eight saw mills in operation within the present city limits and with a yearly output of thirty million feet of lumber. The nearest banking house was in Detroit, which could be reached only by the Gratiot Turnpike in winter and by boat in summer.

Such a situation and the volume of business done in the village demanded better banking facilities. The first to see this need and to open a banking house was William L. Bancroft, who in 1856 furnished the capital for the company, and with Cyrus Miles, a forceful and industrious young lawyer whom he put in as manager, operated under the name of Cyrus Miles & Company. The partnership lasted only a short time, until Bancroft retired to engage in lumbering in Sanilac County; he did, however, keep an interest in the company and continued for several years as a director, even after the firm joined in 1871 with the banking house of John Johnston & Company (organized in 1865) to form the First National Bank.[8]

Mr. Bancroft helped to organize the city government of Port Huron (1857) and was the city's first mayor. In 1858 he was elected representative in the state legislature, and in 1864 was elected to the state senate. In the meantime, despite great misfortune — a

[8] For a history of banking in Port Huron and St. Clair County see Jenks, *op. cit.*, I, Chapter 28, and also *Fifty Years of Banking in Port Huron, Michigan, First National Exchange Bank,* 1871-1921. This work is undated, with no author or publisher listed, but was undoubtedly written by W. L. Jenks.

fire which destroyed his law office, his law library and all his papers, and a serious eye ailment which threatened him with blindness throughout most of his adult life — he managed, with all his other activities, to interest himself in railroads.

He conceived and carried to completion a railroad from Port Huron to Valparaiso, Indiana — a railroad which originally started out as the Port Huron and Lake Michigan Railway [9] — overcoming obstacles which would have discouraged almost any other man.

First, the governor vetoed bills which had persuaded the state legislature to pass in favor of his road.[10] Added to this, rights of way were disputed all across the state and were the cause of constant litigation, and, to further retard his efforts, there occurred the financial panic of 1837, when the road was obliged to go into bankruptcy. However, he finally carried the road to completion, even to buying the rails himself and hiring and supervising the men who did the actual work of laying them.

But before the railroad was completed and at a time when his company wanted to purchase lands in Port Huron for a terminal, Bancroft had had the foresight to realize that Chicago was to be the great railroad center and that connection there was vastly more important than with Lake Michigan. He therefore successfully negotiated a merger of his road with the Peninsula Railroad, and those negotiations finally culminated in the formation of the Chicago & Northwestern, which extended the line to Chicago, and which was later known as the Grand Trunk Western. This was the final link in the chain of long and complicated events from which the Grand Trunk Western emerged as a part of the great Grand Trunk system.

William L. Bancroft,[11] like Daniel B. Harrington, had interests that were many and varied—interests in which his shrewdness, intelligence, and general ability brought success to him and economic growth to the community. Bancroft Street in Port Huron perpetuates his name.

[9] Bancroft got up all the rights of the Port Huron & Lake Michigan Railway Company and the Port Huron & Milwaukee Railway Company and united them.

[10] Governor Henry H. Carpo vetoed a number of such bills, but they were later carried over his veto. For a complete history of railroads concerning Port Huron and district, see Jenks, *op. cit.*, I, 287-396.

[11] Mr. Bancroft died at Hot Springs, Ark., May 1, 1901.

Chapter XXXIII

MICIAH WALKER,
A NINETEENTH-CENTURY HEZEKIAH

And the rest of the Acts of Hezekiah, and all his
might, and how he made a pool, and a conduit, and
brought water into the city, are they not written
in the book of the chronicles of the kings of Judah?

—II Kings 20:20

We of the present day, who with but a twist of the wrist can
produce sufficient water for all our needs, cannot conceive of the
hardships experienced by our forebears before the advent of
municipal waterworks. The people of Port Huron, Michigan bore
with these hardships until the fall of 1873 when on a day of
great rejoicing and celebration, the Holly water engines, sup-
planting the town pump, drew in the sparkling, cool waters from
Lake Huron and sent it coursing underground through the city
and up into their homes, not only supplying all their needs but
also finishing forever the use of the brackish waters which had
caused the prevalence of ague.

To one man is due most of the credit for this civic improvement,
for so early and so successfully establishing waterworks in Port
Huron. The city was fortunate at that time to have among its
citizens one Miciah ("Mac") Walker,[1] a merchant who dealt in
jewelry, books and stationery, and sundry other articles.

To escape the confining demands of his store, however, he
developed, among other things, his natural talent for salesmanship,
and traveled, when circumstances permitted, as representative for
the firm of Clapp & Jones which manufactured "pumping plants"
and steam fire engines.

---

[1] Miciah Walker, it will be remembered, also had the local telegraph office
in his store, and it was he who, when his operator left to join the U. S. Telegraph Corps at the beginning of the Civil War, gave the job to young Tom
Edison.

Surprisingly enough, this merchant was also a self-taught hydraulic engineer, and his mastery of the subject was recognized by the city officials when, split into two warring factions over whether to have the Clapp & Jones or the Holly system, and finally deciding on the latter, the Board of Water Commissioners voted to have Walker superintend its installation even though he was a representative of the rival company.

Walker left his store in charge of his clerk, R. S. Patterson, and went about the business of installing the water works and laying the water mains. While the great engines were being assembled in a new building in Pine Grove Park,[2] ditches were dug along proposed lines of the then populated districts, and a network of iron piping was laid to a depth of four feet. Water gates and hydrants were installed, and the water main, which was being fitted for laying across the bottom of Black River near Military Street Bridge, took on the aspects of a great sea serpent, squirming this way and that way as the men worked on it along the north bank of the river.

The way the workmen excavated the sand and clay on the river bed when the twelve-inch main was ready for laying, was considered remarkable. A fire hose was attached to a hydrant and the diver took the nozzle and went down below. In the meantime the hydrant was opened and the Holly machinery, nearly a mile away, sent a powerful stream of water to blow away the sand and clay from the place where the pipe was to be sunk, four feet—and in some places five feet—below the bed of the river.

The old Military Street Bridge soon grew used to holding the crowds—the "sidewalk superintendents"—who hung over the rails to watch the divers at work, and among them were many women. Dressed in braided basque, with double-breasted jacket, or red-ingote, and for a head covering a nubia—the forerunner of the babushka?—or a little beribboned bonnet set atilt and well over the front of a chignon coiffure, the women seemed to be as curious as the men who were standing around in cut-away-coat, winged collar, and generous cravat, and the usual cap of the period—although some were still wearing the beaver, or silk "stovepipe,"

[2] Pine Grove Park had been a gift to the City of Port Huron two years earlier, by an Act of Congress, March 18, 1870.

which showed conpicuously above the other heads in the crowd.

All were fascinated by the divers' weird-looking submarine armour and by the bubbles which rose on the water indicating the spot below where the divers were working and making all their calculations on the bottom of the river by the sense of touch alone.

Then it was Mac Walker himself—the non-professional diver— whom the spectators watched intensely, for he had to go below and give the final inspection and okay to the work.

Encased in his armour the diver descends,
wrote the local poet, one E. P. Wycoff, in the *Sunday Commercial.*
Fathoms down neath the dark restless waves;
Where the song of the deep in harmony blends
With the gloom of lost mariners' graves, . . .[3]

When the job of inspection was over Walker no doubt appreciated the cheers of the crowds when he safely emerged from the inky depths of Black River and announced that all was well.

The day of the formal demonstration of the Holly engines' power was one of great celebration, and spectators coming into the city from all over the district filled the cedar-block-pavements and dirt streets long before the ringing of the city bells, at noon, announced the beginning of the official program. At that signal, great clouds of black smoke issuing from the tall chimney of the Water Works began curling above the trees in Pine Grove Park.

The Eagle Hose members of the Volunteer Fire Department (of which Walker was the leader) donned their suits of rubber, armed themselves with hose, nozzle, and other necessary implements, and together with their Sarnia "buddies" who had come to help and to do them honor, now marched to their specified hydrants along the main thoroughfare in town, accompanied by several bands, and were ready for action.

The hoarse whistle at the "Works" gave the signal and almost instantly great streams were leaping from the nozzles held by the firemen, and flooding Huron Avenue and Military Street for some seven or eight blocks. The air was filled with the flying spray and through it the solid streams could be seen criss-crossing, or bending in graceful curves over the tops of the buildings.

---

[3] *Sunday Commercial* (Port Huron, Mich.), December 27, 1874.

The second test was made at the City Hall where streams were sent up through different size nozzles, the highest stream reaching forty feet above the ball of the flag staff, which was 170 feet above the ground, and which was considered "fine throwing." Water had come to Port Huron.

There was one other particularly colorful episode in the life of Miciah Walker. In 1871, by his heroic assistance in Chicago during the great fire, Mac Walker focused national attention on Port Huron.

It so happened that when the fire broke out in Chicago on that fateful Sunday evening of October 8, 1871, Walker was at the Adams House, having stopped there enroute to Racine, Wisconsin, where he was to deliver two Clapp & Jones fire engines which were on cars in the Burlington & Quincy R. R. yards some blocks away. By early morning of the next day the unimpeded fire, carried on with unbelievable rapidity by hurricane-like winds, had jumped the south branch of the Chicago River and was eating its way into the heart of the city. Field & Leiter's store (later Marshall Field & Company), the Opera House, and the City Hall were already burning, as were thousands of other buildings, and every piece of the city's fire equipment, including engines and hose, was fast being destroyed or put out of commission by the intense heat of the spreading fire.

By Monday noon the raging inferno had leaped the main stem of the river and was advancing across the southeastern part of the city. It was then that the wind changed to the south, sending the flames northward, thus completing the fire's vicious arc of destruction.

In the midst of the holocaust—and despite the defeatist attitude of the officials—Walker decided he could save the great Elevator A standing in the Michigan Central & Illinois Central R. R. yards. With a final desperate appeal he persuaded the president of the Michigan Central to run a locomotive to the Burlington yards (where the depot was already burning) and draw out the cars which held the two Clapp & Jones fire engines and one thousand feet of hose, and run it back to the Michigan Central yards where stood the famous elevator, which would soon be in the line of fire.

229

Working one engine, with his helper (a diminutive Irishman, Michael Walsh) working the other, Walker saved the great Elevator A, the largest elevator in the world, and the only one left standing in the city of Chicago after the fire.

In the meantime Walker had sent to Port Huron for the old fire engine, Torrent 1, to be shipped by steamer to Chicago to help fight the fires still burning in the huge coal piles; it is estimated that Walker and his engines saved the city of Chicago many millions of dollars. In fact, his savings to the Illinois Central Railroad alone, it is said, was three million dollars.

The city of Chicago was grateful for the initiative and hard work of Mac Walker, and *The Chicago Sunday Mercury* at the time said, in part, "The citizens of Chicago will never forget the immense amount of property saved through the exertions of Mr. Walker of Port Huron, Michigan, and his little engineer, Michael Walsh."[4]

After this eventful interlude, and the installation of Port Huron's water works system, Walker became more and more engrossed in hydraulic engineering. He soon sold his jewelry store to Patterson, his long-time clerk, and gave all his time to designing and building engines in a factory he set up in Fenton, Michigan.

He invented what was known as the Walker System of Water Works, and installed those works in more than fifteen cities and villages—some of them as far away as North Platte, and Kearney, Nebraska, and Wichita, Kansas, then known as the "Boom City of the Great West."

In the meantime, however, this man of many talents retained his residence in Port Huron, dying in 1919 at the age of ninety-two, and was long remembered there as the city's own nineteenth-century Hezekiah.

---

[4] In this connection it is of interest to note the assistance given to the fire victims of Chicago by another St. Clair River district pioneer, Eber Brock Ward, formerly of Marine City but then living in Detroit, and with steel plants operating in Wyandotte and Chicago. The following was printed in the *Port Huron Weekly Times*, Oct. 12, 1871: "On Tuesday, large numbers of people were fed at E. B. Ward's rolling mills in the north part of the city (Chicago). The 1000 employees served at the tables, made of boards, which were spread in the establishment, and the hungry fed."

Chapter XXXIV

JAMES EDWARD O'SULLIVAN,
THE MAN WHO SPARKED THE BUILDING
OF GRAND COULEE DAM

What was described, at the time, as the world's largest man-made structure and one of the most successful ventures in American history — the Grand Coulee Dam — owes its existence to a small group of visionaries led by a tall, lean engineer-lawyer-educator from Port Huron, Michigan, who had gone west in 1909 to practice law in Seattle, Washington. He was James Edward O'Sullivan, son of James O'Sullivan, a building contractor and one-time mayor of Port Huron.

"Jim" O'Sullivan attended St. Stephen parochial school and Port Huron High School and after graduating with a law degree from the University of Michigan opened a law office in Port Huron, but due to his father's ill health he was obliged to help in the office of the O'Sullivan Construction Company before moving west with his wife and family.

He had hoped to practice law in Seattle, but when he eventually arrived there he found so many other lawyers already established that he moved to Ephrata, Washington, and there, before finally setting up his practice, he made a living for his family doing construction work and teaching in the State Normal School.

Some time later, in the little town of Ephrata, a lawyer by the name of William Clapp casually suggested to some farmers who were complaining about the lack of water that it might be a good idea to build a dam across the Columbia at the head of the Grand Coulee and pump the water from there. The editor of *The Wenatchee* (Wash.) *World* emblazoned Clapp's suggestion across the front page of his paper. Perhaps the idea would have died there had it not been seen by James E. O'Sullivan, who had also thought about the reclamation of the sagebrush wasteland. He quickly joined the little group of "big dam" boosters.

Back in his home town of Port Huron, where he was to remain for the next fifteen years, O'Sullivan had taken over the management of the family business when his father died in 1915. There he started his file on the Grand Coulee, a file which was in time to fill twenty large steel cabinets.

As head of the O'Sullivan Construction Company he was erecting many buildings. These included the Mueller Metals Company plant (now Mueller Brass Company), substations for the Detroit Edison Company in several cities, additions to the Diamond Crystal Salt plant (St. Clair), the St. Clair High School, and a five hundred thousand dollar warehouse for the Morton Salt Company, Port Huron.

His work at that time involved engineering, estimating, financing, and the supervision of actual construction. Because of this experience the little group of dam boosters considered his opinion important, and he became their leader.

When he returned to the west the first thing he did was to buy a book [1] on dam building, and he then began writing a series of newspaper articles on the practicality of a dam across the Columbia River. Some of these he clipped out and sent to the Director of the Reclamation Service in Washington, D. C., who was interested enough to telephone O'Sullivan to say that he was sending his engineers to look over the proposed Grand Coulee dam site and asked O'Sullivan to join them.

O'Sullivan stood with the engineers high over the mighty Columbia River and had question after question hurled at him concerning the building of the dam. Although he had ready answers for them they were not convinced, and on returning from the site he was the target of much good-natured "kidding from the commission party" because he even considered such a fantastic scheme. [2]

While the others were enjoying dinner at the hotel that night, O'Sullivan, a little disheartened, took from his car the book on dams and with the aid of the little arc of light under the dashboard again examined the principles of dam-building. Reassured by what he read, and convinced that his ideas were right, he made

---

[1] F. H. Newell & Daniel William Murphy, *Principles of Irrigation Engineering* (McGraw, 1913).

[2] George Sunborg, *Hail Columbia* (New York: Macmillan, 1954), p. 34.

up his mind at that moment to continue to work until his dream of a dam across the Columbia was a reality.

To that end, for the next quarter of century he sacrificed his personal fortune, his comforts, much of his family life, and all outside interests. He became evangelist, lobbyist, consultant engineer, and a doer of any and all jobs that furthered the ultimate success of that dream.

He continued writing articles on the dam for newspapers and magazines; he rode back and forth over the Columbia Basin country in an old Ford in hot summers and below-zero winters talking Grand Coulee dam; he hitchhiked across the west organizing farmers into "big dam" groups and addressed opposition-group meetings even when threatened with lynching. At one point, he crossed the country in a day-coach travelling to Washington, D. C., ate two scant meals a day and lived in a dollar-a-day hotel room, while he was asking Congress for hundreds of millions of dollars and arguing about the dam before congressional committees.

He even preached a sermon about it. One Thanksgiving Day, when the Presbyterian minister was away from Ephrata, the members of the congregation, well aware of his "eloquence and sincerity," asked O'Sullivan, a Catholic, if he would not "fill in and take the pulpit for the day." [3] He accepted and started out with a typical Thanksgiving sermon, exhorting the congregation to be thankful not only for the blessings they had but also for the great things the new West had in store for them — meaning great things like the Grand Coulee dam, of course — and spent the rest of the sermon extolling its ultimate benefits. And it had its effect, for the next day five members of the congregation joined the Columbia River Development League and remained the dam's staunch supporters.

He enlisted the aid of America's greatest engineers, he interested Presidents and Cabinet members and sold the dam idea to senators and to Congressmen. He fought politicians, private utilities, editors, and chambers of commerce, and through it all, especially during the depression, received hardly any subsistence for himself.

[3] *Ibid.*

But after untold and unbelievable hardships and disappointments, ridicule from both friends and enemies, he finally won out. The Grand Coulee Dam became a reality.

Then honors came to him. One was from the United States Government, when, by an Act of Congress, one of the irrigation dams was renamed OSullivan Dam in his honor. When Julius Krug, then Secretary of the Interior, went to Ephrata on O'Sullivan Day to formally dedicate the dam, he presented the guest of honor with a photostatic copy of the congressional resolution designating O'Sullivan Dam and bearing the signatures of President Harry S. Truman, Speaker Joseph Martin, and the late Senator Arthur H. Vandenberg.

Less than a year later, in 1949, James E. O'Sullivan died. But the great work of his lifetime — the Grand Coulee Dam — stands as a monument to his efficiency, and, especially, to his incorruptible tenacity of purpose.

Chapter XXXV

CROCKET McELROY,
THE MAN WHO DEVISED THE FIRST
HYDRAULIC SALT WELL

Marine City, Michigan was probably the first city in the United States to mine salt with the hydraulic, or water mine method. This process is solution mining and proved to be the cheapest of all methods at the time; yet one can look in vain in the books on the history of salt for the name of the man who first made this process possible — the name of Crocket McElroy.

Shipbuilder,[1] stave and salt manufacturer, timber ranger, mayor (St. Clair, Mich.), and state senator, Crocket McElroy was one of the St. Clair River district's most illustrious and energetic pioneers, and his activities in the mining and manufacture of salt were among his greatest achievements. In fact, it was due to his judgment and ingenuity, and, most of all, his persistence, that the salt industry was established in St. Clair County.

The story of salt in the St. Clair River district is as old as it is interesting, and it is on record that salt was actually made there commercially as early as 1815, or shortly after the War of 1812.

There were numerous salt licks (better known as deer licks) in the district where a weak brine oozed to the surface, which attracted wild animals and which became the favorite places of the pioneer hunter. The prevalence of those salt licks was also one of the reasons that, for centuries the Indians had come here in great numbers in the hunting season, and regarded this section of the country as one of their favorite hunting grounds.

The existence of salt springs was also known, and salt was actually made from one of these springs by the mill firm of Meldrum and Park, which had taken over the land and mill formerly owned by Patrick Sinclair, builder of Fort Sinclair (1763–64) on

---

[1] HcElroy built and operated the popular excursion steamer *Mary,* and the steamer *Unique,* both noted for their speed.

Pine River. According to William Goodwin, a pioneer blacksmith who lived along Black River in Port Huron and shod horses and oxen for lumbermen, the "Meldrums sunk a hole within a mile of New Baltimore and found brine, from which they manufactured salt by boiling the salt water in kettles." He said that the people "were starving for salt" at the time of the War of 1812, and that the Meldrum salt "sold for one dollar a quart." [2]

In 1859 the Michigan Legislature passed an act to encourage the manufacture of salt and offered a bounty of one cent a bushel. This instigated the beginning of the industry in Saginaw, where, in 1860, several hundred tons were made. From that time the industry there grew rapidly, chiefly because the manufacturers found an unlimited supply of cheap fuel in the waste from the saw mills. In fact, salt in those days was facetiously referred to as a "by-product" of lumbering.

In the meantime (1860) a company was formed in St. Clair to put down a well, and the brine, which tested well, was made into salt. But after a few years it became evident that the St. Clair company could not complete with Saginaw and the plant was abandoned. Hope was not entirely given up, however. When it was found that cheap coal could be obtained from the Ohio fields, a public meeting was held in St. Clair at which twelve hundred dollars was raised by subscription to repair the old well and re-establish the business.

The matter was put into the hands of Crocket McElroy, president of the Marine City Stave Company, who had recently moved from Marine City to St. Clair to live, and who, earlier, had become convinced that a solid bed of salt underlay the eastern part of St. Clair County at a depth of some 1,500 feet. But after preliminary work had eaten up the twelve hundred dollars, further capital to bore into the salt rock and erect a plant could not be raised in St. Clair, so McElroy persuaded his directors of the Marine City Stave Company to finance a deep well in Marine

---

[2] William Goodwin, quoted from reminiscences in a paper read at the annual meeting of the St. Clair County Pioneer Society in 1887. From clipping (undated) in *St. Clair Co. Pioneer Society Scrapbook, No. 10,* inside flyleaf.

City, and finally, in July of 1882, at a depth of 1,633 feet, he struck a bed of rock salt.[3]

It soon became evident that an ordinary form of pump would not work in such a deep well, so McElroy devised a process of his own which became known as the hydraulic, or water mine method. Water was introduced to dissolve the salt, and when saturated was forced back to the surface. This was done with a double pipe — one inside the other — where water was pumped down between the two to the salt rock, forming a brine which was forced up the inner pipe by the pressure of the water coming down. Then by evaporation the brine was again turned into salt — that magic "white sand," as the Indians called it. Not only did this process give a saturated brine, and one with fewer impurities, but also produced it at a lower cost.

One book on salt credits a George Smith of Saltvale, N. Y., with first using this process (in 1883), but Crocket McElroy had already successfully used it the year before, and by May of 1883 a "modern" salt block was begun, and where, incidentally, for the first time in the State of Michigan, coal was used as fuel in the mining and manufacture of salt.

This salt block continued with varying fortunes for nearly fifty years, when it was burned in 1910. But in the meantime the success of this industry had enthused the citizens of St. Clair to have a salt block of their own. After several abortive attempts at successful output,[4] the St. Clair Rock Salt Company was organized (1886) by Charles F. Moore, his brother Franklin Moore, and Justin R. Whiting, with Mark Hopkins as the first president. The company made a high grade of salt, which chemical analysis showed to be of the purest quality. Soon after the organization of the company,

---

[3] The well was put down on property known as Catholic Point (section 12), land purchased by Father Gabriel Richard in 1818, in trust for the Catholic inhabitants of Marine City (St. Agatha's parish). Mr. Jenks, in his *St. Clair County, Michigan,* says, "The title to this property has never been conveyed from the church, although a large part of it was occupied for many years by the Marine City Stave Company, and it was upon this property that the first well to the salt rock was put down under the auspices of Mr. Crocket McElroy, president of that company," I, 145.

[4] The Thompson Brothers (John and Thomas) Salt Company, later The Port Huron Salt Company, and The International Salt Company.

Charles F. Moore succeeded Hopkins as president, and the name was changed to the Diamond Crystal Salt Company.

From 1929 until 1953 the firm was a part of General Foods Corporation, and Diamond Crystal salt was advertised along with such famous food products as Jello and Post Toasties. In 1953, however, Charles F. Moore, grandson of one of the original incorporators of the company (and long active in selling salt and other General Foods products), with his family, bought back the company, and today, with plants in St. Clair, Mich., Akron, Ohio, Jefferson Island, Louisiana, and Wilmington, Massachusetts, it ranks third largest in sales among the nation's salt producers.

Salt and its manufacture,[5] still one of the vital and leading economic forces in the St. Clair River district, was one of the industries which helped the towns along the river make a graceful and successful transition from the era of lumbering and shipbuilding to the later commercial enterprises and manufactories, and to the era of automation.

---

[5] For a complete list of salt manufacturing concerns at various times in the St. Clair River area, see Jenks, *op. cit.*, I, 374-77, and to which should be added the Morton Salt Company which took over the Port Huron Salt Company in 1910. The Morton Salt plant in Port Huron is one of eleven plants in the United States operated by the company.

PART NINE

THE TWIN CITIES OF
PORT HURON, MICHIGAN AND SARNIA, ONTARIO

Chapter XXXVI

MUNICIPAL BEGINNINGS OF PORT HURON

The municipal beginnings of the City of Port Huron in the St. Clair River district are not only rich in historical lore, but unique in the annals of American cities.

The archaeologist, in excavating the site of an ancient city frequently finds evidences of several cities, one below the other in the strata beneath, and with each stratum giving indications of its relative age. Similarly, the historian studying the founding of the City of Port Huron finds records of no less than seven villages or city plats covering much of the same ground.

Four of these plats, founded in the land boom years of 1835 to 1837 and known as the villages of Peru, Desmond, Gratiot, and Huron, merged and formed the village of Port Huron in 1837. But on the same ground as these overlapping plats was still another village, which had been platted almost twenty years before.

Capitalists of Detroit, as well as of New York and Boston, it seems, had never ignored the Port Huron site and its natural advantages. Joseph Watson, prominent in Detroit and one-time Secretary of the Territory under Governor Hull, was one of the first to realize its possibilities and to actively speculate. He purchased from the Government eighty acres of land on the south side of Black River which was bounded, roughly, by Black River and by what are now Third, Seventh and Griswold streets.

Watson immediately made provisions for the incoming multitudes he expected and envisaged, anxious to establish homes where Black River flowed into the St. Clair. To survey and plat his land he hired no less a personage than William Smith — the same engineer and surveyor who, after the Detroit fire of 1805, replatted the town according to a draft devised from L'Enfant's plan of Washington, D. C., which Judge Woodward had borrowed from his friend Thomas Jefferson. When the platting of Watson's land

241

was finished, he called his village by the astonishing name of Montgats.[1]

The expected multitudes, however, did not materialize, and it was not until almost ten years later that Watson found interest stirring again. One lot was sold. This was in 1827, when he agreed to sell Michael Kerley of Detroit a parcel of land one hundred feet square on "Delude, or Black River," adjoining the Indian reservation, on condition that Kerley would build a good wharf and erect upon it a three-story warehouse or store, Watson to retain the ferry privilege across Black River and the right to land passengers or teams upon the wharf.[2] The proposition was accepted and Watson built the store and wharf.[3]

In 1835 came the great fever of western land speculation which lasted for several years, when nearly twenty million acres of public lands were sold to promoters in Michigan, Ohio, Indiana, and Illinois.

In New York and New England this land boom was known as Michigan Fever, and it was due to a prominent New York State judge, Fortune C. White,[4] who caught the fever, and Daniel B. Harrington of Port Huron, that another village plat came into being.

Daniel's brother, Ebenezer B. Harrington, was studying law in Judge White's New York office at the time, and in the letters that passed between the brothers Daniel no doubt wrote of the opportunities to be had in desirable lands in Port Huron if one had the money to buy. At any rate, Daniel made a visit to his

---

[1] The origin of the French name is one of the local historical mysteries. The inland channel indicated through "gats" must refer to Black River. In those days Black and St. Clair Rivers were much lower than they are today, and the banks considerably higher. In fact, the land south of Black River was often referred to as "The Hill"—a land feature which may have given rise to "Mont," thus Montgats.

[2] In a letter (1827) to Kerley from Watson, then in Sandusky, Ohio, and mentioned by W. L. Jenks in a newspaper article on the villages of Montgats and Peru. Newspaper clipping in *Jenks Scrapbook, No. 1*, Mich. Room, Port Huron Public Library.

[3] The store and wharf were later used by Joseph B. Comstock and his brother Alfred Comstock (grandfather of Governor William A. Comstock) when they first came to Port Huron (1835) and before they moved farther out Black River to their farm in a section now known as Comstock Hills.

[4] White lived in Whitesboro, N. Y.

brother with the result that Judge White decided to invest in land in Port Huron with Harrington — White furnishing the capital, and Harrington the knowledge and management for one-fourth interest.

White and Harrington, in 1835, bought Watson's eighty acres and increased their holdings to a line bounded on the west by the diagonal line of the Indian reservation (which White later took up to add to his plat when the reservation was ceded back to the Government) and which stretched southwesterly from Seventh Street near Black River as far as Tenth Street. They called their plat the village of Desmond [5] (known more familiarly as White's Plat), and Watson's City of Montgats went into oblivion.

In that same year of 1835 Edward Petit platted the land owned by his father, bounded by White's Plat and St. Clair River and stretching from Black River to Griswold Street, and he called it the Village of Peru.[6]

In 1836 John Thorn acquired a patent on a section of land north of Black River and south of present day McMorran Boulevard, which he platted and called the Village of Gratiot; while also in 1836 a New York real estate firm, The Huron Land Company, bought the old Bonhomme and Lasselle claims (land lying between the Military Reserve and Holland Road, and comprising the McNiel Tract) and platted it into the Town of Huron. This "town" in its origin and its ambitious prospectus, was probably the most interesting of all the early plats that made up the city of Port Huron.

The men who were associated in the Huron Land Company were generally leading business men in New York and Boston — Charles Butler, William Bard,[7] Edward A. Nicoll, Joseph D.

---

[5] The name was taken from the Township of Desmond in which it was included. The origin of the name is lost, but it is said the township was named for the Irish insurgent James Fitzgerald, the Earl of Desmond.

[6] The source and relevance of this name remains a mystery.

[7] William Bard was the scion of a noted medical family. His grandfather was the first doctor in America to dissect the human body; his father was retained as physician to George Washington and his family during Washington's residence in New York. Bard himself was the practical founder of life insurance in America. At the time of his investment in Port Huron lands he held the office of President of the New York Life Insurance and Trust Company.

Beers,[8] Federal Vanderburgh, Thomas Suffern,[9] James B. Mower, John Moorehead, and James McBride — all of New York — and John Borland, Samuel Hubbard, and John McNiel,[10] of Boston. Other associates were Erastus Corning of Albany, N. Y., Edward Willett and Benjamin Stephens of New Brunswick, N. J., Benjamin W. Butler (Attorney General under Presidents Jackson and Van Buren, and brother of Charles Butler), and Nicholas Ayrault of Geneva, N. Y.

Charles Butler, noted advocate, counselor, railroad promoter,[11] and realtor, was trustee for the company and the largest stockholder, eventually owning two-thirds of the company's stock. This was the same man who made a large fortune when he invested one hundred thousand dollars in lots in what is now the heart of Chicago, and who started his brother-in-law, William Butler Ogden, on his way to fame in that city when he sent him to Chicago to manage his investments.

---

[8] Joseph D. Beers, one of Wall Street's noted bankers, was the son of Andrew Beers, the renowned maker of De Beers Almanack.

[9] Thomas Suffern was a wealthy and distinguished merchant of New York City, and an importer of Irish drygoods. He was the son-in-law of William Wilson, importer of British drygoods, whose affiliate in Manchester was the first Sir Robert Peel, father of the great Prime Minister.

Port Huron streets carried the names of four associates of the Huron Land Company—Butler, Bard, Beers, and Suffern—but only two remain, Beers and Bard Streets. Suffern Street is now Glenwood Avenue, and Butler Street is Grand River Avenue.

[10] General John McNiel, who as Major McNiel was in Command at Fort Gratiot in 1817, was cited for notable services at the battles of Chippewa and Niagara, having been severely wounded in the Battle of Lundy's Lane. After his resignation from the army in 1830 he was appointed surveyor of the port of Boston by President Jackson, a position he held for many years.

[11] As a railroad promoter, it is said that there was scarcely a railroad leading to or from Chicago with which Charles Butler did not have important associations as founder, president, or director. It was also Charles Butler who came to Detroit for the purpose of meeting with the legislature and inducing it to take some proper steps with regard to the five-million-dollar loan which had been issued by the state in order to obtain funds to build railroads and canals, and in the sale of which it had been greatly defrauded. He did this service under great difficulties and hardships, making the journey from New York to Detroit in the cold month of January, often riding night and day in an open wagon over frozen rivers and rutted roads to reach his destination. In persuading and aiding the Michigan Legislature to meet its bonded debt—as he had in other states—Butler was successful and obtained a national and even international reputation.

Nicholas Ayrault came to Port Huron as the company's agent, under direction of Butler, and remained for several years, being active in business ventures as well as civic and church affairs.

One of the intriguing features of the Town of Huron — a plat which contained more than eight thousand lots, enough to care for a population of forty thousand souls — was the canal called for in its prospectus. In their conception of the town the proprietors took into consideration the fact that, due to the Rapids at the foot of Lake Huron, vessels were often delayed from ten to fifteen days or more waiting for a strong enough wind to overcome the eddies and resistance of the current. They naturally considered that detention of vessels "a severe drawback upon, and injury to, the commerce of the lakes."[12] They decided that the construction of a ship canal [13] to by-pass the Rapids, built from the lake to Black River, would obviate effectually the detention of vessels and at the same time would act as "one of the finest and safest harbours in the world . . . at the foot of one of the largest and most important lakes in the chain of western waters." [14]

The expectations of the proprietors of the Huron Land Company were only partially realized, due undoubtedly to the panic and financial depression of 1837, and the town plat was amended — in what is known as Butler Plat — and later changed in several real estate deals, part of it becoming the Village of Fort Gratiot.[15] In 1857 Butler had bought and platted the land known as Butler Plat, the plat to which his holdings in the Town of Huron were added, and had called it the Town of Port Huron. A great portion of this land had been owned by John McNiel, and his holdings became known as the McNiel Tract.[16]

It was inevitable that much agitation and confusion would arise because of the numerous plats bearing different names, and it was

---

12 From text of the *Prospectus of the Town of Huron*. Copy in Jenks Collection, Port Huron Public Library.

13 More than three-quarters of a century later the City of Port Huron was actually beginning the construction of a canal, from Lake Huron to Black River and almost in the exact spot planned by Butler and his associates, but it was to be a canal for a much different purpose—merely to put a supply of pure lake water into Black River.

14 From the text of the *Prospectus of the Town of Port Huron.*

15 The Village of Fort Gratiot was annexed to Port Huron in 1895.

16 In addition to the McNiel Tract, McNiel Creek (in the north end of Port Huron) perpetuates John McNiel's name.

finally agreed by the owners to give the aggregation of plats one name. A petition was sent to the Circuit Court in August of 1837 to that effect and praying that the name be made Port Huron.

The court evidently heard the prayer, for thereafter the name of the community south of the Military Reserve on both sides of Black River was Port Huron.

Automobile Manufacturing Era

Port Huron's metropolitan area has always been a trading center for a major portion of that section of Michigan known as the Thumb district, an area where some 173,500 or more people reside. It has also served the shopping needs of her Canadian neighbors from Sarnia and other Lambton County centers.

This trade helped greatly in the successful expansion of many manufacturing concerns between the eras of lumbering and ship-building, and present-day industries. But the manufacture of three products in particular — automobiles, agricultural implements, and road-building equipment — gained nation-wide prominence.

The Studebaker Corporation's decision in 1964 to discontinue building automobiles in the United States brought memories to many of the days — long before the 1920–1927 Wills Ste. Claire era in Marysville — when the Studebaker and several other automobiles were manufactured in Port Huron.

Before going into the story of automobile manufacturing in the St. Clair River area, however, it is appropriate to mention here, that the first self-propelled vehicle on record built in Michigan was constructed in a machine shop in Memphis, St. Clair County, in the winter of 1884–1885.

At that time John Clegg and his son Thomas Clegg built a single cylinder car, driven by steam produced in a tubular boiler carried in the rear of the car. Large chunks of soft coal, or cannel coal, which burned with a bright flame, was the fuel, and the vehicle had a seating capacity for four people. Its rate of speed was about twelve miles an hour.

The car was driven by Thomas Clegg on perhaps thirty or thirty-five tests, covering some four or five hundred miles. The longest of these tests was probably to Emmett, Michigan in the summer of 1885, where, on the Fourth of July, Clegg took the

246

Rev. Father John Lynch, pastor of Our Lady of Mt. Carmel Church of Emmett, for a ride in the parade marking the holiday.[17]

Those who saw that parade were never to forget the sight of that first horseless vehicle, but the vehicle itself was soon out of circulation. It had no place to go, for its power could not cope with the incredibly bad roads of that day. Its destiny was to rust away for a generation in the Clegg machine shop, it is said, before it passed into oblivion. In the meantime the gasoline-powered motor vehicle[18] was to develop and advance rapidly in the phenomenal history of the automotive industry in Michigan.

The earliest automobile manufacturing concern in Port Huron was the Northern Motor Car Company. William E. Metzger of Detroit, who in 1898 established the first independent automotive dealership in the country, and who was considered the motivating force in the organization of the Automobile Club of Michigan, organized the Northern Motor Car Company, together with William Barbour and George M. Gunderson.

This was in 1900, and six years later arrangements were made by that company to establish a factory in Port Huron. The corporation successfully reached an agreement with the Port Huron Chamber of Commerce, whereby the Chamber of Commerce would erect a building for the plant and office, and, in the company formed, Port Huron would hold one-fifth of the capital stock of five hundred thousand dollars, and have one resident director.

Pine Grove Avenue at Elmwood Street (near the American entrance to the Blue Water International Bridge) was the site chosen for the factory, and the manufacture of the "Silent and dustless Northern" was begun in 1907.

In the meantime the Northern Motor Car Company had merged with the Wayne Automobile Company to form the E-M-F Com-

---

[17] Interview with Mr. George W. Hartson, Port Huron, ninety-five years old, who saw the parade that day with four of his young friends who had gone to Emmett from Memphis—Fred and Lewis Fitz, John Krause, and Will Sullivan. Mr. Hartson said that "Tommy" Clegg was a friend of R. E. Olds and had worked with him on a steam-propelled vehicle in Lansing, but that he had "beat Mr. Olds in making one."

[18] The first automobile company in Michigan was the Olds Motor Vehicle Company, organized in Lansing, August 21, 1897, by Ransom E. Olds. Olds' second company, the Olds Motor Works, was established in 1899, and operations were moved to Detroit in 1901.

pany (Barney Everett, William E. Metzger, and Walter E. Flanders), and in 1908–1909 the plant on Elmwood Street was known as the Everett-Metzger-Flanders Company. Later, the Studebaker brothers contracted to market the entire E-M-F output, and the two firms merged to form the Studebaker Corporation. The plant on Elmwood Street was known as E-M-F Factory No. 2 of the Studebaker Corporation [19] until 1912, when manufacture of the Studebaker car in Port Huron was discontinued.

It might be of interest here to note that it was in the Port Huron Studebaker plant that the late Harold S. Vance, a native son — who attained to the presidency of the company, and also served as chairman of the board — got his start with the corporation shortly after his graduation from Port Huron High School.

In the meantime two other automobile manufacturing concerns were formed in Port Huron. The Cass Motor Truck Company was one. In 1910 production of Cass one- and two-ton motor trucks was begun on Lapeer Avenue (the site of Mueller Brass) by a Port Huron company composed of Frank J. Haynes, Oscar L. Baer, and Henry B. Hoyt, with A. W. Frantz as general manager. Trucks were manufactured until 1916, although by 1915 the firm was under the name of The Independent Motors Company.

The year 1910 also saw the founding of the Havers Motor Car Company. Albert D. Bennett was president, Herman L. Stevens, vice-president, and Andrew J. Murphy, secretary-treasurer and general manager. The plant, situated on Twenty-eighth Street, manufactured Havers 4-cylinder cars, but when Studebaker discontinued their No. 2 factory on Elmwood Street the Havers Company moved its plant to that address and commenced the manufacture of the Havers Six.

But then on the evening of July 8, 1914, a spectacular fire which started in the varnish and paint room destroyed the Havers plant, along with stock and machinery and about twenty automobiles in process of construction, at an estimated loss of $135,000. And although the Independent Motor Company continued to build

---

[19] Studebaker merged with the Packard Motor Car Co. in 1954, to form Studebaker-Packard Corporation. Name changed to Studebaker Corporation, July 2, 1962.

trucks on Lapeer Avenue through 1915 — when it went out of business — it was with the Havers fire in July of 1914 that the real era of automobile manufacturing ended in Port Huron.

In 1918, however, neighboring Marysville, then a village of about two hundred people, received the news that C. Harold Wills, a prominent engineer and metallurgist, and former production manager and chief engineer for the Ford Motor Company, had selected that place on the St. Clair River as the site for a new automobile plant.

The Wills interests formed the Marysville Land Company and acquired 4,200 acres of property. The city of Marysville was platted, streets and sidewalks were built, sewers and water mains were installed, and the construction of houses and stores was begun. The cornerstone of the factory was laid in June of 1919 — marking the real start in Marysville industrial fortunes — and in 1920 the manufacture of the Wills car was started.

But later in that year a depression, felt by all the automobile manufacturers in the country, forced the then C. H. Wills Company into receivership, and in July of 1923 the plant was sold to Kidder, Peabody & Company, a Boston banking firm. The name of the company was changed to the Wills Ste. Claire Company, with Wills [20] remaining in charge, and production of the eight-cylinder Wills Ste. Claire car was begun.

The new concern was never particularly successful, probably because the Wills Ste. Claire, considered a luxury car, was much too expensive for the average person to own. Finally the company failed, suspending operations in 1926, and the plant was permanently dismantled in 1927.

Although the Wills enterprise itself was unsuccessful, it acted as a magnet, attracting other concerns associated with the automotive industry, such as the Athol Manufacturing Company, now the St. Clair Rubber Company; and the American Bushings Company, later the Pressed Metals of America, Inc., and now the Midwest Machine Company of Indiana, Inc.

In 1935 the Chrysler Corporation purchased the old Wills plant for use as a parts distribution point, and since that time the

---

[20] C. Harold Wills later became the chief metallurgist for Chrysler, a position he held until his death. He died December 21, 1940.

Chrysler plant has been an important cog in the industrial life of Marysville and the vicinity.

Nationally Known Builders of Agricultural Implements and Road-Building Equipment

The fascinating story of the automotive industry in Michigan and the nation shows how the rise and growth of the automobile paralleled the rise and growth of good roads, and to Port Huron goes the honor of being a leader in the country in the movement for those good roads.

The chief reason for Port Huron's supremacy in city, state, and national road improvement was due largely to the city's leading industry of some fifty years ago, the Port Huron Engine & Thresher Company.

The parent company, the Upton Manufacturing Company of Battle Creek, Michigan came to Port Huron in 1884 and established a plant in the southwest section of the city (west of Twenty-fourth Street near the end of Railroad Street) to manufacture agricultural implements and other equipment. The district comprising the property owned by the company became known as Uptonville;[21] it was not until 1891 that the name of the company was changed to the Port Huron Engine & Thresher Company.[22]

The company had its own printing house (as well as its own post office) which issued extensive varieties of illustrated catalogues, covering all types of its farm power and road-building machinery — catalogues which, today, are eagerly sought as collectors' items.

---

[21] The district still has an Upton Street.

[22] Many familiar names of early residents of Port Huron were found among the first officers of this company—C. F. Harrington, president, and F. A. Peavey, vice-president and general manager, while others included D. C. Kinch, H. B. Hoyt, F. B. Whipple, E. H. Moak, and E. D. Vanness. Directors of the company in its earlier days included Nelson Mills, F. L. Wells, H. G. Barnum, F. A. Peavey, H. W. Stevens, J. W. Goulding, C. F. Harrington, J. H. White, and W. L. Jenks. Later officers included A. E. West, who served as president and general manager, H L. Stevens, vice-president, and E. L. Wilson, secretary.

The Port Huron Engine & Thresher Company first became noted for its threshing machines[23] — the "World's Greatest Thresher," so the slogan went — as well as for corn machinery and plowing, sawing, and hay-bailing machinery. The company grew so fast that the name of PORT HURON ENGINE & THRESHER CO. was soon emblazoned on warehouses in such cities as Peoria, Ill., Des Moines, Ia., Wichita, Kan., Minneapolis, Minn., and in Winnipeg, Manitoba.

However, it was probably its road-making equipment which really put this company on the map — equipment which ranged from rollers to dump carts. The first spreading dump carts ever made by a manufacturer, made suitable for hauling in "trains" on dirt roadways, and also the first of all road rollers having power sufficient for hauling such trains, were built by the Port Huron Engine & Thresher Company before 1900.

On the Fourth of July in that same year (1900), this company was instrumental in having the initial International Good Roads Congress in the United States, also the first practical convention of road builders in Michigan, held in Port Huron.

On that day, on Twenty-fourth Street in front of the plant's location was built the historic mile of hard surface macadam road, the first of its kind in the nation, using the Company's road-building equipment. The macadamizing was done under the supervision of Colonel E. G. Harrison of Washington, D. C., road expert for the United States Government, before a great assemblage of citizens and dignitaries from many states and from Canada.

At that time was shown the first train made suitable for hauling, dumping, spreading, and compacting road-building materials, all at once. The Port Huron Engine & Thresher Company that day proved the truth of the company's famous advertisement, that it had "'The Most Complete Macadamizing Outfit in the World,"

---

[23] The Port Huron Engine & Thresher Company was one of the manufacturing concerns with which Henry Ford worked in developing the Ford farm equipment. He bought their threshing machines and tested them out on his farm. Later he acquired some of their tractors, as he did the tractors of every available make, to test and study, and in 1916 the Fordson Tractor was announced by the Ford Motor Company.

and it was not long before those road-building monsters were rolling in every county in Michigan, in other states from Michigan to Texas and from Maine to California, and in Canada.

The giant rollers [24] of that company, making the roads adequate for the automobile in that era of accelerated road building, were almost as familiar a sight on America's highways as the automobile itself.

In 1914 the plant was moved farther south on Twenty-fourth Street, to a section in Port Huron known as South Park; but shortly afterwards the company, like so many other industries throughout the country, felt the impact of the First World War. Completion of any loan was almost impossible. In addition, the U. S. Government put an embargo on freight passing through Chicago, causing the company to lose its western market, and it was eventually forced out of business.

The era of the manufacture of automobiles, agricultural implements, and road-making machinery in Port Huron marked the transition of the industrial era of Thomas Edison's day to the present era of automation. In the Edison years there were the beauty of white sails and the discordant screeching of the little steamboats' whistles, the crunching of surging log rafts in the rivers, the shouts of the rivermen, and the whining clamor in the busy saw mills. There were the clear notes of the bugle and the martial music of the regimental band at Fort Gratiot, the booming of the fort cannon morning and evening, and the pounding of the caulker's mallet in the shipyards. And there was the whir of wild pigeons migrating by the thousands and casting darkening shadows over the countryside as they passed.

In Edison's own words, "The town (Port Huron) in its pristine youth was a great lumber center, and hummed to the industry of numerous saw mills. An incredible quantity of lumber was made there yearly until the forests nearly vanished and the industry with them. The wealth of the community, invested largely in this business and allied transportation companies, was accumulated

[24] In 1961 when the TV Spectacular, "Merrily We Rolled Along," reviewed the fascinating history of the automobile, the sequence portraying the development of good roads showed one of the Port Huron Engine & Thresher Company's huge rollers as part of the road building equipment.

rapidly, and as freely spent during those days of prosperity in St. Clair County, bringing with it a high standard of domestic comfort." [25]

In Edison's day Port Huron had a population of less than five thousand. Today its estimated population is 36,625 — the metropolitan area, which includes Marysville and three contiguous townships, reaching 60,330. From a town of saw mills, shipbuilding and ship-repairyards, tanneries, and cooper shops (kept busy with the exporting of whitefish, pickerel, and perch), Port Huron developed into a city of foundries and factories.

Today the Blue Water area hums with approximately 77 industries, including 36 major manufacturing concerns, with the greater outputs being in brass products, magnet, automotive and aircraft wire and cable, auto parts and marine engines, paper manufacture, small-boats building, and salt manufacture — listed in the order of their importance with regard to the number of people employed.

In the last years great strides have been made in urban development in Port Huron. A handsome new auditorium-arena complex [26] adorns the central business district; and the new Civic Center, replacing an old slum area, has been well established with a County-City building, County Jail, St. Clair County Library, Y. M. C. A., Marian Manor, [27] and several commercial buildings. Presently under construction are a filtration plant, two new Port Huron Junior College buildings, [28] and several public housing units; and in prospect are additional bridges across Black River, pedestrian arcades and malls, and a program to provide adequate parking space, especially in the central business district which would promote a greater flow of traffic, rectifying the early city-planning which, as with other older cities, was not geared to and did not provide for the automobile. All are but a part of the great Urban Renewal Plan which has been planned for completion by the year 2000.

[25] C. F. Ballentine, "The True Story of Edison's Childhood and Boyhood," *Michigan History Magazine*, IV, No. 1, January, 1920, 177.

[26] Henry McMorran Memorial Auditorium and Junior Sports Arena.

[27] League of Catholic Women's 'Home for girls away from home."

[28] The Al J. Theisen Vocational and Technical Center and the Clara E. Mackenzie Library and Science Building.

Chapter XXXVII

SARNIA AND SOME CANADIAN NEIGHBORS

Across the St. Clair River from Port Huron is Canada's "Chemical Capital," Sarnia, Ontario — a fascinating industrial panorama by day with its giant pipes, tubes, tanks, towers, and refineries, and a fairyland of lights by night, myriad lights reaching up into the heavens in numerous heights and patterns, their beauty reflecting in the river below along a five-mile shore line.

Chemical Valley, the greatest concentration of the petro-chemical industry in the Dominion, covers thousands of acres along the Canadian shore of the mighty St. Clair River, and within the City of Sarnia, which has experienced a phenomenal industrial development. Acquiring city status in 1914, Sarnia now has a population of some fifty-three thousand people.

In the same era which found many of the pioneers settling along the St. Clair River on the Ameican shore, a number of noted Englishmen established homes on the Canadian side of the river, especially in the townships of Sarnia and Moore in Lambton County.

Some of these men were retired British naval officers who were first impressed with the beauty and the potential of the district while still in His Majesty's service, and who, later, established their homes in this new country, beginning in the early eighteen thirties.

Among these men — often referred to as Old Country Gentlemen — were Admiral Thomas Alexander Vidal and Captain Richard Vidal, who were brothers and who had seen service around the world in the Royal Navy, and Captain William E. Wright, who had commanded one of the warships that guarded Napoleon while he was on the Island of St. Helena. One of these men was destined to make an indelible mark in Lambton County. He was Captain Richard Emeric Vidal, who, together with George Durand and Malcolm Cameron, were to found the city of Sarnia.

Captain Vidal, perhaps the first English-speaking settler in what is now Sarnia, came to the St. Clair River area in 1832. He arrived on the little steamer Red Jacket, then plying between Detroit and Port Huron and stopping, when necessary, at The Rapids — as Sarnia was then called — before going on into Black River to tie up at the Kerley dock near present-day Military Street Bridge in Port Huron.

Impressed by the beauty and the possibilities of the district, Vidal took up his Crown grant of two hundred acres at The Rapids, and after leaving instructions for a log house to be built, sailed for England for his family. He returned in 1834 to begin his career as a town official, road builder, and railroad promoter.

In the meantime George Durand had come (1833), opened the first shop at The Rapids, and four years later built a saw mill. This latter industry was a great advancement for the settlement, for until then lumber had to be brought from the Black River Steam Mill in Port Huron. Also in Port Huron was the post office through which the settlers at The Rapids got their mail, until Captain Vidal arranged to have it brought on horseback, and then by stage, from London, Ontario, with Durand as postmaster.

Malcolm Cameron came to The Rapids in 1835 and bought 100 acres adjoining Captain Vidal's land, then laid it out in town lots. He built a second saw mill, a grist mill, operated a general store, and was a ship owner in conjunction with his lumber business, shipping lumber from Canada to Great Britain.

These three men, with Vidal as the promoting force, founded Sarnia, giving it that name in deference to the suggestion of Sir John Colborne, then lieutenant-governor of Upper Canada — Sarnia being the Latin name for the Channel island of Guernsey, where Colborne had been governor.

Captain Richard E. Vidal's coming to the St. Clair River district marked the turning pont in the history of that tiny backwoods settlement. Today, his name and those of Durand and Cameron are preserved in the street names of Sarnia.

Admiral Alexander Thomas E. Vidal,[1] while not as permanent a resident of Lambton County as his brother, was certainly a more spectacular one in his associations with the Blue Water district.

The admiral first saw the St. Clair River in 1815 as a young lieutenant in the Royal Navy, while assisting Lt. Henry Bayfield

---

[1] Vidal Shoals above the Sault commemorates his name.

in charting the river and lower Lake Huron. While in the district he must have been impressed with its beauty and natural resources, for in 1834, when he received his grant of two hundred acres, he chose a spot on the St. Clair River in Moore Township, where he built a house and started farming. He was recalled to service in 1835, however, and for the next eleven years served in the Royal Navy in many parts of the world.

In 1850, after he was gazetted vice-admiral, he returned with his family to Moore, and finding the old house in ruins built a second one, often referred to as the "Castle." This house and its locally made walnut furniture, seemed to intrigue residents on both sides of the river — it was once owned by Baron Von Jasmond, a one-time resident of St. Clair, Michigan — and has often been the subject of those reminiscing about the early days. Included in the many oddities of the house — described as a "fit house for a sailing man" — were "knees" under the massive beams and in the corners, ship-fashion, to stand a gale without twisting. Vidal's washstand and chest of drawers, which he had used on shipboard, were fastened, or ironclamped, to his bedroom wall.

With the exception of serving one year as the first township treasurer, Vidal shunned politics and spent his time in supervising his farm and enjoying life on the St. Clair River, until he returned to England in 1862, where he died three years later.

It was while on duty charting the St. Clair River and lower Lake Huron in 1815, that one of Vidal's more spectacular episodes connected with the St. Clair River district (an episode having international connotations) occurred. In September of that year the H. M. S. *Confience* — formerly the U. S. S. *Scorpion,* captured by Lt. Miller Worsley of the Royal Navy the year before after the destruction of his own ship, the *Nancy* — with Vidal in command, was anchored in Sarnia Bay when one night several of the crew plundered part of the *Confience's* stores and deserted down the river in two of the ship's boats.

Commander Vidal, in an "armed canoe" went in pursuit the next morning and eventually caught up with the deserters in an inn on the American side of Lake St. Clair, near Grosse Pointe. The sailors were arrested and ordered back, under guard, to the *Confience,* but in the meantime an angry mob had gathered — a mob still bitter against the British since the recent war, and resentful of a British commander ordering men around on American soil. As a result, Vidal himself was arrested by Captain John Meldrum of the Michigan Militia and confined in jail for a week before he was finally released on bail. He was later convicted and fined $778.85.

In many of the accounts of this incident there is implied that President James Madison, urged by Vidal's friends, through the British envoy in Washington, to pardon Vidal and remit his fine, finally wrote to Governor Cass, saying that, everything considered, he felt that the cause of justice had already been served and asking the governor to remit the fine. However, when President Madison through his Secretary of State, James Monroe, sent the official pardon to Governor Cass and asked that Vidal's fine be remitted, Cass replied that it was too late — that "the fine imposed by the Court (had) been paid to the Sheriff of the County and by him to the Territorial Treasury," and Cass returned the pardon to the President.[2]

Captain William E. Wright was perhaps the most colorful of the distinguished British naval officers who were Lambton County's earliest pioneers. Like the Vidals, Captain Wright, while in the Royal Navy, had seen service in many parts of the world, including the East Indies, the Atlantic Coast of North America, and New Orleans.

Shortly before his retirement from the Royal Navy Captain Wright had commanded the man-of-war, *Griffon,* one of the warships guarding Napoleon during his enforced stay on the Island of St. Helena. The two became well acquainted, and Wright in later years treasured a tortoise-shell snuff box which the Emperor had given him.

While at St. Helena Wright married Jane Leech, a daughter of one of the members of the governing committee on the island, who was also the governor of the East India Company's stores, and a man of great wealth. A story is told of the time, when at a ball given in honor of Napoleon at St. Helena, the Emperor showed marked attention to the then Miss Leech, one of the belles of the Island. While dancing, so the story goes, she remarked to the

---

[2] Letter to James Monroe, dated at Detroit, February 2, 1816. *Pioneer and Hist. Coll., Mich.,* XXXVI, 338. The Supreme Court records also show the trial.

Emperor that she had a favor to ask of him. When he replied that he would certainly grant the favor if it were in his power to do so, she asked him for a lock of his hair. He assured her that it would give him great pleasure to grant the request but that she would have to honor him by cutting it off herself and with his sword, which she did.

The lock of hair was preserved in a beautiful brooch and brought by Mrs. Wright when she came with her family to Canada. Near the turn of the century the brooch was reported in the possession of the widow of Dr. Henry Wright, of Ottawa, a son of the one-time belle of the Island of St. Helena.

The Wrights came to Canada in 1833. The voyage took seven weeks, stopping first at Toronto, and then at Amherstburg, where they spent nearly a year before the retired naval officer came on to claim his Crown grant in Moore. At Amherstburg tragedy befell the family. Mrs. Wright was stricken with cholera and died within a matter of hours. That same year (1834) the family moved to their farm, just south of Corunna, where a log house had been built for them.

They arrived from Detroit at nine o'clock at night — after travelling for eighteen hours — on the steamboat *General Gratiot,* which landed in front of their house, and where thick bushes reached to the water's edge. Two planks were laid from the gangway to the shore, and down those planks walked Wright, his seven children, his sister, a servant girl, and a governess. The steamboat also brought all their household goods, including a grandfather's clock, fine china and rare treasures from the East; and also aboard ship and the last to go down the gangplank was a veritable menagerie of farm animals and household pets, including a cat and a dog, chickens, pigs, a goat, a cow, and a calf. By midnight both the menage and menagerie were settled in their home in a new country.

Captain Wright lived on his farm for some thirty-five years before he died in 1869, at the age of eighty-four. During that time he interested himself in many village and township affairs. His activities as captain of the Moore Militia during the Mackenzie Rebellion [3] are well known, but not quite so familiar, perhaps, is the fact that he commanded one of the earliest steamboats to

---

[3] See PART FIVE, Chapter XVII.

run on the St. Clair River. This was the 250-ton *Minacetunk*, sometimes spelled *Minnessetunk* — an Indian word meaning "Spirit of the Wave." Captain Wright ran her between Sarnia and Malden (Amherstburg), her average time being four days by steam and sail; it is said that she sometimes tied up over night to a tree, and that she would stop and take on passengers at any dock at the flutter of a handkerchief.

Many streets in Moorestown perpetuate Wright family names, and St. James Street and Napoleon Street also reflect Wright's association with the great Emperor on the Island of St. Helena.

There were other distinguished Old Country Gentlemen besides the retired British naval officers who settled in Lambton County on the St. Clair River. Contemporary with the Vidàls of Sarnia and with Captain Wright of Moore, where the Talfourd brothers, Froome and Field.

The Talfourds were born in London, England of a well-to-do family, and prior to emigrating to Canada in 1832, where they operated a farm in Caradoc, Field was employed in an engineer's office. Froome, who had been serving on merchantmen, was clerk to Captain Frederick Marryatt of the frigate *Ariadne*—the same Captain Marryatt who wrote the sea stories, *Mr. Midshipman Easy*, *Peter Simple*, and *Masterman Ready*. One of Froome's duties, it is said, was to copy that author's writings.

Of adventurous spirit, and wanting to see Lake Huron, the Talfourd brothers left Caradoc on horseback, and on the second day out, following a trail through Plymton—which had been blazed by George Durand, one of the founders of Sarnia—they reached Errol and caught their first sight of the beautiful blue expanse of water that Champlain had named the Freshwater Sea.

They continued traveling south, and impressed with the economic possibilities of the area they bought some lots, and later secured additional government land in Moore Township, south of the Sarnia Reserve. The following year they sold their property in Caradoc and settled in Moore. There, in what was later known as Froomfield, named for both brothers, they cut down the huge trees—"to let in the sunlight," as the Michigan pioneers would say —and further cleared their lands.

Field Talfourd, however, after a short time found the arduous tasks of making a home in the wilderness too much for him, and he moved first to the United States and then back to England, where he followed his natural bent, sketching and painting. That he was successful in his field as an artist is evidenced by the fact that two of his works—charcoal sketches of Robert Browning and Elizabeth Barrett Browning—hang today in the National Gallery.

His career as an artist may have been greatly aided by his association with the friends of his influential older brother, Sir Thomas Noon Talfourd, the distinguished English jurist and writer. Sir Thomas was the author of the Copyright Bill, and of the tragedy, *Ion*, but was better known, perhaps, as the friend of Charles Dickens, who dedicated his *Pickwick Papers* to him, and of Charles Lamb, whose letters Sir Thomas edited and published.

Froome Talfourd became a more permanent resident in Lambton County, continuing to reside in Froomfield for more than thirty years before returning to England. During that time he operated a flour mill on his farm, and divided his brother's property (which he had acquired) into village lots. He served as justice of the peace and as a magistrate, was a lieutenant-colonel in the Moore Militia which guarded the river front between Sarnia and Sombra, and also held the important post of Visiting Superintendent to the Indians.

At the age of sixty Froome Talfourd sailed for England, presumably on a visit, but for some reason not given in his biographical sketches, he never returned to Canada. He spent the rest of his years in London, no doubt in association with the literary circles of his brothers' friends, and died there at the age of 95.

Talfourd Creek and Talfourd Street in Sarnia perpetuate his name.

PART TEN

LEGENDS
AND A TALL TALE OR TWO

I cannot tell how the truth may be;
I say the tale as 'twas told to me.

—Sir Walter Scott

Chapter XXXVIII

TALES OF EXPEDIENCY AND INGENUITY

Stranded Brothers Show Their Ingenuity

The ingenuity of the pioneer was never better demonstrated than by two of the sons of Andrew Westbrook of East China Township, while on an important mission for their father.

When several valuable horses were stolen from Westbrook's farm, Ebenezer Westbrook and his half-brother, William, volunteered to intercept the thieves and bring back the horses. The trail of the thieves led the brothers, on horseback, over the Fort Gratiot Turnpike to Detroit and then on over the old Sauk Trail, now U.S. Route 112—the same trail used by traders, soldiers, and settlers following in the footsteps of the Indians, who had used it for centuries. At the time of the incident the trail was known as the Chicago Road, an uninviting but semi-passable stagecoach road, over which emigrants from the east thronged westward toward Lake Michigan and beyond.

The brothers knew well this Indian trail, which by-passed the swamps and lakes and other natural obstacles, and they made good progress. Inquiries at different points along the way indicated evidence of the route taken by the thieves—through Ypsilanti, Tecumseh, and Moscow, the latter a main stopping point for travelers on the long journey between Detroit and Chicago and where the Kalamazoo River could be forded.

At each stopover, however, the thieves seemed always to be a step ahead of their pursuers, but the brothers continued on in the pursuit, which took them through most of the southern counties. In fact, the chase took them almost to Chicago before they finally caught up with the thieves. Unfortunately, the thieves managed to elude their pursuers and made their escape, but were obliged to leave behind the horses, which were recovered.

From all indications the recovery of the horses was made some distance from Niles in the little hamlet of Bertrand, and without a doubt it was at the old Higby Tavern where the Westbrook brothers spent their last night before returning home. But there a new dilemma confronted them. The long trek and unexpected over-night stops in so many towns had used up their money, and they were without funds for the journey back home. Their decision on how to finance the trip was quickly made, however, and, according to friends and relatives of the brothers, quite illustrative of their characters.

Ebenezer, a religious man and with leanings toward a ministerial career, decided to preach his way home. William, who was adept at cards, chose to get his money by gambling. This they did at each town where they stopped overnight.[1] One can imagine Ebenezer riding over to Niles to preach at the mission there, while William raked in his winnings in the old Higby Tavern, that very first night.

That the plan to recover their resources was successful is evident from the fact that the Westbrook brothers arrived home not only with the recovered horses, but with more money than they had when they first started out.

The Captain Found a Way

The ingenious and practical way our pioneer forebears met crises in their everyday lives was never more clearly or delightfully shown than in the story concerning Captain John Clark (also of East China Township) and his famous slab of salt pork.

Captain Clark, remembered for his good sense and decisive action—as in the Canadian sloop incident in the Patriot War—was often called upon by those in trouble to help them out of their predicaments, even after his retirement to his farm.

The story is told of a Great Lakes skipper, on his way from Green Bay with a cargo for Detroit. When a storm came up on Lake Huron, his vessel struck against some object which stove a hole in her bow. The captain ordered his men into one of the small boats to cover the hole with canvas. Working in the heavy and angry seas the crew managed to place the canvas and hold it with guy ropes, but the operation was only partially successful

---

[1] This story was told to the author, in a letter, dated November 30, 1957, written by Mrs. Julia H. Finster, great-granddaughter of Andrew Westbrook.

and there was still an inflow of water. Toward morning, as the steamer made its way into the St. Clair River it was apparent that the inrushing water was increasing, and to keep the pumps going was taxing the men to the limit of their strength. When the boat steamed past St. Clair the captain put in at Captain Clark's wood dock and sent a messenger up to his house to ask him if he would help take the steamer into Detroit.

Captain Clark was eating his breakfast when the word came to him, but he immediately accompanied the messenger back to the dock. After getting details of the trouble he descended into the hold of the boat to examine the hole for himself. After his examination was finished he went back to his house and down into the cellar to his pork barrel.

Selecting the largest slab of pork that he could find in the great cask, he wiped the brine from it, put the slab into a piece of canvas, and after tying the ends of the canvas together he threw the sack over his shoulder and left the house. Trudging back to the wood dock he again went into the hold of the vessel and instructed the men how to wedge the slab of pork firmly into the hole.

After the boat was bailed out Captain Clark told the exhausted captain and crew to go to their cabins for a rest and that he would take the boat into Detroit, and when they arrived safely at their destination the slab of pork was still firmly wedged in the hole.

William T. Mitchell and Zachariah Chandler
Prove an Old Saying

The old saying "Politics makes strange bedfellows," figures in this next tale. There have been times when the saying, so often a figure of speech, became literally true. Take for instance the incident concerning Judge William T. Mitchell of Port Huron, a prominent Democrat, and Detroit's Zachariah Chandler, an ardent Whig and one of the founders of the Republican Party.

A Democrat of the old school, Judge Mitchell was one of seventeen Michigan Democrats who journeyed to Washington in 1857 to see James Buchanan inaugurated President. Coming from Michigan, where there were still frontier conditions, with a minimum of travel and communication between their home and the

265

Capitol—Mitchell and his party did not realize the necessity of engaging quarters in Washington in advance. As a result, when they arrived in the Capitol there was not a room to be had in any hotel or home.

Finally, after much hunting around, Mitchell and his fellow Democrats came upon a small, dilapidated hotel on Pennsylvania Avenue which had been closed for some time—a hotel so run-down and so inadequate that not even the crush of the inauguration would warrant its reopening.

In desperation the men hunted up the former proprietor of the hotel and with much persuasion succeeded in making a deal with him to open the building so they could sleep there for the two weeks for two dollars a day each, a charge they thought exorbitant considering one could get first-class accommodations at such fine hotels as the Biddle House in Detroit for only a dollar and a half a day. Besides that, there were only nine beds, which meant that sixteen of the men would have to share a bed with his fellow traveler. Lots were drawn for the odd bed and Judge Mitchell won.

In the meantime, Zachariah Chandler, one-time Whig mayor of Detroit, and now newly elected to the Senate (to succeed Lewis Case) arrived in Washington to be sworn in for his first term as senator. One would have thought that Chandler, or at least his Whig party members, would have arranged for his stay in Washington but he, like many other Michiganders, was without accommodations and was desperate for a room when he met up with Mitchell with whom he was acquainted.

Chandler asked Judge Mitchell where he was staying, and when Mitchell told him of the rooms for which he and his party had arranged, Chandler immediately proposed that he stay with them. But Mitchell, somewhat taken by surprise, said that he did not think the idea was a good one. In fact he told Chandler that the thought of seventeen Democrats harboring a Republican during a Democratic inauguration was preposterous. Chandler pleaded with Mitchell—begged him—and offered to be as good a Democrat as any of them until the inauguration was over if they would only take him in. It was either that or he would have to walk the streets all night, he told Mitchell. Mitchell finally agreed to put it up to the vote of the rest of his party.

Those were the days when political feeling was intense and when all sorts of ruses and abuses were indulged in, such as publicly challenging voters and "snatching" them at polling places on one pretext or another, and trumping up charges to warrant arrest and jailing until after election day. In fact, so heated was the political feeling at the time, that it was only by the barest majority that the men voted to take the Whig in, and as a result Chandler shared Mitchell's bed for the two weeks of the inauguration.

One can imagine how dearly Chandler paid for his two weeks lodgings—a lone Republican and the barbs of seventeen Democrats —but Judge Mitchell said that, considering everything, he and Chandler got along fine, and that ever after that time, although each one adhered strongly to the tenets of his own party, they remained good friends until Chandler's death some twenty years later.

A Pioneer Lawyer's Expediency

Expediency was a trait well developed from necessity by many of our pioneers, but none acquired the art with more finesse than did the adroit Omar D. Conger, lawyer, lumberman, and politician, and the only resident of the St. Clair River district to hold the office of United States Senator.

Omar D. Conger, born in Cooperstown, N. Y., and a graduate of Western Reserve University first came to the St. Clair River district in 1847 to be associated with his uncle, Jonas Titus of Detroit. The latter had a water mill in Lakeport, which was then a village plat under the name of New Milwaukee. Previous to his arrival in Port Huron, where he made his home, Conger served two years (1845 and 1846) as a member of Dr. Douglass Houghton's party engaged in exploring and surveying the Upper Peninsula.

Conger was state senator from 1855 to 1860, representative in Congress from 1869 to 1881—where he was known as "The Great Objector" because of his familiarity with parliamentary law and his fondness for raising points of order to harass his opponents— and United States Senator from 1881 to 1887.[2]

[2] After the expiration of his last term as U. S. Senator, Conger continued to live in Washington, until his death in 1898, at the age of eighty.

It was due to Senator Conger's persistence in Congress that the Harbor of Refuge at Harbor Beach was built, as well as the Lake St. Clair Ship Canal and the Port Huron Custom House, among many other important governmental enterprises.

Previous to serving in these public offices, however, Conger practiced law in Port Huron and throughout the county—in addition to his working in the lumber woods and saw mill—and there are probably more stories told about the habits of this man in his practice of law than of any other St. Clair County pioneer lawyer.

Conspicuous in his habitual dress of swallow-tail coat and stovepipe silk hat, with flowing beard, Conger was noted for his caustic wit, his skill as a debator, his shrewd analysis of character, and his great power over juries.

Pioneers, it seemed, were always comparing Conger with Judge William T. Mitchell, as a lawyer. Mitchell, according to some, cultivated the court, Conger generally disregarded it and relied on his skill to bring the jury to his way of thinking. Conger was credited with the great ability of reading upon the faces of jurors the thoughts which were passing through their minds, and of presenting his arguments in such a manner as would meet the pecularities of each member. In this respect he was considered the finest lawyer in the state.

The story is told of the time a Detroit man by the name of Bernard was prosecuted for obstructing Mill Creek, an important stream in lumbering days running down from the northwest part of St. Clair County and emptying into Black River in the vicinity of Abbottsford in Clyde Township.

Bernard was defended by Dewitt C. Walker (founder of Capac, Mich.), Daniel W. Goodwin of Detroit, and William T. Mitchell of Port Huron, considered a formidable trio at the time. Conger was the prosecuting attorney. He was determined to convict Bernard, but there was one juror who remained obstinately unmoved by his arguments throughout most of the trial. He decided to find out something about this juror—especially about his background.

He learned that the man, before coming to Michigan, had run logs in his home state of Maine. The man was fond, it seemed, of telling stories of the log drives on a certain stream near his old home—of how, after being away from home for weeks and months, the raftsmen would come to a certain turn in the stream and suddenly see, on the eminence overlooking the stream, their wives and children waiting to catch a glimpse of them, and then, how the raftsmen, hurrying over the rapids, would soon be with their loved ones.

Conger, on the last day of the trial, described this scene with all the eloquence he could command, especially dwelling on the anxious impatience with which a husband and father hurried over the shoals and rocks, and the joy with which he was greeted by his family. Before he was through Conger detected the glimmer of a tear in the eye of the once unmoved juror—an effect which the advocate alone understood.

Then with a fierce and swift invective Conger described such a man as Bernard obstructing Mill Creek, delaying the drive by weeks, and preventing the happy reunion of a father with his beloved family.

The jury that evening brought in a verdict of guilty.

Chapter XXXIX

THE WIND BLEW FAIR FOR CAPTAIN SAM WARD

Up anchor! Up anchor!
Set sail and away!
The ventures of dreamland
Are thine for a day.

—Silas Weir Mitchell

When Charles Butler, the New York capitalist, made his trip in 1833 to estimate the possibilities of land speculation at the Rapids in what is now Port Huron, and also at the little frontier settlement on Lake Michigan which was later to be the great metropolis of Chicago, he urged many of the St. Clair River pioneers to consider investments in these lands.

Lots in the four plats, which were eventually to make up the Town of Port Huron, and which included Butler's Town of Huron, platted in 1837, were rather slow in moving. But in the meantime, Butler had gone on to take stock of the settlement on the Chicago River, and had satisfied himself of Chicago's future—that that "germ of a city" would become the "largest inland commercial emporium" in the United States.

The rest of the history of that most hectic land boom the western country ever experienced is well known, as is Butler's ultimate investment of one hundred thousand dollars in the swampland that was then Chicago—one-third of which Butler auctioned off the same year (1835) and sold for more than the original cost.

Not quite so well known, perhaps, are the stories of some of the other individual speculators, or would-be speculators, among the thousands who descended on that frontier settlement at the foot of Lake Michigan. Take for instance the story of Captain Sam Ward's planned investment in the lands in Chicago.

In 1835 Captain Ward had just finished at Newport (Marine City) the building of his fourth schooner, *General Harrison,* and had taken her with a cargo, on her maiden voyage, to Detroit.

270

She made the trip for trading, and it was Captain Ward's intention on her return to pick up along the way cargo bound for Green Bay.

Posted in the taverns and hotels in Detroit were the promoters' maps and pictures of the growing city of Chicago, and the town was rife with stories of land auctions and of fortunes in the making. Captain Ward decided he would try his luck, too, after he had finished his business at Green Bay, and he took with him from Detroit a thousand dollars, of which six hundred dollars was earmarked to bid for city lots at an auction in the embryo metropolis.

Leaving Detroit he sailed through the Detroit River and Lake St. Clair, stopping for cargo at ports along the way, and set sail up the St. Clair River, through Lake Huron to the Straits of Mackinac and around to Green Bay, and then down Lake Michigan to Chicago. The weather had not been good—there had been adverse winds and many squalls—and the trip took almost a month, much longer than Ward had expected.

When he finally reached Chicago, in the late afternoon, the streets were crowded with land speculators, hurrying from one sale to another. A man dressed in scarlet, carrying a scarlet flag and riding a white horse with scarlet trappings, announced, like a town crier, the times of the auction sales, and everywhere he went crowds gathered around him.

Captain Ward made note of the time of the auction sales, looked over the land packages, made some decisions and waited for the morrow. But the next day was beautiful, and a wind had sprung up. As the captain put it, the wind was "blowing fair" for him, and he just could not resist the temptation of a good run. He ordered the sails hoisted on the *General Harrison* and started home, letting his contemplated land purchases go with the wind.

In referring to the incident some twenty years later and just before he died, Captain Ward commented that had he gone ahead with his planned purchases and had invested his six hundred dollars in the lots he had picked out, he would have made more money out of them—at the "average rate at which the lots were sold"—than he had made from all his years of sailing and ship-building—and that was a good-sized fortune.

271

Chapter XXXX

GLIMPSES OF PIONEER LIFE

A Fearless Hunter and a Gracious Host

Hunting, from the pioneer's standpoint, was more a matter of livelihood than sport. The pioneer could ill afford to spend his time in pure fun. He hunted for food; and deer hunting, especially, was a serious matter with him since it meant not only food for himself but food to sell. A saddle of venison always brought a fine price, particularly in Detroit markets.

The pioneer also hunted for skins, and even after the era of the fur trader, he still hunted the deer, bear, wolf, and lynx, as well as the wildcat, fox, coon, badger, beaver, rabbit, and mink. He got five dollars bounty apiece from the Government for wolves, and he found a ready market for any of his skins.

Judge Zephaniah Bunce, early mill operator and owner, merchant, postmaster,[1] holder of important county and territorial offices,[2] and one of the most noted pioneers of the St. Clair River district, was also one of the most courageous of hunters. There is a story told about him concerning the time he set out for Harsen's Island to buy some hay.

It was early one winter's evening when he started out, and, dressed in his great coat, buckskin pants and beaver cap, he climbed into his French train (a sort of boarded-up sled), tipped the Indian pony with his whip, and started down the ice of St. Clair River.

A short distance from St. Clair Judge Bunce saw in the distance ahead of him, silhouetted against the snow, a number of animals

---

[1] Postmaster of Desmond (1831-33), as the settlement at the mouth of Black River was then known.

[2] In 1820 Governor Cass appointed Judge Bunce Associate Justice of the county court, and in 1822, Chief Justice. He held the office until it was abolished in 1827. In 1824, when the territory passed under the second stage of government consisting of governor and legislative council, he was selected as a member of that body, and in 1833 appointed Associate Judge in the circuit court of the Territory.

clamber up a steep bank and disappear into the woods beyond. When the judge finally reached the spot he found on the ice by the side of the path ahead of him the body of a deer which the wolves had just killed. It was still bleeding from the wounds in its throat and the ice and snow were discolored with blood.

It so happened that the winter was one when wild game had been particularly hard to find, and when the judge saw the deer he thought of what a treat a venison steak would be and decided to appropriate the deer for himself. He grasped the antlers and with almost unbelievable strength he pulled and heaved until he got the deer into the sled. He then put the whip to the pony and started down the trail.

But he had not gone far before the wolves he had robbed came yelping after him, and as they came they seemed to increase in number. Judge Bunce succeeded for awhile in beating them off with his great whip, but presently he came to a rough place on the ice which slowed him down and then it was that he began to fear that the wolves would have him as well as the deer, so he compromised by tumbling the deer out of the sled. The pack of wolves closed around the body of the deer, and the Judge, again putting his whip to the pony, left them to their carnival. It was one of the few times when a prize venison steak eluded that pioneer hunter.

Better luck was had on another occasion when the judge was crossing Lake St. Clair on the ice and saw a large animal in the track ahead of him, and so gave chase. The snow was deep on each side of the track and after a time the animal, tired out, jumped into the snow and stood on his haunches. The judge raised his heavy hickory whip-stock and struck the animal's head and so stunned the beast that he could cut its throat without difficulty and then put it in his sled.

When reaching the opposite shore he inquired of a French settler what it was that he had captured. The astonished man asked Judge Bunce where it came from. "O, I got him back there on the ice," replied the judge.

"Got him!" shouted the Frenchman. "Got him *alone?* Mon Dieu! You must thank the Virgin that he did not get *you!*"[2]

---

[2] O. C. Thompson, "History of Judge Zephaniah W. Bunce," *Pioneer and Historical Coll., Mich.*, I, 442.

And the judge found out that the huge prize he had captured was a wildcat.

Those were the days when weary travelers in stage coaches or wagons often mistook log houses along trails for inns. Many of the private homes did function as inns where hotels and inns were not likely to be situated, and their owners were licensed innkeepers. In any event, most pioneers, whether or not they kept an inn, were obliging hosts, having experienced themselves the feeling of relief at seeing such a refuge as a log house after having been jostled and shaken for miles over rutted or corduroy roads.

But many a pioneer's hospitality was put upon to the extreme, as is shown in one of the several experiences that Judge Bunce had with unexpected guests when the St. Clair River district was still a frontier country.

One November evening as the judge sat at his mahogany table, under the light of the camphine lamp and made entries in the little ten-penny notebook-diary, he heard the staccato beat of horses' hoofs and the rumble of wheels on the frozen road, and the "Whoa—!" of the driver as the house was reached.

When the judge unlatched the door he saw a group of men—six in all—emerge from the stagecoach and come up the path. He learned from one of them that all had come up from Mt. Clemens where they had spent the night before and had expected to reach Port Huron on their way north to see some timber land, but that their horses were tired out and the driver had refused to go farther without resting them. Could the owner of the house, the man asked courteously enough although slightly pompously, give them dinner and lodgings for the night.

The judge without hesitation said of course he could, and if there was a twinkle in his eye the men were not aware of it. He invited them in, and the weary and hungry travelers, obviously grateful for what they thought was a most comfortable inn, divested themselves of their greatcoats and woolen caps and mufflers and made themselves at home.

Judge Bunce put an extra leaf in his mahogany table and placed his cane-bottom chairs around it, and the men were soon enjoying the turtle soup the judge warmed in a kettle in the fireplace. While they enjoyed the soup the judge took down a ham of venison from

274

the rafters in the shed, cut slices of it and cooked that too in the fireplace and served it with tea, cornbread (made without salt), and maple syrup—all of which the men seemed to enjoy thoroughly.

The next morning the judge raided his pork barrel, fried generous slices of the salt pork in his large iron skillet and served it to the men with more cornbread and maple syrup and great mugs of tea.

When the judge's hired man brought around the horses, the well-fed and well-rested men asked for their bill, and were quite surprised—and some a little embarrassed—to discover that Judge Bunce was not running an inn and would not accept payment. He had never before taken money for his hospitality, he told them, and certainly did not intend to take any from them.

One of those guests, Josiah B. Frost, a very young man at the time, never forgot Judge Bunce's kindness and generosity, and many years later, on the occasion of the judge's one hundredth birthday,[3] November 14, 1887—and when there was a celebration at his home attended by some three hundred friends and well-wishers, including ex-Governor David H. Jerome and Senator Thomas W. Palmer—Josiah Frost rode all the way from his home in Ypsilanti, Michigan in a sleigh, most of the way in a blinding snow storm, to do honor on that occasion to his one-time gracious host.

The Glorious Carouse

Our pioneers, when occasion provided, were likely to engage in considerable horseplay, and in a style which exhibited the utter unconventionality of the day. The occasion in this particular instance was a party given by a group of realtors called the Pontiac Company (1819), celebrating the opening of the first mill and mercantile establishment in what is now the city of Pontiac, as well as the opening of the road from Detroit to Pontiac, now known as Woodward Avenue Superhighway.

The Pontiac Company consisted of many noted Detroiters, including Judge Augustus Woodward, Colonel Stephen Mack (brother of Andrew Mack, proprietor of the Mansion House, who settled on the St. Clair River after he retired from the hotel business), Judge Solomon Sibley, John L. Whiting, Austin E.

---

[3] Judge Zephaniah W. Bunce died in 1889 at the age of one hundred and two.

Wing, and Alexander Macomb, as well as James Fulton and David C. McKinstry who with Thomas Palmer founded the city of St. Clair.

The celebration included an elaborate dinner, the drinking of innumerable toasts and afterward various sports; and present at the party were not only the members of the Pontiac Company but also nearly every male Detroiter of business or professional rank, or social consideration, including Governor Lewis Cass, Judge George A. O'Keefe, and John Roberts.

Also present was Dr. Harmon Chamberlain, the popular, skilled, first resident physician of the city of St. Clair, a man of affairs and well known in the Territory, a founder of the St. Clair County Medical Society, and one-time mayor of St. Clair. As it turned out, Dr. Chamberlain became one of the key figures of the celebration.

That year the question of electing a delegate to Congress, for which no nomination had as yet been made, was to come up before the people in the fall election, and the gentlemen of the Pontiac party, in their happy frame of mind following the abundance of liquid refreshments required for the numerous toasts, resolved themselves into a committee to nominate a candidate for the honorable office.

It was Judge Woodward's idea, or so the story goes, for the men to be put through the mill, so to speak—that the one whose skill in the hopper could produce the best meal should be the candidate —and he, (Woodward) as miller, and Colonel Mack, dressed as an Indian Chief, would be the judges. The candidates, Governor Cass and Judges David Leroy, Solomon Sibley, and George A. O'Keefe, were then put in the hopper, one coming out as bran, one as shorts, and one as middlings, and so on, and as none met the necessary qualifications all were given ridiculous punishments. Judge O'Keefe, for instance, who came out of the hopper as a mere bushel of hulls—according to Indian Chief Mack—was made to scrape with his teeth an ounce of pitch from the bark of a nearby pine tree.

Later, on the way back to Detroit and in the afterglow of the numerous toasts enjoyed, the hilarious party, still "whooping it up all the way and making the woods echo with their yells,"[4]

---

[4] Robert B. Ross George B. Catlin, *Landmarks of Detroit,* (*Evening News,* (Detroit), 1898), pp. 357-358.

stopped near Royal Oak at the home of a Frenchman and tried to persuade the man to join the party. When the man obstinately refused, court was immediately convened, and the Frenchman, for his so-called contumacy, was convicted and sentenced "to be hanged by the neck until he (was) dead."[5]

A rope was put around the man's neck and attached to the shafts of one of the reveler's carts. Some of the men then climbed onto the rear of the two-wheeled cart so that the Frenchman was actually suspended for several seconds before the men got off the cart, and when the man was let down he slumped, insensible, to the ground.

Dr. Chamberlain hurriedly examined the prostrate form, and although, as he soon discovered, the man had only fainted—and no doubt from fright—still, to keep up the ghastly joke, he pronounced him dead. At that awful announcement the men rushed forward to try and resuscitate the victim, but Dr. Chamberlain grandly waved them away and "revived" the man himself. He then warned the men that had he not been a physician of unsurpassing skill the Frenchman would never have been brought back to life, and that all who had participated in maltreating him would certainly have been hanged for murder. The revelers, somewhat sobered, thoughtfully made their way back to Detroit.

But before leaving the Frenchman's place the men showered their victim with gifts of money in repentence, and it is said that the Frenchman afterwards declared he would almost be willing to be hanged again for the same considerations.

That hilarious celebration of the Pontiac Company has gone down in the annals of Michigan history as the Glorious Carouse.

The Future Wife of General McClellan
Gets a Lesson in Retreat

When Harriet Shippey[6] left the Fort Gratiot enclosure one afternoon in the spring of 1839 and said goodby to the blue-coated sentry, she had no idea that the trip back home would be any more eventful than previous ones. She had just given a music

---

[5] *Ibid.*

[6] Harriet Shippey was the sister of Martin H. Shippey, one of the early residents present at the town meeting in 1837 who voted to unite the four plats at the confluence of Black River with the St. Clair, and give the new town the name of Port Huron.

lesson to the daughters of the handsome and popular Lieutenant Randolph Marcy, and, as usual, was being accompanied a short way by her chattering, lively little pupils, Mary Ellen Marcy and her sister Frances.

It was a lovely, warm March day and the trio sauntered happily down the trail that is now Fort Street to their usual place of parting, a few blocks away.

The little girls had just said goodby to their music teacher and were walking backwards, still waving farewell, when to her horror, Miss Shippey saw a bear emerging from a thicket about fifty feet from where the little girls had to pass.

Once over the first paralysis of her fright, Harriet, yelling for help, rushed to the now screaming little girls and pushed them to a clump of trees along the walk and commanded them to stand there and face the bear that was coming slowly toward them.

The bear, distracted momentarily by the yelling and screaming, had stopped her loping progress, moving her head up and down and back and forth inquiringly, and then slowly ambled toward the plank walk again.

The valiant Harriet held her ground and did her best to protect her pupils. Well trained in the pioneer ways of self-preservation concerning wild animals, it had been impressed on her that if one stood with his back to an object, such as a tree, and faced the animal, it would not attack. To run, she had been told, could be a fatal mistake.

Whether this method would actually have worked in Harriet's favor or not, history will never know, for as the bear moved toward them a rustling was heard in the thicket and at the same time a bear cub jumped friskily into the clearing and ran playfully to its mother. At this, the bear disregarded the girls and began to push her cub back toward the woods. Determinedly, almost crossly, she kept nuzzling her cub to safety until both were out of sight.

Taking advantage of the mother bear's concern for her young, Harriet grabbed each girl by the hand, and, yelling still louder for help began to run with them back toward the fort enclosure as fast as her flounced skirt and starched petticoats would allow. By this time her cries for help had been heard inside the stockade and soldiers came running to their rescue, and one of them, well in

278

advance of the others, was the tall, broad-shouldered Lieutenant Marcy himself.[7]

Bear episodes were, of course, common enough in pioneer days, but the participants in this one made it worthy of note. Mary Ellen Marcy was the same Miss Marcy who later married General George B. McClellan of Civil War fame, who ran for President but was defeated by Abraham Lincoln.

Harriet Shippey's nephew, John A. B. Shippey, more than half a century after the episode, wrote to the Michigan Historical Society, gathered together in their annual meeting, and suggested, rather facetiously, that the Shippey bear incident on Fort Street "no doubt furnished Mary Ellen with some special pointers to give her husband in the tactics of retreat, for which the General was famous." [8]

The Pioneer With a Big Heart

There is a little street called Runnels near the west end of the city limits of Port Huron, only three blocks long, which has since 1900 perpetuated the name of a man who was prominent for more than fifty years in the marine, lumbering, and civic interests of the city and the district.

He was Daniel N. Runnels, who was twice mayor of Port Huron, and who also served on the City Council and held other important offices. Aside from his political offices, he was engaged in the lumber business for more than twenty years and has been remembered as a raftsman who brought some of the largest loads of pine timber down Black River.

Daniel Runnels was also actively engaged in the steamboat and ferry business with Captain James Moffat. Probably the best known boat that he and Captain Moffat owned was the 92-foot Omar D. Conger, considered one of the finest ferry boats on the Lakes. This same Omar D. Conger met a grievous end one Sunday afternoon in March of 1922, when her boiler exploded while she

---

[7] Marcy, later a Major-General and Chief-of-Staff for his son-in-law, General McClellan, also became famous as a big-game hunter, and was the author of several books, including his popular *Border Reminiscences.*

[8] Clipping from *Port Huron Weekly Times,* March 21, 1895.

was at her dock in Black River, killing four of the Conger crew and injuring several of the townspeople.

But it was as a marine contractor and builder of docks and bridges that Runnels was perhaps best known and best remembered. "Dan, the pile driver," he was familiarly called. An early resident, reminiscing at an annual meeting of the St. Clair County Pioneer Society, remarked that Runnels had built nine-tenths of all the docks from Marysville to the Fort Gratiot Lighthouse at the foot of Lake Huron, and had driven nearly all the piles for wharves and buildings in the same territory.

Daniel Runnels was equally well known for his generosity and his kindness, especially where the needy were concerned. Typical of his acts of charity is the story they tell about him of an incident that occurred when he was building the approaches to the third Military Street Bridge (1869) over Black River.

He had his scow in the river and was directing his crew of men who were driving the piles for the south approach to the bridge, when in the near distance the workmen saw a funeral procession coming up Military Street. As the hearse came nearer, drawn by sleek horses with their heads handsomely tasselled in black plumes, the men stopped working and each one removed his hat and held it over his heart.

Slowly the horses, held severely in check by the somber looking driver in plug hat, drew the hearse up to the corner near the bridge and turned into Water Street, as the men continued to stand motionless in respect for the dead.

But as they watched, Runnels suddenly threw down the long iron rod he was holding and with great strides was over the side of the scow and onto the bank of the river and running up the incline to Water Street. He had quickly realized that the hearse was the only vehicle in the funeral cortege and that the little group of mourners, about six in number, were trudging along behind the hearse, evidently too poor to hire a hack to carry them to the cemetery.

With a commanding gesture Runnels stopped the funeral procession and hurried over to a hack standing near the corner. He took out his wallet and handed the driver what was evidently the necessary fare and the driver turned the hack around and drew up alongside the mourners. Mr. Runnels opened the hack door and after directing the mourners to get in, closed the door and the procession moved on.

Runnels then returned to the scow as the men resumed working, and the "put-put" of the steam engine, the screeching of the machinery that lifted the great iron weight high in its frame, and the metallic thud of the monkey as it was let fall on the pile, went on without further interruption.

An Errand of Mercy

Many dramatic stories have been told about the centuries-old Straits of Mackinac, but no single reported incident is more illustrative of the courage and fortitude of our pioneers than the night trip over the ice of the Straits by William Roberts of Emmett, on an errand of mercy.

In the late fall of the unusually cold winter of 1881–1882, Kittie Sheehan, the niece of William Roberts was visiting in St. Ignace when she was taken ill. She became steadily worse, and the girl's mother, Roberts' sister, was summoned and was with her when, later in January, she died. The mother immediately telegraphed her brother to come to St. Ignace and arrange to bring the remains back to Emmett for burial.

Roberts started out at once for St. Ignace, but arriving at the Straits of Mackinac he found that the ice and great drifts of snow had blocked up the channel and that the steamer *Algomah* had ceased running.

By this time it was almost ten o'clock at night, and as he was anxious to cross without delay he set about going from door to door in Mackinaw City, until he was able to secure the services of two Chippewa Indians who would guide him across the ice of the Straits to St. Ignace.

In order to guard against any of the party drowning by falling into an air hole in the ice the Indians procured a heavy rope similar to a hawser, and all were fastened together, somewhat like mountain climbers who are roped together before an ascent. They then started out over the ice in single file, one of the Indians taking the lead.

The night was bitterly cold, but Roberts was hardly aware of the low temperature so determined and so preoccupied was he on

281

his errand of mercy. They made it safely enough for the first few hours, but then when about half way across the frozen waste the lead Indian fell into an air hole. He managed to grab hold of the edge of the ice and hold on until his two companions hauled him to safety, but not before he had been submerged almost to his shoulders and his clothes soaked with the icy water.

The Indian must have been suffering greatly, but still he urged his companions to continue on, and to run, saying that he would get warm as soon as his clothing had frozen. The men obeyed— the soaked Indian still taking the lead — and the trio without further mishap, arrived at St. Ignace at three oclock in the morning.

Roberts soon found the house where his sister was sorrowfully keeping watch over the dead body of her daughter, and as the body was already in a coffin the decision was made to recross the Straits immediately. Roberts secured the services of a third Indian with a sort of bobsled to which the coffin was roped, and, in the meantime, the lead Indian, having secured dry clothing, was ready to recross with them.

Roped together as before, but with the added burden of the heavy coffin, the mournful party silently picked its way over the treacherous ice. The weather had grown continuously colder, and the Indian guides, hauling and pushing the coffin through constant drifts, lost, for a time, the use of their hands. Roberts and his sister then took their turns drawing and steadying the coffin as best they could, and finally, at eleven o'clock that same morning — seven long hours from the time they had left St. Ignace — they reached the opposite shore.

From Mackinaw City the funeral party made the rest of the trip by train, and, arriving in Emmett, the body of the young girl was finally laid to rest in Kenockee Cemetery.

Rogues Among the Pioneers

Roguery among the pioneers, it seems, was more prevalent than formal history records, and this fact was especially apparent during the Civil War after the Draft Act went into effect.

In that act there was a provision which made it possible for the draftee to avoid service either by paying the Government three hundred dollars, or by providing a substitute, and the official registers show — as in all other sections of the state and nation — a substantial number of substitutes among the Civil War soldiers from the St. Clair River district.

Often times the substitute was hired by the draftee for a financial consideration, but there were times, too, when he was coerced — even tricked — into substituting. In regard to this latter practice there is the story told about how a farmer in the district avoided his draft service by base skulduggery — only one of the acts of rascality reportedly perpetrated by him during his lifetime in the district.

When this farmer was eventually drafted he was reluctant to go to war, but the only way out of the situation was to pay the Government the three hundred dollars or to hire a substitute, and he was disinclined to do either.

It so happened that strangers, a young man and his wife, were passsing through the district, and since night overtook them when they were near the rogue's farm, the couple stopped and asked him if he would give them lodgings for the night. The farmer affably agreed. He told the hired man to take care of the strangers' horse, and he himself helped to carry in their bags, which were placed in the front hall of the farmhouse. After supper the travelers were shown to an upstairs bedroom and they took with them the smaller of the two bags.

Late that night the farmer did a peculiar thing. He took several sterling silver knives and forks from a chest in the dining room, and untying the straps of the travelers' carpetbag, placed the silverware between some layers of clothing and then carefully closed the bag and fastened the straps securely.

The next morning when the travelers came downstairs the farmer served them a substantial breakfast of hot bread, strips of sidepork with milk gravy, eggs, applesauce, and coffee, and when the couple asked the farmer how much they owed him for their room and meals he played the genial host and refused to accept anything.

The grateful couple made their farewells and started on their journey. The farmer waited until he thought they were about a mile away and then he called his hired man and told him some of his silverware was missing and that he suspected the couple who had spent the night with him. He told the hired man to hitch up the wagon and then taking the hired man with him he started in pursuit of his erstwhile guests.

He caught up with the travelers after about two miles of rapid travel over dusty roads and then the farmer, in rather an apologetic manner, told the couple that some of his valuable silverware was missing and that he was investigating everyone who had been in the neighborhood, themselves included since they had stayed at his house. The surprised couple naturally protested their innocence, whereupon the farmer, quite suavely said that if they were telling the truth they certainly would not mind having their bags searched. To this the couple willingly acquiesced — even going so far as to help untie the bags.

The farmer ordered his hired man to go through the bags, and of course he found the silver knives and forks. The man, astonished, looked at his wife, and she equally astonished, looked back at her husband. Each was indignantly aware of his own innocence. But then, an infinitesimal seed of doubt — each of the other — began festering in the minds of the man and his wife, for there, for all to see, was the silverware, and there, too, was the hired man as witness that it was found in their luggage.

The farmer, in a position to bargain, magnanimously agreed not to prosecute if the young man would take his place in the draft, and the result was that the erstwhile guest was forced to act as substitute for the conniving farmer for the duration of the war.

Chapter XXXXI

A GREAT LAKES TALE OF TOW AND
OTHER UNUSUAL FEATS

Michigan history, of course, has been deliciously spiced with many yarns of such supermen-lumberjacks as Paul Bunyan, and such fabulous sailors as Charles Brown's Old Alfred Bulltop Strongalong — tales of engrossing factual interest even though topped with a generous icing of incredibility.

Certainly the St. Clair River area sailors, well known to all the port towns, had their yarns too, and while their stories do not quite match up to those of the Yankee deep-water sailors in the magnitude of their feats, they do a magnificent job of stretching the belief of the listener.

These stories usually came out of the get-togethers of the Great Lakes captains in Port Huron, St. Clair, Detroit, Cleveland, and other port towns, for instance the time a group of them met in Detroit in the late eighteen eighties to tell of their experiences. Among them was Captain L. R. "Tod" Boynton.

Tod Boynton, who originally hailed from Port Huron, was the same Captain Lewis R. Boynton, it will be remembered, who made history by helping to design, and then navigating as master, the famous Mackinac ferry, *City of St. Ignace,* the ferry that Admiral Makaroff of the Russian Navy came here to study in 1900 and to copy for service on Lake Baikal in Siberia.

Well, sir, it was Captain Boynton who won the prize that day for the story of the greatest wrecking feat performed by any of the old skippers. Several of the other stories sounded incredible, but Tod's seemed literally true with only a modicum of doubt about it, and so he received an engraved whale's tooth — the engraving said to have been done by Old Alfred Bulltop Stormalong himself.

It all happened while Tod was master of the Tug *Mayflower,* when he was delivering a tow of lumber to a Lake Erie port. On passing Peach Island one of the barges in his tow got hard

285

aground. For two hours he wrestled with the barge but couldn't budge her. At that point most skippers would have given up, but not Captain Tod.

He called to those on the barge to let go his line and then he steamed to the other side of the island. Here he hitched to a large stump and for two hours endeavored to pull the island out from under the barge. At the end of the two hours he went back and found the barge afloat.

Now there were the disbelievers — and naturally they were not present at the accomplishment of this great feat — who said that the skipper must have heaved the barge off with the anchors, but there were others who stoutly maintained that Captain Tod moved the island ten feet nearer Canada, and the suggestion is on record — they say — that the lake charts should have been changed accordingly.

If you think that tale a bit too tall to take — at least without a glass of port — consider the true story of the harrowing and almost unbelievable experience of another St. Clair River area skipper, Captain S. H. Burnham of Sombra, Ontario. It seems that a group of retired tug captains got together for a reunion in 1910, reminiscing about the days of such famous tugs as the *Mocking Bird*, the *George E. Brockway*, the *Champion*, and the *B. B. Jones*, and one of the stories concerned Captain Burnham, who, during his long years of sailing, had had many interesting and unusual experiences.

The particular experience related at that time occurred when Captain Burnham was master of the *B. B. Jones* and when the *Jones*, moored at the foot of Court Street in Port Huron, exploded her boilers, killing seven of her crew and injuring three others including Burnham who was blown sky high. The only reason the captain was not more seriously injured, he reported, was that he was able to catch hold of a low-lying cloud and thereby ease his fall.

Of course that feat was not too extraordinary when you consider the true facts of the experience of Amos Stiles,[1] one of the crew of the propeller *Independence*, when that steamer's boiler

---

[1] Several sources give as the man who caught hold of the bale of hay and made the descent unharmed, Jonas W. Watson, the purser.

exploded in the St. Marys River and crew and cargo were flung high in the air.

While up in the air Stiles came in contact with a flying bale of hay, and, grabbing hold of it, fell with it to the river below. He finally managed, in the rushing, turbulent waters, to climb aboard the bale of hay, and using it as a life-raft found himself hurled down the raging St. Marys Rapids. To navigate the rapids was a dangerous feat, to say the least — a feat, for the most part, executed only by the Indian in his canoe — but Stiles made the trip, still hanging onto the bale of hay, and was rescued at the foot of the rapids.

After recovering from his ordeal Amos Stiles was able to work for many years as assistant superintendent at the Sault Canal, but the shock of the experience, and injuries sustained, had evidently affected his facial muscles, for he was never known to laugh — at least in public — after the incident, and has since been known in marine lore as " the man who never laughed." [2]

With reference to the *Independence,* it was Laughlin P. Morrison (son of Captain L. M. Morrison of Corunna, Ontario, a notable skipper on the Great Lakes for over fifty years) who more than forty years later was the engineer in charge of dredging the channel where the *Independence* still lay. The *Independence,* according to Morrison, sank on Vidal Shoal less than two miles above the Sault Ste. Marie Rapids. As boats continued to increase in draft, the Vidal Shoal came to constitute a menace to navigation and had to be removed, and in the process Morrison's equipment brought up what proved to be the twin propellers and remaining hulk of the *Independence.*

The vessel had been loaded with a cargo of trade goods for barter with the Indian fur trappers, and Morrison and his crew of workers secured many curious souvenirs, including round wooden

---

[2] Lauchlin P. Morrison, who later brought up the wreck of the *Independence,* says in his memoirs that at the time of the raising of the steamer "old man Stiles" was one of the observers, and that although he had the reputation of never laughing he noticed that when some particularly funny story was told Stiles would disappear for awhile behind some machinery shelters and when he reappeared he would have "all the earmarks of a man who had had a good, hearty laugh." L. P. Morrison, *Memories of the Great Lakes,* typewritten (no date), p. 53, in Jenks Collection, Port Huron Public Library.

match boxes filled with old sulphur matches (the smell of sulphur still strongly evident), brass rings that had been gilt at one time, and beads of all sizes and colors.

Also salvaged were nine bottles of Indian trade whiskey, two of which Morrison secured for himself. The whiskey proved to be "terrible stuff," as Morrison later wrote in his memoirs, but it gave him the idea to play a joke on his friends. He let the word get around that he had some whiskey "forty-four years old at least," and then invited some of his friends to dinner, intimating that he would serve some of the liquor, and managed, too, to find out what was the "favorite tipple of those several friends in the whiskey line." He had no refusals to his dinner party.

In the meantime he carefully removed the ancient green wax from one of the bottles, emptied out the Indian trade whiskey and, refilling it with the best brand of whiskey he could buy, resealed it with the old wax.

Before the dinner was served he brought forth the treasured bottle and was particular in letting his friends examine it carefully. He then removed the wax from the bottle in the presence of all and poured each member of the party a "stiff jolt."

"I can still hear today," Morrison wrote in his memoirs, "the sips of appreciation and awed expressions of '44 years old!' 'Some whiskey, boy!' " So entranced were the guests at the age of the liquor that they overlooked the fact that it had been in glass bottles all that time and that whiskey stored in glass did not improve with age. They were all cognizant of that fact, Morrison declared, but had completely forgotten for the time being — either that, or, as he added, they "were the most courteous guests that ever graced a dinner table." [3]

---

[3] *Ibid.*, p. 53.

Chapter XXXXII

PAUL BUNYAN,
LEGENDARY HERO OF THE ST. CLAIR RIVER AREA

Now let's have no more nonsense about the true origin of America's great legendary hero, Paul Bunyan. It was bad enough when Maine claimed him and when Wisconsin and Minnesota tried to show cause of rightful ownership, but when the Russians appropriated first rights to Paul — asserting that Paul was none other than Paulenovitch Bunyanevskii—well, that's going too far.

The truth of the matter is that Paul Bunyan first became famous in Michigan. And not only in Michigan but right in the beautiful Blue Water region of the St. Clair River.

And we have to laugh, too — tolerantly, of course — at some of the assertions of our own Michiganders that the Paul Bunyan stories originated in the Saginaw lumber camps. There is no more truth in that claim than there is in the stories that Saginaw had the first saw mills in Michigan. The St. Clair River area had saw mills almost a century before Saginaw did, and if there were tales circulated in the Saginaw camps they were stories of exploits which occurred in the St. Clair County lumber camps years before and which drifted Saginaw way.

Of course it is true that Paul, a one-time chef in Montreal, Quebec, browsed around the great primeval forests of the Northwest, as a looker, that is, before he came upon the great white pine belt in Michigan. When he saw the fine stand of cork pine in the Black River and Mill Creek regions, however, he reckoned that that was the right place to begin operations in a serious way. How do we know? We got it straight from an old time lumberman who knew Paul — who, in fact, really discovered Paul for what he was. Our friend wasn't given to embellishing or enlarging on his tales — too much. He always left the erroneous stories, like the one about the Great Lakes being formed from the footsteps of Paul, to the literary tall-tale tellers. And he always told his stories in an offhand, flat, factual sort of way, with a rapid flicker of his eyelids

289

which added credence to his reminiscences — that honest-to-lumberman's-truth sort of way that no one could gainsay.

But to get on with the story. The first time Paul Bunyan appeared in the St. Clair River area was in the early days of Port Huron, when Black River was called Little River and the St. Clair, Big River, and when the settlement at the mouth of little River was known as Down-at-the-Mouth — no reflections meant.

Paul appeared in February, and it was a winter of extreme cold and great privation. The snow was deep and the ice in the rivers was two feet thick, with no prospect of a thaw. The inhabitants were destitute of provisions, and there were no means whereby supplies could be obtained. Things certainly looked bad.

While two men were sitting in the Halstead & Thornton store (corner of Huron Avenue and Quay Street) consoling themselves with a game of checkers and some of Whit's brandy—"Whit" being Whitcomb, who ran a hotel nearby — the door opened and a giant of a young man entered. He couldn't have been more than sixteen years old and hadn't yet got his full growth, but he had to stoop over double to come in the door. When he straightened up, which he had barely room to do between the floor and ceiling, one of the chess players who was 19-hands-horse-measure tall himself, said that the lad was the tallest and strongest man in Michigan.

"You can eat again," Paul told the chess players, and when they looked at him in disbelief, he told them he had broken through Big River, down at the mouth of Little River, and they could now have all the fish they wanted until supplies could move again. That wasn't exactly the way Paul expressed himself, but his way is not for a history book.

Evidently he convinced the chess players enough so that they followed him, and they saw, to their amazement, a great gaping hole in Big River near the mouth of Little River. Paul had taken a fifty-foot log, two feet in diameter, and, handling it as another man would a piece of cord wood, had used it to break through the thick ice.

Now straddling the hole, he began to swing in and out of the water a huge net he had ingeniously made out of a bull chain and choker he had found in the yard of a nearby saw mill. At every revolution of the net, great, beautiful whitefish and silvery pickerel

290

and fat little perch came flying out of the water and landing on a pile which grew bigger and bigger until it reached as high as the second floor of the saw mill chandlery nearby.

News of Paul's great feat spread like a balsam woods fire and people began coming from as far south as Belle River, as far west as Brockway, and as far north as Burtchville to carry home the fish. The whole district was fed.

Now Paul was naturally a modest fellow; he didn't perform his great exploits just to show off. In every instance he showed his cleverness and skill only when expediency was necessary—as on this occasion. When everyone seemed to have enough, anyone but Paul would have called it a day. But not Paul. He kept right on heaving out the fish onto the fast growing pile, and as the water flew out with the fish it froze in a glaze over them. As he worked he directed some men to keep throwing shovelfuls of sawdust on the pile to act as insulation, and before the day was over there was a pile of fish high enough and frozen hard enough to feed the whole district until spring. It is believed that this instance is the first case on record of deep-freeze refrigeration.

When Paul appeared again, lumber was king, and he really began his lumbering exploits in a big way.

A local cruiser, then boss of a camp up Wadhams way, was in need of a good cook, and when a man of gigantic proportions wandered into camp looking for a job and asserted that he had been a chef in the Prince Edward Hotel in Montreal, he was hired right there on the tote road. The stranger was a French-Canadian, Paulette Cicero, by name. "Dey call me Paul," he said.

"You the feller that passed through here that winter of the great famine and made the big haul?" asked the Boss.

"Eet was not'ing!" insisted Paul, modestly, shrugging his shoulders which measured two ax handles and three plugs of Spearhead in width.

The Big Boss liked Paul, and when the work was done and there was a time for relaxation Paul and he did a lot of reminiscing. One day Paul was telling of how he could trace his ancestry right back to one Antoine Auclaire, apothecary in early Quebec and physician to Count Frontenac, when all of a sudden his great curly black beard began to itch his chin. Leaning lazily against one of the smaller sugar maples — one about one hundred feet tall —

he reached up nonchalantly to bend down the top fringe of it to scratch the itchy spot when he unexpectedly sniffed the scent of the grayfish fungus growth hanging like a tangled web over the uppermost tip of the tree.

"Pulmonaria officinalis!" he shouted in astonishment, and right there that revelation of knowledge proved that he was related to the learned apothecary of ancient Quebec.

"Lungwort!" corrected the Big Boss.

"Mertensia Virginica," went on Paul, further breaking down the special classification of the plant.

"Lungwort, we called it," insisted the Big Boss.

"Same t'ing!" snapped Paul. "She make fine yeast! We have finest bread in countree, by gar!"

And so not only was baking revolutionized in the lumber camps from that time on, but Paul's bread dough was also a miracle worker in more than one emergency. There was the time when the ten-feet-high Big Wheels with a load of twenty-four logs — each twenty feet long and four feet in diameter — got mired in the tote road. The possibility of ever getting the load of big sticks to move again seemed hopeless. The tote teamster cussed and alternately coaxed and threatened the six span of horses to a mightier pull; the scalers cussed and heaved at the logs with their iron-lipped springboards; the hookers cussed and pulled on the choker chains; the yard crew cussed and dug mud away from the mired Big Wheels, the Straw Boss cussed and chewed snoose; and the Big Boss, standing around fuming, cussed them all. But to no avail. Everything they did served only to settle the load of big sticks that much deeper in the mud. The crew was ready to give up in despair.

But they had reckoned without Paul who had been lounging cross-legged against the load, thinking. Now, slowly, he uncrossed his legs, saying quietly, "I feex heem, by gar!" and strode off toward the cookhouse.

Pretty soon he came back carrying one of his huge 4' by 8' baking pans filled with a fresly mixed batch of bread dough. He directed the yard crew to shovel away the mud from under the load between the wheels and then he pushed the great pan of dough into the excavation they had made. As the yeast began to work the dough began to rise and with such force that the Big Wheels with their load of logs were lifted right out of the mud. The six span of horses heaved to, and soon the great load was cleared of the mire. The cheers of the loggers could be heard as far away as Lexington, Michigan.

It was about this time that Paul performed another great feat — or two, we should say. One raconteur in relating some of Paul's exploits said that he invented grindstone. Paul didn't invent grindstone, he discovered it. He discovered it right up in what is now Grindstone City, and this is the way it happened.

Paul was a great advocate of exercise. After a big, hearty meal of his famous bread, beans, salt pork, and tea, he liked nothing better than to take a walk before retiring to his grass-and-hay-lined bunk. A walk up to the tip of the Thumb and back on an evening was nothing for Paul. He'd sit on the heights overlooking beautiful Lake Huron, swing his feet in its cool waters and lean back on his elbows and do his thinking. Paul was a great thinker. And while he thought he would doodle. His doodling was often tracing fantastic patterns in the sand or gouging out great fistfuls of sand to make miniature houses and saw mills.

On this particular evening of which we speak, while Paul was doodling in the sand, his great, strong fingers heaved up a piece of flat abrasive stone. Curious, Paul went on digging, and slab after slab of the sandstone was unearthed until he had enough quarried to pave a courtyard. Suddenly Paul remembered that he had heard one of his French-Canadian cousins, living in Detroit, telling of how they were hard-pressed to find a suitable kind of paving material for the streets of the town. This stone was just the thing.

Hurrying back to the Wadhams camp Paul put his "cookee" on one of the wild ponies he had broken in — the literary tall-tale tellers hadn't as yet invented Paul's Blue Ox — and sent him to Detroit with the news of his discovery and his bid for the paving job. By ten o'clock the next morning the cookee returned with the glad tidings that the Common Council would accept the stone on Paul's terms.

Paul immediately went to work quarrying the stone — forming it into large disks with his thumb nails — and when they were worn down he sent to camp for his huge doughnut cutter to do the work, and then sent the disks rolling down to Little River. And as he

293

rolled them toward Little River—rolling them so fast that they were held up by their own swift momentum—an idea came to him. Paul was one to kill two ideas with one grindstone if he had the chance. He sent word to all the men in camp to stand by the grindstone line with their axes, and, as the disks rolled by, the whirling abrasive sandstone sharpened them.

Paul was also smart enough to plan the quarrying of the grindstones for just the time when great cribs of cork pine were being rafted from Port Huron to Detroit. The rafts of pine acted as a perfect float for the heavy grindstone, thereby saving Paul half the cost of transportation.

That's how Woodward and Jefferson Avenues in Detroit were first paved — they say — and how sandstone, or grindstone as it became known was first discovered for sharpening tools. Incidentally, Paul's quarrying of the sandstone started an industry that lasted for nigh on a century up in the little Thumb town of Grindstone City.

EPILOGUE

High in the autumn moonlit sky wild geese in V-shaped formations, with military precision make steady progress over the St. Clair River in their migration from the Canadian north to the American southland. The faint honking of the geese which precedes their appearance, and which makes one eagerly scan the heavens, grows raucously louder as the flocks pass overhead, only to grow fainter again as the vision disappears.

The annual flights of the wild geese have been as constant as the arrival of the seasons of the year in the great plan of the Universe, and they have been crossing and recrossing the St. Clair River from time immemorial, hailing, as it were, the beauty and the nobility of that majestic waterway.

Many changes have taken place in the region of the "charming streight" since first the wild geese observed its habitation by the white man. The face of the countryside has slowly changed, as have the activities on land and on water. The towering pines have disappeared as farms and hamlets replaced them. The sprawling saw mills and lumberyards, the dry docks and shipyards, the tanneries and cooper shops and breweries have all made way on both sides of the river for the fantastic architecture of the age of formulae and steel. They have made way for the pulsating factories designed for the manufacture of synthetic rubber, of plastics and fiberglas and carbon black, of brass and copper fittings, of automobile parts and marine engines and small pleasure craft, and of innumerable other mechanical, chemical, and petroleum products to satisfy the demands of modern living.

The once almost invisible trails that were roads and highways are now great ribbons of concrete freeways crisscrossing a countryside geared to the automobile age. Through urban renewal projects the public squares as well as older, run-down sections of towns are fast becoming useful shopping, cultural, educational, and recreational centers, complete with handsome buildings, well-planned, artistic malls and pedestrian arcades, public housing complexes, and adequate parking facilities.

295

The St. Clair River, which once knew only the canoe and the bateau, has carried on its heavenly blue waters the succession of sea beauty that was the sailing vessel, the trim steamer and the saucy little tug, the speed boat and the elegant yacht, and the great, long — unbelievably long — freighters. And now the same blue waters of the St. Clair River, a midway link on the St. Lawrence Seaway, carry also the trans-oceanic vessels of foreign countries — ships from Great Britain, France, Italy, and Germany, from Norway, Sweden, Holland and Denmark, and from Japan, Israel, Liberia, and many other countries. The wild geese, in fact, have seen the commerce of the St. Clair River grow from the arrival of La Salle's *Griffin* — and from the passage of the little schooner *Gladwin* on the first through trip from Detroit to Mackinac *and back* — to the mighty ships carrying more tonnage during the eight-month season of navigation than is transported in a full year on many of the world's great waterways combined.

As the wild geese now wing their way in the jet-age heavens, their formation a salute to the grandeur of the scene below, one wonders if their calls are not also hailing the accomplishments of the succeeding generations of men who made use of the resources of the St. Clair River region for the betterment of those who, in the words of the immortal Hennepin, would one day "be so happy as to inhabit that Noble Country."

BIBLIOGRAPHY

Manuscripts

BHC, DPL = Burton Historical Collection, Detroit Public Library, Detroit, Mich.

JC, PHPL = Jenks Collection, Port Huron Public Library, Port Huron, Mich.

Black River Steam Mill. Day Books and Ledgers. 8 Vols. (1832-185?) (Last date illegible.) JC, PHPL.

Bradstreet, John. Letter to Patrick Sinclair, Sept. 12, 1764. William L. Clements Library, University of Michigan, Ann Arbor.

Beard Papers. JC, PHPL.

Butler, Charles. Papers. JC, PHPL.

Brakeman Papers. JC, PHPL.

Clarke, John C. Papers. JC, PHPL.

Facer, W. D. "Reminiscences" in letter form. n.d. JC, PHPL.

Harrington Papers. JC, PHPL.

Harrow, Alexander. "Journal" (Feb. 3, 1791—Aug. 18, 1800). BHC, DPL.

——————. Log Books. BHC, PHPL.

Heintzleman, Samuel P. "Diary" (Aug. 2, 1826—Dec. 28, 1829), while stationed at Fort Gratiot. U. S. Military Academy Library, West Point, N. Y.

Howard, Mrs. John. "Reminiscences of Fifty-four Years Spent in Michigan." Pages bound. JC, PHPL.

Jenks, William Lee. "The Fort Gratiot Turnpike." Typewritten. JC, PHPL. (Also in Michigan History Magazine, v. 9)

——————. "History of Port Huron Street Railways." Typewritten. JC, PHPL.

——————. Papers. JC, PHPL.

——————. Scrapbook. JC, PHPL.

——————. "Samuel Ward." JC, PHPL.

Morrison, Lauchlin P. Memoirs of the Great Lakes. JC, PHPL.

Palmer Papers. JC, PHPL.

Porteous, John. "Diary." BHC, DPL. Excerpts of Diary are also in JC, PHPL.

Quaife, Milo M. "Letters." In Jenks Papers. JC, PHPL.

St. Clair County Pioneer Society. Minutes of Annual Meetings (1875-1926) and Reminiscences. JC, PHPL.

U. S. Coast Guard, Washington, D. C. Official Report, Nov. 9, through Nov. 15, 1913, by George W. Plough, Keeper of the Lake View Lifeboat Station (now Port Huron Lifeboat Station), District No. 11.

Van der Linden, Rev. Peter. "Alphabetical List of Ships Built in St. Clair County, Michigan." Typewritten, 1965.

Ward Letters. 2 vols. Typed and bound. Privately owned, n.d. (Letters from Nov. 12, 1807 to March 13, 1856.)

Ward Papers. JC, PHPL.

Maps

Bayfield, Henry W. "Western End of Lake Erie," copied from "Survey of Lake Erie, in the years 1817 and 1818," by Lieut. Henry W. Bayfield, R.N.

Del'Isle. Carte Du Canada Ou De La Nouvelle France. Paris, 1703. BHC, DPL.

Lahontan. "A General Map of New France," in New Voyages to North America, v.1. London, 1703.

——————. "Map of the Great Lakes," in Memoires de L'Amerique. Hague, 1706.

Newspapers

Commercial Tribune (Port Huron)
Daily Times (Port Huron)
Daily Tribune (Port Huron)
Detroit Free Press
Detroit Gazette
Marine City (Mich.) *Independent*
Port Huron Commercial
Port Huron Observor
Port Huron Press
Port Huron Times
Port Huron Times Herald
Port Huron Tribune
Port Huron Weekly Times
St. Clair County Press (St. Clair, Mich.)
St. Clair Republican (St. Clair, Mich.)
Sunday Commercial (Port Huron)
Sunday Herald (Port Huron)
Weekly Herald (Port Huron)

Books, Magazines, Collections, Booklets

M.H.M. = Michigan History Magazine. Michigan Historical Commission.
M.P.H.C. = Michigan Pioneer and Historical Collections.
Achievements of Crocket McElroy of St. Clair, Michigan. Booklet. n.d.
Ballentine, Mrs. Caroline F. "True Story of Edison's Childhood and Boyhood." *M.H.M.*, IV, 168.
Bancroft, William L. "Graphic Pen Pictures," printed in *Sunday Herald* (Port Huron) Dec. 20, 1897. Now in Scrapbook. JC, PHPL.
————. "Memoir of Capt. Samuel Ward," *M.P.H.C.*, XXI (1882), 336.
Bates, George C. "By-gones of Detroit, 1832-1836." *M.P.H.C.*, XXII, 305.
————. "Reminiscences of the Brady Guards," *M.P.H.C.*, XIII, 530.
Beasley, Norman. *Freighters of Fortune.* New York & London: Harper, 1930.
Before the Bridge, A History and a Directory of St. Ignace and Nearby Localities. Pub. by Kiwanis Club of St. Ignace, Mich. Inc., 1957, commemorating the opening of the Mackinac Bridge.
Beers, J. H. & Co. *History of the Great Lakes.* 2 vols. Chicago, 1899.
Bryan, George S. *Edison, the Man and His Work.* London and New York: Knopf, 1926.
Bryant, William Cullen. *Letters of a Traveller, or Notes of things seen in Europe and America.* New York: Putnam, 1850.
Burr, E. D. "Navigation VS Banking," *M.P.H.C.*, XXVIII, 652.
Burton, Clarence M. "The Building of Detroit." Booklet. 1912.
————. *The City of Detroit, Michigan, 1701-1932.* 4 vols. Detroit and Chicago: S. J. Clarke Pub. Co, 1922.
————. "Detroit in 1832," *M.P.H.C.*, XXVII, 163.
————. *Early Detroit, A Sketch of Some of the Interesting Affairs of the Olden Time.* Booklet. n.d.
"Burton Historical Leaflets." *Detroit Biographies.* vols. I to X, 1922-1931.
Campbell, James V. *Outlines of the Political History of Michigan.* Detroit: Schober & Company, 1876.

298

Cass, Lewis. "Letter to James Monroe, February 2, 1816." *M.P.H.C.*, XXXVI, 338.

Catlin, George B. *The Story of Detroit*. Detroit: The Detroit News, 1926.

Channing, Edward and Lansing, Marion F. *The Story of the Great Lakes*. New York: Macmillan, 1909.

Clark, William A. "Memorial Report," *M.P.H.C.*, III (1881), 605.

Crampton, Mrs. Emeline Jenks. *History of the St. Clair River*. St. Clair (Mich.), 1921.

Cuthbertson, George A. *Freshwater; A History and Narrative of the Great Lakes*. New York: Macmillan, 1931.

Cyclopedia of American Biography. New York: D. Appleton, 1891.

Davis, Marion Morse. *Island Stories; Straits of Mackinac*. Lansing, Mich.: Franklin DeKleine Company, 1947. (Stories also appeared in *Michigan History Magazine*.)

Densmore, Frances. *Chippewa Customs*. Washington, 1929.

Diary of the Siege of Detroit in the War with Pontiac. Ed. by F. G. Hough. Albany: J. Munsell, 1860.

Dictionary of American Biography. New York: Charles Scribners Sons, 1928.

Dyer, Frank Lewis and Martin, Thomas Commerford. *Edison, His Life and Inventions*. New York: Harper, 1910.

Disturnell, John. *The Great Lakes, or Inland Seas of America*. New York, 1863.

Eldridge, Robert F. *Past and Present of Macomb County, Michigan*. Chicago: S. J. Clarke, 1905.

Farmer, Silas. *The History of Detroit and Michigan*. 2 vols. Detroit: Silas Farmer Company, 1889.

Fifty Years of Banking in Port Huron, Michigan; First National Exchange Bank (1871-1921). Privately printed. n.d.

Fuller, George N. *Economic and Social Beginnings of Michigan: a study of the settlement of the lower peninsula during the territorial period, 1805-1837*. Lansing: Wynkoop, Hallenbeck, Crawford Company, 1916.

"Gladwin Manuscripts" (Charles Moore). *M.P.H.C.*, XXVII, 605.

Goodrich, Calvin. *The First Michigan Frontier*. Ann Arbor: University of Michigan, 1940.

Grant, Ulysses Simpson. *Personal Memoirs of U. S. Grant*. 2 vols. New York: Charles B. Webster, 1885.

Gwinn, Florence McKennon. *Pioneer History of Huron County, Michigan*. Huron County Pioneer and Historical Society, 1922.

"Haldiman Papers," *M.P.H.C.*, VIX (1886), 343.

Hamlin, Marie C. W. *Legends of Le Detroit*. Detroit: Thorndike Nourse, 1884.

Hatcher, Harlan. *The Great Lakes*. New York: Oxford University Press, 1944.

—————. *Lake Erie*. Indianapolis and New York: Bobbs-Merrill, 1945.

Havighurst, Walter. *Land of Promise*. New York: Macmillan, 1946.

—————. *The Long Ships Passing*. New York: Macmillan, 1942.

Hemans, Lawron T. *Life and Times of Stevens T. Mason*. Lansing, Michigan, Historical Commission, 1920.

Hennepin, Father Louis. *A New Discovery of a Vast Country in America*. Reuben G. Thwaites Edition. 2 vols. A reprint from the second London issue of 1698. Chicago: McClurg, 1903.

Hinsdale, Wilbert B. *The First People of Michigan*. Ann Arbor: George Wahr, 1930.

History of Bay County, Michigan, with Illustrations and Biographical Sketches of Some of its Prominent Men and Pioneers. Chicago: Page, 1883.

History of Huron County, Michigan. Chicago: Chapman, 1884.

History of St. Clair County, Michigan. Chicago: Andreas, 1883.

History of Sanilac County, Michigan. Chicago: Chapman, 1884.

History of Macomb County, Michigan. Chicago: Leeson, 1882.

Holbrook, Stewart H. *Iron Brew.* New York: Macmillan, 1940.

Hubbard, Bela. *Memorials of a Half-Century in Michigan and the Lake Region.* New York: Putnam, 1887.

Hurlbut, Frances. *Grandmother's Stories.* Privately printed. Cambridge: Riverside Press, 1889.

Jameson, Anna. *Winter Studies and Summer Rambles in Canada.* 2 vols. New York, 1839.

——————. *Sketches in Canada.* London: Traveller's Library, 1852.

Jenks, William Lee. "The Diary of the Siege of Detroit." *M.H.M.*, XII (1928), 427.

——————. "Fort Gratiot and Its Builder, Gen. Charles Gratiot." *M.H.M.*, IV (1920). 141.

——————. *Patrick Sinclair.* Michigan Historical Commission Bulletin and Collections. Lansing, Michigan: Wynkoop Hallenbeck Crawford Co., 1914.

——————. *St. Clair County, Michigan; Its History and Its People.* 2 vols. Chicago and New York: Lewis, 1912.

Johnson, I. A. *The Michigan Fur Trade.* Lansing, Michigan History Ser., 1919.

Josephson, Matthew. *Edison, A Biography.* New York, Toronto, London: McGraw-Hill Book Company, 1959.

Karpinski, Louis C. *Bibliography of the Printed Maps of Michigan, 1804-1880.* Lansing: Michigan Historical Commission, 1931.

Kinzie, Mrs. J. H. *Wau-Bun.* Chicago: Donnelley, 1932. (Lakeside Press.)

Lahontan, Baron de. *New Voyages to North-America.* Ed. by R. G. Thwaites. Chicago: McClurg, 1905.

Landon, Fred. *Lake Huron.* Indianapolis and New York: Bobbs-Merrill, 1944.

Lanman, James Henry. *History of Michigan.* New York: French, 1839.

Lauriston, Victor E. *Lambton's Hundred Years, 1849-1949.* Sarnia (Ontario): Haines, n.d.

Laut, Agnes G. *Cadillac; Knight Errant of the Wilderness.* Indianapolis and New York: Bobbs-Merrill, 1931.

Lossing, Benson J. *The Pictorial Field Book of the War of 1812.* New York: Harper and Bros., 1868.

Lyon, Lucius. "Letters of Lucius Lyon." *M.P.H.C.*, XXVII, 412.

Mackintosh, Alexander. "Letter to Richard Bullock." *M.P.H.C.*, XV, 412.

Marine History; The Lake Ports. Port Huron. Descriptive and Historical Review. Detroit. Historical Publishing Company, 1877.

McKenney, Thomas L. *Sketches of a Tour to the Lakes.* Baltimore: Fielding Lucas Jr., 1827.

Michigan: A Guide to the Wolverine State. New York: Oxford, 1941.

Michigan Archaeologist (Michigan Archaeological Society), December, 1958, v. 4, No. 4.

Michigan History Magazine.

Michigan Pioneer and Historical Collections. 39 vols. Michigan Historical Commission: Lansing, 1877-1915.

Moore, Charles. *History of Michigan.* 3 vols. Lewis Publishing Company, 1915.

Nute, Grace Lee. *Lake Superior.* Indianapolis and New York: Bobbs-Merrill, 1944.

————. *The Voyageur.* New York and London: D. Appleton-Century Company, 1931.

Palmer, Friend. *Early Days in Detroit.* Detroit: Richmond, Backus, 1906.

Palmer, Thomas W. *Detroit in 1837; Recollections of Thomas W. Palmer.* Detroit; Printed for the Burton Abstract and Title Company, 1922.

————. "Mr. Thompson's School at St. Clair in 1842;" Address by Thomas W. Palmer, Pioneer's Day, June 25th, 1907. Booklet.

Paré, Rev. George W. *The Catholic Church in Detroit, 1701-1888.* Detroit: Gabriel Richard Press, 1951.

Parke, Hervey. "Reminiscences," *M.P.H.C.,* III (1881), 572.

Parkman, Francis. *Conspiracy of Pontiac and the Indian War . . . ,* Boston: Little, Brown, 1887.

————. *Count Frontinac and New France Under Louis XIV.* Boston: Little, Brown, 1905.

————. *La Salle and the Discovery of the Great West.* Boston: Little, Brown, 1897.

————. *The Old Regime in Canada.* Boston: Little, Brown, 1902.

Pontiac Manuscript. *M.P.H.C.,* VIII (1885), 266.

Pound, Arthur. *Once a Wilderness.* New York, Reynal, 1934.

Proudly We Record; the Story of Wyandotte, Michigan. Sponsored by the Rotary Club of Wyandotte, Michigan, 1955.

Quaife, Milo M. *Chicago and the Old Northwest, 1763-1835.* Chicago: Chicago University Press, 1913.

————. *Lake Michigan.* New York: Bobbs-Merrill, 1944.

Robertson, John. *Michigan in the War.* Lansing: W. S. George and Company, State Printers and Binders, 1882.

Ross, Robert B. and Catlin, George B. *Landmarks of Detroit.* Detroit Evening News, 1898.

Rutherford, John. Narrative of a Captivity. In the Siege of Detroit of 1763, The Journal of Pontiac's Conspiracy. Ed. by M. M. Quaife. Chicago. 1958. Donnelley. (The Lakeside Classics)

Sagendorph, Kent. *Stevens Thomson Mason, Misunderstood Patriot.* New York: Dutton, 1947.

St. Bernard, Alexander. "Murder of King Strang" (As told to O. Poppleton), *M.P.H.C.,* XVIII (1891), 626.

Schoolcraft, Henry Rowe. *Narrative Journal of Travels.* Ed. by Mentor L. Williams. Lansing: Michigan State College Press, 1953.

————. *Personal Memoirs of a Residence of Thirty Years with the Indian Tribes on the American Frontiers.* Philadelphia: Lippincott, Grambo and Company, 1851.

Sheldon, Mrs. Electa Maria. *Early History of Michigan.* Chicago: Barnes, 1856.

Sheridan, Philip Henry. *Personal Memoirs of P. H. Sheridan.* 2 vols. New York: Webster, 1888.

Simonds, William Adams. *Edison; His Life, His Work, His Genius.* Indianapolis and New York: Bobbs-Merrill, 1934.

Stockton, C. M. "Reminiscences of Port Huron," *M.P.H.C.,* XVIII (1897-1898), 110.

Stoddard, Francis Hovey. *Life and Letters of Charles Butler.* New York, 1903.

Sunborg, George. *Hail Columbia.* New York: Macmillan, 1954.

Thompson, O. C. "History of Judge Zephaniah W. Bunce," *M.P.H.C.*, I (1874-1876), 434.

Town of Huron at the Foot of Lake Huron, St. Clair Co., Michigan. A Circular addressed to Capitalists, and Those Who Design Removing to the West. Published by the Proprietors. New York: E. B. Clayton, Printer, 1837. (A prospectus bound in hard cover.)

Utley, Henry M. and Cutcheon, Bryon M. *Michigan as a Province, Territory and State*. New York: Publishing Society of Michigan, 1906.

War of the Rebellion Records. Washington: Government Printing Office, 1897.

Walther, Florence H. *A History of Lexington*. 1934.

Ward, David. *Autobiography of David Ward*. Privately printed, 1912.

Ward, Eber. "Autobiography." *M.P.H.C.*, VI (1883), 471. Incidents in the Life of Mr. Eber Ward, Father of Capt. E. B. Ward of Steamboat Fame As Related to Mrs. E. M. S. Stewart in the Summer of 1852; Read at the Annual Meeting of the State Society, June, 1883.

_____. "The Remarkable Family of Ward. Interview with Capt. Eber Ward." *Inland Seas*, v. 17, No. 1, Spring, 1961, p. 58. First appeared in *Marine Review and Marine Record*, v. 26, Sept. 11, 1902, p. 27.

Williams, Ralph D. *The Honorable Peter White*. Cleveland: Penton Publishing Company, 1907.

Women's Canadian Historical Society of Toronto. Annual Report and Transaction, No. 13 (1913-1914).

Wood, Edwin O. *Historic Mackinac*. 2 vols. New York: Macmillan, 1918.

Woodford, Frank B. *Lewis Cass, The Last Jefferson*. New Brunswick, New Jersey, 1950.

Woolson, Constance Fenimore. "St. Clair Flats," in *Constance Fenimore Woolson*, Ed. by Clare Benedict. London: Ellis, n.d. First appeared in Appleton's *Journal*.

Young, William T. *Sketch of the Life and Public Services of General Lewis Cass*. Detroit: Markham & Elwood, 1852.